RULING
THE ROOST

RULING
THE ROOST

THE MANAGERS OF
SHEFFIELD WEDNESDAY

RICHARD CROOKS

pitch

First published by Pitch Publishing, 2025

1

(pitch)

Pitch Publishing
9 Donnington Park,
85 Birdham Road,
Chichester, West Sussex,
PO20 7AJ
www.pitchpublishing.co.uk
info@pitchpublishing.co.uk

A CIP catalogue record is available for this book
from the British Library.

ISBN 978 1 83680 182 5

Typesetting and origination by Pitch Publishing

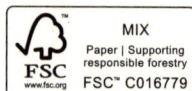

MIX
Paper | Supporting
responsible forestry
FSC
www.fsc.org   FSC™ C016779

Printed and bound in the UK on FSC® certified paper in line
with our continuing commitment to ethical business practices,
sustainability and the environment.

Printed and bound in India by Replika Press Pvt. Ltd.

Contents

For Dad, Norman Lewis Crooks; sons Ben, Sam and Tom; grandsons Charlie, Edward, Cameron and William; and granddaughter Dorothy

Acknowledgements

MY GRATEFUL appreciation to Jennifer Ann Wiles for her support in the writing of this book – her thoughts, comments and suggestions on the narrative have been once again unerringly helpful.

A particular thank you to Chris Turner and Alan Biggs for their time and for providing such illuminating insights.

A thank you to Trevor Braithwait at Sheffield Wednesday for giving me permission to quote from the club's programmes.

And to Claire Lewis, editor of the *Sheffield Star*, thank you for giving me permission to quote from the *Sheffield Star Green 'Un* and the *Star*.

To the staff at the British Library who have been unfailingly helpful in assisting my research – thank you.

Jason Dickinson, Sheffield Wednesday's club historian, thank you for your assistance with information and for the use of several images in this book.

Thank you to Duncan Olner for the design of the cover, and to Gareth Davis for editing the book.

And thank you particularly to Jane at Pitch Publishing for continued support and advice in producing this book.

Quotations used are referenced by their source – newspapers, magazines, books with the author and publisher referenced. Permission has been sought from the publishers.

Preface

WHY WRITE a book about the managers of Sheffield Wednesday?

Firstly, Wednesday is my club – I've supported them since the first time I heard their name, and no doubt well before that as Dad and my whole family are staunch and passionate Wednesdayites in the football hotbed that is the city of Sheffield.

Secondly, while there have been several books that have provided a profile of Wednesday managers as part of a larger historical narrative on the club, there has not been a book dedicated to the men at the helm.

I've written six books; five on football including one on the Sheffield derby: *Wednesday v United: The Sheffield Derby*. And I want this book to be focussed on Sheffield Wednesday.

And finally – Danny Röhl. He's the manager who has made the greatest impact on the club in the last 30 and more years – he performed a football miracle by masterminding the club's retention of Championship status from a seemingly impossible position when he was appointed in October 2023.

Röhl is passionate, energetic, meticulous, engaging and inspirational. He has single-handedly galvanised the supporters, he has given them belief, real belief that Wednesday are moving forward in the right direction – the hopes and aspirations of Wednesdayites have been ignited by the German.

He reminds me of the arrival and impact of Bill Shankly as manager of Liverpool. At a low ebb, the Merseyside club owe a huge debt to the Scotsman who transformed their fortunes – winning the Football League and the FA Cup – and laying the foundations for their success-laden future. For some, Shankly's relationship with the Liverpool supporters was close to messianic.

In Röhl's short time in charge at Hillsborough there are clear parallels to be drawn with the former Liverpool boss.

Introduction

ALL THE men – and to date it has only been men – who have had responsibility for the Sheffield Wednesday first team are covered in this book, whatever their title: manager, secretary-manager and latterly head coach,

While those overall responsibilities have evolved and changed over time the core responsibility for the Sheffield Wednesday team – its performance and results – has remained.

The staff supporting the man in charge have changed substantially over the years. The first man at the helm, Arthur Dickinson, took charge in Victorian times, and he would find the manager's support staff of today to be wholly outside the scope of his understanding of the resources available to a manager.

Operating in the late 19th century and into the first two decades of the 20th century, Dickinson handled a range of tasks totally outside the remit of the latter-day managers and head coaches. The latter group are now supplemented by assistant managers, coaches, recruitment analysts, performance analysts, dieticians and the like.

The game in the 2020s is hugely different to that of 100 or even 50 years ago.

Manager turnover has increased substantially during the last 50 years – 27 managers for Sheffield Wednesday over that period, 14 over the last 20 years.

The book is laid out in chronological order of permanent managers – a chapter on each man, detailing their background, the duration of their tenure in charge, key features of their time at the helm and their statistical record.

In those instances where a temporary appointment led to the incumbent becoming the permanent manager, the statistical record includes all the games in his charge.

In the statistical record I have maintained the convention of recording the result after any extra time in cup competitions and not recording the result following penalty shoot-outs.

The entry for 'Best league season' is identified for managers who have completed a full league season and reflects the highest league placing for the club at the season's end.

The
Managers

1

Arthur Dickinson

ARTHUR JOSHUA Dickinson – manager of The Wednesday?

In his book, *Sheffield Wednesday: A Complete Record 1867–1987*, respected author Keith Farnsworth has a chapter titled 'Owls Managers'. Dickinson is not mentioned; the chapter starts with Bob Brown in 1920 – the latter described as the 'first professional secretary-manager in Wednesday's history'.

In similar vein, Farnsworth's earlier book, *Wednesday!*, makes no mention of Dickinson in the narrative covering the club in the late 19th and early 20th centuries.

For his part, Wednesday's club historian Jason Dickinson states in *Sheffield Wednesday FC: The Official History*, 'Although not a team manager or head coach in the modern sense of the terms … [he] was without doubt the main figure behind team selection and the overall management of Wednesday FC from the late 19th century until 1920.'

In Jason Dickinson and John Brodie's book, *Sheffield Wednesday: The Complete Record*, Arthur Dickinson is identified as 'manager' from 1880 to 1920.

The *Rothmans Football Yearbook* identifies Arthur Dickinson as 'secretary-manager' from 1891 to 1920.

Interestingly, the seminal work on Wednesday history, *The Romance of the Wednesday 1867–1926* by Richard Sparling, has no reference to Dickinson as the manager.

In *The Remarkable Story of Fred Spiksley: The First Working-Class Football Hero*, author Mark Metcalf observes that in 1891

Dickinson's title of financial secretary 'was slightly confusing as he effectively picked the side at Wednesday for many years, and in 1899 oversaw the club's conversion to a limited company … and [he] joined the Wednesday committee in 1876 and stayed until 18 May 1920'.

No doubt the role Dickinson fulfilled was nothing like that of a modern manager or head coach – he was much more focussed on running the totality of the football club.

Underlining the breadth of Dickinson's responsibilities, it was he who wrote a letter to Fred Spiksley in 1907 that stated his contract would not be renewed, writing a reference for him in support of his application to be Watford manager in 1910. The letter included, 'I can say with confidence that you will not find yourself a better judge of a professional football player. If you can get him to give up his on-course horseracing activities you will have secured an excellent football manager.' Spiksley was not offered the position at Watford.

To illustrate that responsibility for the players, at a celebration meal at the Carlton Restaurant in Sheffield for the 1902/03 First Division title winners he praised the players and is quoted as stating they are a 'credit to the club' and 'I am proud to take them anywhere'.

For a dinner on 24 August 1903, at the Masonic Hall on Surrey Street 'to commemorate the winning of the Football League Championship' the invitations were sent out by 'A.J. Dickinson Hon Sec'. 'Your reply not later than Wednesday August 19th will oblige' with a return address of 5 Pool Square Sheffield.

Ambrose Langley, Wednesday's warrior-like defender of the late 19th and early 20th centuries, wrote a series of 15 weekly articles published in the *Sheffield Telegraph Saturday Sports Special* from 29 August to 5 December 1925.

He stated that Dickinson was part of the team selection committee and directly involved in tactics to be employed in games. On one occasion the team were at Saltburn preparing for a game against Sunderland and Langley observed, 'The 'Wednesday Selection Committee was headed by Club chairman, Mr John Holmes, and included the great Mr A.J. Dickinson,

Jack Earp the Club Captain, Bill Johnson the Club Trainer and Fred Spiksley.'

Dickinson spoke to the committee, 'It seems to me that having lost twice already to Sunderland this season, we need to understand why, so that we can work out what we need to do differently to win the cup tie.'

Certainly, Arthur Dickinson's role involved scouting for players – indeed on one such visit to Dumbarton in Scotland, in September 1891, intending to sign two players, Dickinson was attacked by a 'howling mob' intent on preventing any such transaction. As Sparling put it in *The Romance of the Wednesday*, 'Wednesday have an official who actually faced a bloodthirsty mob, who really underwent a rough handling in Scotland and who is the only man who has ever shed blood for the cause of Wednesday ... Mr Dickinson was bleeding from the mouth and the nose, and felt just about used up. When his face "developed" he had two black eyes and was generally bruised...for two days he stayed at his hotel in Glasgow.'

Perhaps the best description of Dickinson's role is provided in *Sheffield Wednesday: The Complete Record*, 'Although Arthur Dickinson was never actually Wednesday's official manager, it would be unfair not to include him in this section [on managers] due to his tireless work behind the scenes and sheer unswerving dedication to the club's well-being and progression, both on and off the field of play.'

It is thought that local man Dickinson joined Wednesday initially as a member of the club in the 1870s and joined the committee in 1876.

He played an important role behind the scenes – he was a key figure in Wednesday's move to Olive Grove in 1887, and in the same year was appointed to the position of honorary financial secretary while the club moved to its first permanent home at the Grove. Four years later he had taken responsibility for all secretarial and managerial duties.

Evidently, one of those duties was to keep all the match receipts from a home game hidden under his sofa until the banks opened on the Monday morning!

The move to Owlerton – later renamed Hillsborough – in 1899 saw Dickinson responsible for the purchase of land on which the new ground was built. It was largely down to his organisation and drive that the stadium was ready to stage football in that first season.

During Dickinson's 22 years at the helm, Wednesday's league form for the most part was impressive – very impressive in consecutive seasons in 1902/03 and 1903/04 when they were league champions – and members of the First Division for all but one of those campaigns.

During his tenure the club performed very well in the FA Cup – winning the trophy twice and additionally reaching the semi-final stage on four occasions.

Unquestionably Wednesday had their greatest success while Arthur Dickinson was in charge.

Their first success in the FA Cup came in 1896 against Wolverhampton Wanderers at the Crystal Palace.

The national newspaper, *The People*, describing itself as 'A Weekly Newspaper for All Classes', reported, 'Victory rested with Sheffield Wednesday, after a well contested but distinctly rough affair by two goals to one. This is the first time the Cup has gone to Sheffield Wednesday and the visitors are to be heavily congratulated on their success. It was estimated in the course of the game close upon 30 free kicks were given for fouls.'

After the 1907 FA Cup triumph at the same venue – defeating Everton, 2-1 – the team returned to Sheffield with the trophy and a civic reception. The *Sheffield Daily Independent* reported, 'Last night Sheffield literally went wild with enthusiasm. No other term describes it. Sheffield Wednesday brought home the English Cup. The streets were utterly choked. Seventy or 80 thousand people congregated at the very least.'

The newspaper went on to describe the civic reception at the Sheffield Town Hall, 'Mr Herbert Nixon, the vice-president of the Wednesday club, proposed a vote of thanks ... He would also like to thank their honorary secretary [Arthur Dickinson], the only honorary secretary in the First Division of the league and one of the most loyal adherents of the club that they could wish to have for the tremendous amount of work he had put in towards securing their success.'

Alderman Hughes, a Wednesday director, 'added his tribute to the services rendered by Mr Dickinson who, he said, spared no time nor trouble to further the interests of the team'.

Subsequent seasons saw Wednesday maintain high standings in the First Division albeit progress in the FA Cup was not so readily achieved.

The First World War intervened after completion of the 1914/15 season. Resumption of the Football League in 1919/20 saw Wednesday have a disastrous campaign – they finished bottom of the First Division on 23 points and relegated, a full 14 points adrift of safety and 13 points behind the club next to bottom.

Dickinson resigned on 18 May 1920, albeit he remained a director and was often seen around the ground in subsequent years.

It seems likely that Dickinson played a significant role in the selection of his successor, Bob Brown.

His football activities were not confined to Wednesday – he served on several football committees including the FA Council, Football League Management Committee and International Selection Committee.

He was on league business in London, travelling to an English League vs. Scottish League match at White Hart Lane, when he died suddenly on 4 November 1930 at the Euston Hotel.

The *Sheffield Independent* carried news of Dickinson's death on its front page – he collapsed in the hall of the Euston Hotel in London. Near to him at the time, among others, was Herbert Chapman, the Arsenal manager.

For that subsequent inter-league game both teams wore black armbands as, in the words of the *Athletic News*, 'Football parted company with a quiet, friendly little figure whose loyal and sincere labours will never be forgotten'.

Many tributes were paid to Arthur Dickinson. The *Sheffield Independent* of 5 November quoted Mr W.G. Turner, chairman of Wednesday, as saying, 'A man for whom I had the greatest respect ... he had an uncanny knowledge of the rules of football

... Although he had a peculiar manner at times he was always good at heart. His affection for the Wednesday was his ruling passion.'

Fred Bye, secretary of the Sheffield Union of golf clubs and an ex-Football League referee, said, 'He is a man who has been heart and soul in the Wednesday, and no one has worked harder nor with more success than did he.'

In the same newspaper under the heading 'Wednesday's Great Man' it stated, 'Mr Dickinson has devoted his life to football. It was his great hobby. He had a deep love for the Wednesday and for many years his guiding hand had a great deal to do with the club's wonderful triumphs ... Mr Dickinson inspired trust and devotion. It was his remarkable gifts of organisation that enabled the club to expand and, eventually, in 1892, to gain admission to the Football League. That was the start that led to great things.'

Dickinson's funeral was held in Sheffield on Friday, 7 November and it was a significant occasion, the *Sheffield Independent* reporting, 'Leaders of the Football Association and representatives from clubs from all parts of the country were present to pay their last tribute yesterday, of Mr Arthur J. Dickinson ... the coffin was brought from London to Sheffield by train ... huge crowds had collected [at the station] and police had to clear a way ... the cortege which left the station at 3pm for the burial at the General Crematorium was over half a mile long.'

Dickinson remained a bachelor throughout his life, which perhaps gave him more time to devote to all his work activities.

Someone who never suffered fools gladly, Dickinson was 'a man not prone to small talk, who took praise and criticism with equanimity, Dickinson also loved the country life and cycling, although his main passion in life was Wednesday' according to *Sheffield Wednesday: The Official History*.

And difficult though it is to comprehend in the modern day, all of Dickinson's duties at Hillsborough were part time – his main occupation was running his Sheffield cutlery business.

For Wednesday, Dickinson's contribution was immense – his work and legacy for the club of the highest order.

For Arthur Dickinson's statistical record, I have included all Football League results from the first season in 1892/93 through to his last season in 1919/20, and FA Cup results from his appointment in 1891/92.

Born: 1851 (Date not known), Sheffield
Died: 4 November 1930
Appointed: 1891 (Date not known)
Departed: 18 May 1920
First game: 23 January 1892: Bolton Wanderers (h),
                 FA Cup first round, won 4-1
Last game: 1 May 1920: Oldham Athletic (h), First
                 Division, won 1-0
Best league season: 1902/03, 1903/04 First Division
                 champions; 1895/96, 1906/07 FA Cup
                 winners

Record	P	W	D	L	F	A	Win%
League	840	352	172	316	1314	1247	41.9%
FA Cup	82	42	16	24	139	82	51.2%
Total	**922**	**394**	**188**	**340**	**1453**	**1329**	**42.7%**

2

Bob Brown

APPOINTED ON 24 June 1920 in preparation for Wednesday's first season in the Second Division in the 20th century following relegation, Robert 'Bob' Brown hailed from Hebburn in County Durham.

In his 13 years in charge he took Wednesday back to the First Division and was at the helm for the club's two consecutive Football League title wins of 1928/29 and 1929/30.

Little is known about his early career – he served an apprenticeship in the shipyards and played semi-professional football in his younger days for several clubs including Hebburn Argyle – while his primary occupation was as a qualified cabinetmaker.

He was appointed as a scout for Wednesday in the northeast in 1905 – reportedly paid 10 shillings (50p) a week. And such was the quality of output from Brown's scouting that he was appointed assistant to secretary-manager Arthur Dickinson in 1908.

He and his family – his wife and two sons – moved down to South Yorkshire and he spent three seasons in the role before accepting a position as secretary-manager at Southern League Portsmouth.

Brown made a great impact on the south coast – initially steadying a club in danger of going out of business, then acquiring several quality players which led to Portsmouth winning the Southern League Second Division title.

Following the First World War, Brown was in charge at Portsmouth as they claimed the Southern League title and most importantly their admittance to the Football League as a founder member of the Third Division.

Once the 1919/20 season had finished there were great changes for Brown – despite winning the title and a place in the Football League there were clearly problems behind the scenes and disagreements with the directors on the south coast.

He left Portsmouth for fellow league newcomers Gillingham – being in charge of the Kent club for only four weeks before Wednesday came calling, moving to Sheffield 6 as the club's first professional secretary-manager.

Brown arrived with Wednesday at a low ebb. The recovery and rebuild took time – six seasons – before promotion to the First Division. Legendary names including Ernest Blenkinsop, Jack Brown and Jimmy Trotter were part of that promotion-winning team and would be the core of the team that later went on to claim the two consecutive First Division titles.

A satisfactory first season back in the top flight – finishing 16th – was followed by a downturn in performances and results in 1927/28, Wednesday bottom of the table with only ten games remaining. The inspired signing of Jimmy Seed, made captain on his arrival, resulted in a remarkable change of fortunes. Undefeated in those final ten games (with seven wins), Wednesday climbed to 14th in the table at the season's conclusion.

That run of form continued into the new season, culminating in winning the title for the third time in the club's history, a fantastic achievement given the trials and tribulations of the previous year.

Wednesday issued a souvenir programme for the visit of Arsenal in September 1929 – it opened with 'The Glorious Campaign of 1928/29' and observed, 'The present season has opened with the club on the crest of the biggest wave of success which the followers of the game at Hillsborough have experienced for many years. The championship of the First Division of the Football League, the reserve team captured the Central League Championship.

'These successes were the climax of one of the most remarkable transformations in the history of either the club or the game.

'The preceding season when, for close upon four months, the club stood at the foot of the table facing relegation, has not been forgotten, and, what is more, the wonderful effort on the part of the team, by which they extricated themselves from that apparently hopeless position at the 11th hour will never be forgotten...

'The management of the club, at that time, took the view – and as events have since proved the correct view, that players who could rise to such an occasion had both the ability and the determination to serve the club with every success last season ... the championship was won by the very same team with one exception, Gregg, who established himself as the regular inside-left.

'The spirit which characterised the team is still retained, and it is such that it can be relied upon to stand the club in good stead not only during the present season but in others to come.'

It did indeed – building on that achievement, the following season Wednesday romped home to the title with a record ten-point margin between themselves and second-placed Derby County, this at a time of two points for a win.

That same 1929/30 season saw Wednesday beaten semi-finalists in the FA Cup – unluckily defeated in the eyes of many. Aside from that campaign progress in the FA Cup under Brown was moderate – the fourth round the furthest the club reached.

After the consecutive league titles, Wednesday finished third in each of the next three seasons.

Brown was regarded as a tough disciplinarian and had the respect of the squad while his ability to spot and develop very talented players continued – Mark Hooper, Ellis Rimmer and Jack Allen added during his tenure.

Comparisons were made between the Wednesday man and his counterpart at Huddersfield Town and later Arsenal, the legendary Herbert Chapman. But they were quite different individuals – Chapman had played league football, Brown had not. And unlike Chapman, the Wednesday boss did not welcome personal publicity and was stand-offish with the press.

In his book *Wednesday!*, author Keith Farnsworth made the following observation, 'There is not much doubt that a vital clue to the success was the appointment of Chris Craig [as trainer], who virtually overnight, instilled in the players a spirit and a quality of endurance which provided the basis for a positive, determined attitude … they became a team of great triers, 90-minute men who refused to accept defeat … Craig a Scot from Forfarshire, had the football and medical knowledge, and the personality, which earned him the respect of the players.'

Months later, tragedy – while on holiday in the summer of 1933 Bob Brown's wife passed away. Weeks later early into the new season, after having been diagnosed with high blood pressure, Brown resigned.

On 23 September 1933 the *Star Green'Un* reported, 'Robert Brown had resigned his position as secretary-manager of Sheffield Wednesday and that his resignation had been accepted was the news sprung upon the football world yesterday. Mr Brown lost his wife during the past summer, and he has been ill for some weeks.' A matter-of-fact statement and no more.

For his last game in charge the team received positive coverage in the *Sheffield Independent*, whose reporter had 'never seen Wednesday play such beautiful football for a couple of years – since the great days of the Championship years. Some of the movements were really remarkable … Wednesday's improvement compared to previous home games was marked. There was more sparkle and dash, the play was more open.'

After his departure, Brown's health having shown some improvement, he worked as a scout for several clubs and lived on Wadsley Lane in Sheffield.

Sadly, while working as a scout for Chelsea, he collapsed on a station platform at Leeds railway station and died the following morning in the Leeds General Infirmary.

On a separate note, local club Mexborough FC had cause to be grateful to the Wednesday manager in 1932/33 – he loaned three players to the club, and their chairman commented in the

South Yorkshire Times and Mexborough & Swinton Times on 26 May 1933, 'There would have been no Mexborough Football Club now if it had not been for Mr Bob Brown of Sheffield Wednesday.'

Born:	1872 (Date not known), Hebburn, Co. Durham
Died:	7 March 1935
Appointed:	24 June 1920
Departed:	21 September 1933
First game:	28 August 1920: Barnsley (a), Second Division, drew 0-0
Last game:	16 September 1933: Middlesbrough (h), First Division, won 3-0
Best league season:	1928/29, 1929/30 First Division champions

Record	P	W	D	L	F	A	Win%
League	552	248	126	178	977	823	44.9%
FA Cup	37	16	8	13	70	49	43.2%
Total	**589**	**264**	**134**	**191**	**1047**	**872**	**44.8%**

3

Billy Walker

TOM MUIRHEAD, manager of St Johnstone, was offered and accepted the position to succeed Bob Brown. The Scottish club refused to release Muirhead from his contract and he had to withdraw his interest in Wednesday.

As a result at the age of 36, William Henry 'Billy' Walker successfully applied for the role – making him the youngest managerial appointment at the club.

This was Walker's first managerial position – the *Birmingham Daily Gazette* noted it came 'after he had for a few months studied office routine which goes with the job of managership'.

As a player described as 'a fine tactician and lethal marksman, Walker was idolised at Aston Villa', and considered one of their finest-ever players. A one-club man, he scored a record 244 goals in 531 appearances for the Midlands club and in his debut season, 1920/21, was an FA Cup winner.

He gained 18 caps for England – returning to captain the team after a five-year absence, for the game against Austria at Wembley in 1932.

Walker had his own strong views on management – clearly not courting popularity, he parted company with such established Hillsborough favourites as Ernest Blenkinsop, Jack Leach and Harry Burgess, while bringing in Jack Palethorpe, Joe Nibloe and Wilf Sharp among others.

He tried – and failed – to sign two famous footballers of the day, Tommy Lawton and Stanley Matthews. The move for Lawton – a future England international centre-forward – may well have been successful had it not been for his mother's intervention. Quoted in *Billy Walker: Once, Twice, Three Times a Winner*, Lawton said, 'Mr Walker was very nice to me. He offered me lodgings and to give me ten shillings a week pocket money. My mother thought I was too young to go so far away on my own, so the matter was dropped.'

On his arrival at Sheffield 6 the club were struggling in 19th position in the First Division table – he quickly asserted his own management style and the team went on a 12-game unbeaten run, finishing the season 11th, firmly in mid-table.

In his first full season in charge, 1934/35, Wednesday won the FA Cup for the first time in 28 years defeating West Bromwich Albion 4-2 at Wembley – the game described as 'the most thrilling postwar cup final'.

The front-page headline of the *Sheffield Independent* after the Wembley triumph, 'GALA WELCOME FOR CUP HEROES Victorious Heroes in Triumphant City Procession' – the newspaper reported on the cup winners' Saturday evening banquet at the Russell Hotel in London and in particular on Walker's words, 'Mr Walker said he had had faith in his team all along. He knew they could do it. It was a work of art getting the best out of footballers at times. Some required "the whip" whereas others had to be cajoled into doing the right thing. His captain [Ronnie Starling] came into the latter category. He considered Starling one of the greatest inside-forwards of postwar football and he would not change his team for the Arsenal or any other.'

Coupled with the FA Cup success, Wednesday had a good season in the First Division, finishing third in the table.

The following year brought a marked change of fortunes – a battle to avoid relegation. 'The danger bells really began clanging for Wednesday when the defence, which had been their mainstay, considered by some to be the strongest in the league, suddenly started shipping goals at an alarming rate – 17 of them in three consecutive games,' said author Edward Giles in *Billy Walker: Once, Twice, Three Times a Winner*.

The relegation picture was only cleared up on the last day of the season – with Wednesday on the right side of the line, finishing third from bottom, condemning Blackburn Rovers and Aston Villa to the drop.

That season brought Wednesday's one and only success in the FA Charity Shield – defeating league champions Arsenal 1-0 in October 1935.

Prior to the start of the 1936/37 campaign, an article in the *Sunderland Daily Echo* focussed on team formations, stating, 'We will see more converts to the five forward attack plan and less of the W formation ... Billy Walker the Sheffield Wednesday manager has stated that his team is to be one of those that do it.'

Formation change, or not, things got worse – relegation at the end of 1936/37. And that followed a dramatic decline over the second half of the season – after the first 21 league games Wednesday had achieved 18 points and looked relatively comfortable; the second 21 games were a very different story with four wins, four draws, 12 points and bottom of the division with 30 points.

'Shortcomings in attack were a main reason for Wednesday's downfall [scoring 53 goals] ... Injuries and inconsistencies in team selection were other contributory factors,' continued Edward Giles.

Maybe the manager had been distracted towards the end of that relegation season. An interesting snippet in the local newspaper: Billy Walker was fined 7s 6d (37.5p) for keeping a dog – a fox terrier – without a licence on 21 April 1937. Walker said in the *Penistone, Stocksbridge and Hoyland Gazette* on 5 June, 'I thought the wife had taken one out.'

No consolation in the FA Cup – exiting the tournament at the fourth-round stage.

Into the new season and Wednesday really struggling – after 14 games, 21st in the Second Division with a miserly total of eight points.

Evidently, shareholders directed their anger at the manager after yet another defeat – this time at Barnsley in early November, Wednesday now 22nd and bottom of the Second Division.

Events progressed and chairman W.G. Turner accepted Walker's consequent resignation on 9 November 1937.

In the local *Green 'Un Sports Special* on 13 November, 'The week has been one of the most momentous in the history of Sheffield Wednesday, with the resignation of Mr W.H. Walker, the secretary-manager, and its acceptance. One regrets the parting. During his four years at Hillsborough "Billy" has experienced the sweets of success and the bitterness of failure, but I know he would have liked to have stopped in a last attempt to save the club from relegation.'

The *Leicester Evening Mail* noted, 'It was perhaps unfortunate for Billy Walker that he took up the reins at Sheffield in a blaze of glory, taking his team to a cup final victory in his first season. Thus, he set himself a tremendously high standard to maintain.

'He had whetted the Wednesday fans' appetite for great things and when the slump came – caused more or less by too many players getting old together – the cheers gave way to wholehearted condemnation until manager Walker apparently finds the situation rather intolerable.'

Walker went on to be appointed manager at newly formed non-league Chelmsford City in January 1938 as the Essex club moved from amateur status to semi-professional – one of his first signings: ex-Wednesday player Jackie Palethorpe, a goalscorer for the club in the 1935 FA Cup Final.

His time in this role was short-lived – returning to league football as Nottingham Forest manager in March 1939. He was at the helm when Forest were relegated to the Third Division South in 1949, returning to the Second Division two seasons later, and he led them back into the First Division in 1957, enjoying an FA Cup triumph in 1959.

He therefore achieved a hat-trick of FA Cup wins with three different clubs – as a player with Aston Villa and as a manager with Wednesday and Nottingham Forest.

He finished in football management in 1960, subsequently serving on the committee at Nottingham Forest until his death in 1964.

Born:	29 October 1897, Wednesbury
Died:	30 November 1964
Appointed:	8 December 1933
Departed:	8 November 1937
First game:	9 December 1933: Liverpool (a), First Division, won 3-1
Last game:	6 November 1937: Barnsley (a), Second Division, lost 4-1
Best league season:	1934/35 First Division, third; 1934/35 FA Cup winners

Record	P	W	D	L	F	A	Win%
League	165	53	48	64	236	269	32.1%
FA Cup	17	10	4	3	35	20	58.8%
Total	**182**	**63**	**52**	**67**	**271**	**289**	**34.6%**

4

Jimmy McMullan

SCOTSMAN MCMULLAN started his playing career as a wing-half with Denny Hibs (Stirlingshire), then on to Partick Thistle before moving south to become player-manager at non-league Maidstone United. A successful period with the Kent club before he returned to Thistle in 1923. He joined Manchester City in 1926.

He gained 16 Scotland caps – including one as captain of the famous 'Wembley Wizards' who defeated England 5-1 in March 1928. He was acclaimed as 'one of the finest half-backs Scotland has ever produced'.

An oddity to his international career – he played for England against his native Scotland at Celtic Park, Glasgow in June 1918 before he played for the Scottish national team.

At club level he was regarded as one of Manchester City's greatest-ever players and in 1977 McMullan was one of 11 players who had streets named after them on a new estate in Moss Side – Jimmy McMullan Walk, Moss Side the area where City's Maine Road ground was located.

His managerial career began at Oldham Athletic in 1933 before a brief spell at Aston Villa and then Notts County before having the opportunity to succeed Billy Walker at Sheffield 6.

Rumours circulated that McMullan was in the frame for the positions at Hillsborough and also at Manchester United. It prompted the chairman at Notts County to state, 'There is no change contemplated in regard to the management of the club.

Mr McMullan is under an agreement with the club. There is no question of his going.' The *Sheffield Independent* reported on 29 November 1937 that, when questioned about it, Jimmy said the whole thing had come as a 'thunderbolt', albeit he accepted his chairman's position on the matter.

Less than a month later, in the *Leicester Evening Mail*, the columnist 'Crusader' was intent on making a point, 'Recently in these columns I mentioned that Jimmy McMullan, manager of Notts County, would take over a similar post at Sheffield Wednesday. This was denied by the Notts County club, and manager McMullan wisely kept silent on the matter, but my information was not hearsay. It was based on inside information.'

McMullan had accepted Wednesday's terms to join as manager subject to Notts County agreeing to his release – his release confirmed on 29 December. It had taken almost two months to appoint him as Billy Walker's successor.

At the time of his arrival, Wednesday were struggling in the Second Division – McMullan more than steadied the ship with a record of more than a point a game until the end of the season, albeit relegation only avoided by wins in the last two games of the season, finishing 17th.

The following season – the last before the war intervened to curtail league football – Wednesday made a concerted bid for promotion, pipped at the post by their cross-city rivals in the last game of the season for elevation to the top flight. They finished third and missed out on promotion by one point.

'Looker-On' in the *Sheffield Independent* observed on 8 May 1939, 'There is sympathy for Sheffield Wednesday on missing promotion by one point. They have contributed valiantly to a wonderful season for Sheffield football, and it is quite probable that they will join United in the Upper Circle a year hence. They have the players.'

Wednesday progressed to the fifth round of the FA Cup that season – playing eight games; five of those were replays.

Prior to the start of the 1939/40 season the *Daily Herald* reported, 'In the opinion of Jimmy McMullan, the Sheffield Wednesday team which just missed promotion last season will be good enough to win it next. There is a good mixture of youth and experience at Hillsborough and [he] is not a bit scared of his reserves not coming up to scratch when needed.'

On the Saturday before the season's start, F.G. Walters, in the *Star Green'Un*, wrote, 'Beaten on the promotion push last season by one point, Sheffield Wednesday should be assured of an important part in the struggle to reach the First Division this time around … When I spoke about the possibilities to Jimmy McMullan, I said to him, "I take it you are expecting a good season."

"'I would much rather you said I am hoping for a good season," replied the Wednesday manager. "I have been too long in the game to expect anything."

'In this instance, however, I think the margin between expectation and hope is next to nothing.'

In the event we would never know. Only three league games were possible at the start of that season, one win and two defeats – the start of the Second World War led to McMullan being given a temporary contract at Hillsborough and one where he was effectively Wednesday's part-time manager, taking a full-time job in a local factory.

Fuel shortages and restrictions on travel meant that the makeshift football competitions introduced were played on a regional basis.

Because it was wartime, clubs were all but closed down during the week, with perhaps a couple of evenings training the only sign of activity at the grounds apart from on matchdays.

Wednesday participated in a truncated East Midlands Regional Division, a North Regional League formed for 1940/41 and two competitions for the Football League North held in 1941/42.

And given the nature of wartime, guest players were a common occurrence for many teams – in September 1940, Notts County, the visitors at Hillsborough, had all 'guest players'.

Reports at the time suggested that McMullan may not have had the toughness for the manager's job, being described as a man of 'charm and modesty'– apparently lacking the directness with his older players, wanting them simply to utilise their skills.

For the younger players he wanted them to follow the lead of their older team-mates and in particular to use their energy to tire out the opposition's older players and exploit that tiredness towards the end of the game.

In those first three years of wartime competitions, Wednesday struggled – losing more games than they won. As a result, once McMullan's temporary contract had ended in April 1942 it was not renewed. Vice-chairman William Fearnehough commented, 'We've not fallen out with Jimmy, but feel our decision is in the best interests of everyone in the present circumstances.'

McMullan made a statement to the *Sheffield Telegraph*, 'Wednesday know their business best. The war has caused many upheavals and it is my misfortune that I have become one of the victims, for I believe if there had been no war I should have been with Wednesday for some years. I had a good side together and had some promising youngsters ready to bring in before the war came. In 16 months, I had lifted the team from the foot of the table into the promotion race.

'It is not easy to run a team in wartime. Clubs equally as famous as Wednesday have had bad times and I question whether any other manager would have done better in the circumstances. I admit things have not gone well. Some clubs and managers, however, have been better placed than Wednesday, and have been able to retain – or obtain fairly regularly – the services of first-class men in key positions. I have tried to do my best and have no regrets on that score.'

McMullan was lost to football management after his spell at Sheffield 6.

He passed away on the same date – 28 November 1964 – as his predecessor at Hillsborough, Billy Walker.

Born: 26 March 1895, Scotland
Died: 28 November 1964
Appointed: 3 January 1938
Departed: April 1942
First game: 8 January 1938: Burnley (h), FA Cup third
                round, drew 1-1
Last game: 29 April 1939: Tottenham Hotspur (h),
                Second Division, won 1-0
Best league season: 1938/39 Second Division, third

Record	P	W	D	L	F	A	Win%
League	61	28	15	18	110	82	45.9%
FA Cup	10	2	6	2	11	12	20.0%
Total	**71**	**30**	**21**	**20**	**121**	**94**	**42.2%**

(Wartime football excluded)

5

Eric Taylor

ERIC WOODHOUSE Taylor was born in 1912 at Birley Carr in Sheffield. His working life commenced in a law firm – an advertisement for an office boy at a city football club changed the direction of his career and life. At the time of his job application, he did not know whether the future employer would be Wednesday or United. He was delighted when he learned it was his club – Wednesday.

The new position of office boy was created in 1929 – working for secretary-manager Bob Brown.

Keith Farnsworth observed in *Sheffield Wednesday: A Complete Record 1867–1987*, 'It was said that Brown was given an assistant as reward for winning the league championship.'

In October 1934 Taylor was promoted to assistant secretary to Billy Walker, before succeeding McMullan as secretary-manager in 1942. Taylor had not played professional football.

Interesting to note that the Taylors' wedding reception was held at Hillsborough in 1938 – many decades before any corporate hospitality arrived in football.

When taking over from McMullan, the normal programme of league and cup games had been suspended. During the war Taylor worked part-time at Howell's Tube Works – no doubt focussed on supporting the war effort.

The team, in Taylor's first season in charge, reached the League North War Cup Final, losing 4-3 to Blackpool over two legs – it is worth pointing out that several of the players unavailable to McMullan had returned to play for the club.

The Football League North was created soon after Taylor's appointment – two separate competitions taking place in each of its first three seasons, then one competition in 1945/46. Underlining the priorities of wartime – Wednesday had 40 players in the armed services in 1943/44.

One further anomaly of the time – Wednesday played in blue and white hooped shirts for the first and only time in 1945/46.

After the end of hostilities in 1945 Taylor was formally appointed full-time secretary-manager on 14 June 1945. He demonstrated he was an able manager – albeit he left the day-to-day training, coaching and tactical matters to his coaches – at the outset Bill Knox and later Alan Brown and Jack Marshall (two future Wednesday managers).

Normal league competitions resumed in 1946/47 and it was a difficult time for Wednesday – in the Second Division and finishing one place above relegation. Significant improvement over the next two campaigns – fourth and eighth positions respectively.

Taylor was at the helm when the club were promoted in 1949/50 – finishing in second place and promoted on goal difference; the team they pipped – cross-city rivals United.

The 1950s dubbed the 'Yo-Yo Years' for the club – Wednesday relegated and then promoted three times during the decade. The progression of league finishes from 1950/51 under Taylor underlines that pattern: 21st in the First Division; first in the Second Division; 18th, 19th and 22nd in the First Division; first in the Second Division; 14th and 22nd in the First Division.

Taylor at the helm for Wednesday's worst defeat in the Sheffield derby, a 7-3 reverse at Bramall Lane in September 1951.

An FA Cup semi-final defeat in 1954 the only significant cup campaign during the decade.

That third relegation at the end of the 1957/58 season prompted the board of directors to end Taylor's responsibility as team manager, and enable him to focus on matters off the field as the club's general manager.

The *Star Green 'Un* on 5 July 1958 headlined 'Sheffield Wednesday make dramatic change in policy – Team Manager to Relieve Eric Taylor of Dual Job'.

Chairman Dr Andrew Stephen was at pains to emphasise that 'the directors had complete confidence in Eric Taylor and valued the very fine work he had done'. For his part, Taylor concentrated on the administration of the club and all matters except team affairs.

Interesting to recall the tactics employed by Taylor when he was team manager – definitely long-ball!

An insight is provided by Rob Sawyer's biography of Catterick, *Harry Catterick: The Untold Story of a Football Great*, in which he highlighted that 'a former RAF officer had analysed all the matches played by Wednesday', and added, 'The resultant charts were studied and tactics made to suit.'

In the same book, Catterick said, 'The more often the ball was in the opponents' half, and penalty area in particular, the more often were Wednesday likely to score.

'Players in defence must not hold the ball but get it first-time into the opponents' half or, better still, penalty area. No passes between defenders in their half of the field.

'Forwards were instructed to shoot at goal whenever possible and get X number of shots per match or they would be dropped.'

Wednesday's England international centre-half Peter Swan confirmed to the *Sheffield Star* in 1977, 'I was not allowed to pass the ball more than ten yards. It was big boot, long ball stuff because the plan was to get the ball into the opposition's penalty area as quickly, and as often, as possible.'

Swan's assessment of the manager, in *Peter Swan: Setting The Record Straight* – 'Taylor was a brilliant man who'd worked up from being an office boy to being team manager and general manager. He was a smart man and was never out of a collar and tie and looked like a businessman. He was very shrewd and everybody respected him. But I can't remember him ever giving a bollocking to anybody and he didn't look like the type who could do that.'

And Swan could not recollect Taylor ever giving a team talk – Taylor limited his words to the players before a game to 'go out and enjoy it'. He had limited knowledge of the game from a tactical perspective, Swan confirming that Wednesday's football was 'not pretty to watch'.

Training evidently consisted largely of running. As Swan commented, 'We were sometimes given a ball at the end of the training session and allowed to play five-a-side in a tiny gym underneath the stand, but apart from that, we didn't see a ball until the Saturday.'

Add to this that Wednesday still did not have a training ground of their own – they trained at the local greyhound track at Owlerton, except on those days when the greyhounds took precedence (greyhound time trials for example), so then they trained in Hillsborough Park.

Looking at his time in charge, the manager proved to be an astute dealer in the transfer market – for example Eddie Quigley had been bought for £12,000 from Bury in 1947 and sold for a record fee of £26,000 two years later to Preston North End.

He paid a British record fee of £35,000 for Jackie Sewell from Notts County – a move that Sewell was not at all keen to take initially, wanting to maintain his partnership with fellow England international Tommy Lawton. He changed his mind 'because Eric Taylor was so persuasive, but also that Eric was a gentleman and had treated him impeccably' as written in *Eric Taylor: A Biography*.

The transfer of Ron Springett from Third Division Queens Park Rangers for £10,000 in 1958 had a couple of interesting aspects to it – with interest from several clubs, most notably Sunderland, Taylor matched the terms the Wearside club had offered and agreed to let Springett train in London with his old club QPR and travel to Sheffield for games.

And he made it clear to Springett that with a move to Wednesday he'd become England's international goalkeeper within three years (he achieved that within half the time and went on to make 33 appearances for the national team).

Springett described Taylor as a 'father figure'. Others described him as a perfect gentleman and someone who commanded great respect.

An interesting aspect of Taylor's handling of players he wanted to attract to the club focussed on the route they took from the two city railway stations, Midland and Victoria, to Hillsborough. 1950s Sheffield was an industrial city with smoke belching across the steel mills and factories. Taylor steadfastly avoided this industrial landscape and instead ensured players and their wives saw the picturesque Rivelin Valley on the way to the ground.

As well as transfer dealings, homegrown players came to the fore during the Taylor years – among them Redfern Froggatt, Derek Dooley, Hugh Swift, Albert Quixall, Alan Finney and Johnny Fantham.

Taylor took great pride in his club and considered the second team in Sheffield to be Sheffield Wednesday Reserves. He enjoyed visits to London for away games – staying overnight on the Friday and enabling the players to enjoy a West End show on that night. This contrasted with the club across the city who evidently travelled to the capital on the Saturday morning and returned that evening.

An event that rocked football and particularly rocked Sheffield Wednesday – the betting scandal exposed in 1964 tore into the very heart of the game. It was described as the 'greatest sporting scandal of the century'.

Many players from different clubs were embroiled in the scandal – the highest-profile of whom were Wednesday's England international centre-half Peter Swan and his team-mates David Layne and Tony Kay. They were accused and found guilty of betting on Wednesday to lose a game they were playing in, at Ipswich Town in November 1962, which was lost 2-0.

National headlines when the scandal broke in April 1964 – immediate suspension of the players and a lifetime ban from the game subsequently imposed by the Football Association.

It was Eric Taylor who fielded all the calls and communications to the club from the outside media; Taylor who steadied the ship at Hillsborough when faced with a whirlwind of accusations and recriminations; Taylor who fronted and addressed the supporters at half-time in the first game after the scandal had broken – using the public address system, contemporary reports describe his speech as impassioned and 'Churchillian' in pulling the supporters together.

His club – our club – was reeling and almost on its knees. He made sure that Sheffield Wednesday came together and rode the storm of the greatest scandal.

Derek Dooley, Wednesday player and manager and a legend in the city, observed in *Dooley! The Autobiography of a Soccer Legend*, 'Over the years it was often said that the man they called "Mister Sheffield Wednesday" had too much power, but even his critics admitted he was never guilty of abusing his authority and nobody could ever say he ever failed to give his heart and soul to the club's cause. Eric didn't do what he did for personal gain, he did it for Wednesday.'

After the arrival of Harry Catterick as team manager in 1958, Taylor's great focus was Hillsborough and the development of the ground, and he made a great success of it – the new North Stand opened in 1961, the South Stand paddock converted to all seating in 1965, the West Stand opened in 1966 – hosting four games at the 1966 World Cup and numerous FA Cup semi-finals. At the time Hillsborough was considered by many to be the best-appointed football ground outside of Wembley – the 'Wembley of the North'.

Many observers in the media considered Wednesday's investment in the development of the ground to be of long-term financial benefit for the club.

No doubt Taylor would have been a proud man when Hillsborough was confirmed as the best provincial ground in the 1966 World Cup.

Unfortunately, the very positive off-field developments were not matched by progress on the field. Quite the reverse.

The supporters' views? Given the substantial majority were those who stood on the terraces, no doubt they would have preferred financial resources to be better apportioned to developing the team.

Certainly, that was the view of Dad, Uncle Ray and Uncle Tony – they could not have been clearer on the point. Indeed, it's worth noting the one part of the ground untouched during Taylor's time in charge was the Spion Kop (excepting a new electronic scoreboard installed for the 1966 World Cup) – it remained uncovered and therefore open to the elements.

With Taylor's organisational skills and standing in football administration he was offered, and turned down, the role of executive secretary in the newly formed US professional league under Phil Woosnam.

In 1967 the general manager suffered a near-fatal car crash on Rivelin Valley Road in Sheffield which affected him significantly – many said he was never the same person again. He handed over secretarial duties to his very capable assistant Eric England in 1973 and announced plans for retirement the following year. Sadly, Taylor died in September 1974.

He had given 45 years' loyal service to Wednesday and a testimonial was held for him in October 1974, Wednesday v England XI. Contributions in the testimonial programme underline the esteem he was held in by the football world.

Former Manchester United manager Sir Matt Busby, 'Eric was a great friend and a great organiser, as I knew from personal experience. He always had a sense of humour, and even under stress had a happy disposition. He made a great contribution to football.'

Former FIFA president Sir Stanley Rous, 'He was a man of vision and a most capable organiser … He was proud of his club and always sought opportunities to show its splendid facilities to visitors.'

Ex-Southampton manager Ted Bates, 'As chairman of the Football League SMA [Secretary Managers' Association] he worked ceaselessly on behalf of its members to improve the Football League Pension Scheme … a great champion of managers … he gave a lot of time to people in the game.'

A less positive view of Taylor's contribution to the club came from Wednesday's Scottish international midfielder Jim McCalliog in *Wembley Wins Wembley Woes*, 'I love Sheffield Wednesday, his decisions were to the detriment of the club, so why would he be called Mr Sheffield Wednesday? He and the board have a lot to answer for in the 60s and 70s.'

Undoubtedly, Eric Taylor's contribution to the development of Hillsborough was immense. His impact on the development of the playing side was at the very least problematic. Many supporters of the time would echo McCalliog's view.

In his time at Sheffield 6, Taylor lived in the Fulwood district of the city on Tom Lane.

Born:	22 May 1912, Sheffield
Died:	23 September 1974
Appointed:	Summer 1942
Departed:	26 June 1958
First game:	5 January 1946: Mansfield Town (a), FA Cup third round, drew 0-0
Last game:	26 April 1958: Wolverhampton Wanderers (h), Second Division, won 2-1
Best league season:	1956/57 First Division, 14th

Record	P	W	D	L	F	A	Win%
League	504	182	120	202	874	899	36.1%
FA Cup	35	14	8	13	58	47	40.0%
Total	**539**	**196**	**128**	**215**	**932**	**946**	**36.3%**

6

Harry Catterick

THE 1957/58 season had been calamitous for Wednesday – the 'yo-yo' tag in full swing as the club finished bottom of the First Division and were relegated with a paltry 31 points.

With the announcement that the dual role of secretary-manager was no more, the position was advertised (at a cost of over £100, reported the *Star Green'Un*) and applications invited for the role of team manager – one man responsible for coaching the first team and scouting.

The board's preferred choice for the position was a Yorkshireman, the soon-to-be Tottenham Hotspur manager, Bill Nicholson, and he was offered the job by Eric Taylor.

That offer came after England's early exit from the World Cup in Sweden in 1958 where Nicholson was on coaching duty. Nicholson turned the opportunity down. 'I told him I was happy at Tottenham and did not want to leave,' he said in *Bill Nicholson: Football's Perfectionist*.

Within weeks Nicholson was offered and accepted the manager's job at White Hart Lane – and he became a major rival of Harry Catterick over the next 15 years.

The author Brian Scovell saw similarities between the two men. 'Catterick was a tough disciplinarian who insisted his players should be first to the ball. A student of tactics and an avid reader he shunned publicity,' he wrote in the same book.

With Nicholson not Hillsborough-bound, press speculation on who would take the Wednesday hot-seat went into overdrive.

Managers apparently in the frame included Raich Carter, Ron Greenwood and Tim Ward. The latter was strongly tipped and had beaten Catterick to the position at Barnsley in 1953.

For his part, Catterick had been a player with Everton before taking his first steps in management at Crewe Alexandra – as player-manager in December 1951. Having failed in his quest for the Barnsley job he took the job at Rochdale in June 1953. Five years at Spotland, which he described as 'five happy years', and he was now looking for the next step up in his career, albeit two years remained on his contract.

Evidently it was a shock to most people when Harry Catterick's appointment was announced at a stormy AGM on 14 August 1958. Harry was not the proverbial big-hitter – he had managed two struggling Lancashire clubs.

But he had impressed the board – vice-chairman Mr F. Gardiner was quoted in the *Star*, 'We interviewed a number of people who had experience with the top clubs but felt that perhaps they were on the way down. Catterick impressed us with his positive approach and forceful personality. We had a few problems then and felt that Catterick might be the man to sort them out.'

Catterick informed the *Star* about his appointment, 'I had a tip to apply, subsequently getting on the shortlist. By some coincidence on arrival for the interview I saw Tim Ward who was being interviewed for the same position.'

He was appointed on a reported salary of £1,800 a year. The new Wednesday manager left Rochdale on good terms albeit that club insisted he work his notice period.

Wednesday's first programme of the season commented, 'Let there be a warm welcome for Mr Harry Catterick, who has been appointed team manager and who will enter upon his duties in the next few days.' Those few days meant a 1 September start.

Asked by the *Star* about his priority in the new role he was clear, 'Get Wednesday back into the First Division, that is their proper place … there's nothing more I love than a fight.' His wife Nancy was also interviewed and she observed, 'Whether Rochdale win, lose or draw Harry never shows his feelings. It is the same about this new move but I feel deep down that he is very pleased.'

And for Catterick, a first at Hillsborough – the first manager whose sole responsibilities focussed on the players and the team.

Catterick's first season in charge was a successful one – champions of the Second Division. The programme for the final home game against Barnsley commented, 'In the handing out of bouquets there must be one to Mr Harry Catterick who in his first season as team manager, has had the pleasure of controlling a promotion-winning side. He has had his problems but it must have been satisfying to see our schoolboy signings such as John Fantham, Peter Swan and Tony Kay make the grade and firmly establish themselves.'

Add to that a club record haul of 106 goals in a season. The Second Division championship in 1959/60 remains the last league title won by the club.

Catterick was unhappy with his financial rewards after getting Wednesday promoted and doing well in their first season back in the top flight – finishing fifth; an excellent league season. He requested an increase to his salary. No such increase was forthcoming – an offer of £1,000 instead from the board of directors for progress made.

In mid-April 1960 Catterick requested a release from his contract – in his press statement, 'A Football League club of considerable repute, offered the position of manager with full control of playing matters, a five-year contract and an increase in salary of some 40 per cent.'

The club concerned was never identified, albeit representatives of Everton – one a lawyer – had called at Catterick's home, asking if he'd be interested in the manager's job at Goodison Park.

Wednesday were not prepared to match the offer and not prepared to release their manager from his contractual obligations.

Rob Sawyer, Catterick's biographer, observed in *Harry Catterick: The Untold Story of a Football Great*, 'Complaining to the press was a method he would use at all the clubs he managed.'

In September 1960 Nottingham Forest interviewed Catterick for their managerial position – with an increase to his current salary.

Prior to the board meeting to discuss the matters, Catterick changed his position – commenting in the *Star*, 'I stayed because of my love for the team ... and the public were behind me. I hoped that in future the board would make an offer of a more substantial salary.'

And his love for the team was more than justified – finishing the 1960/61 season as runners-up to the double-winning Spurs, and Wednesday the first team to defeat Spurs that season with a raucous Hillsborough rocking in November 1960 as the home team ran out 2-1 winners.

For good measure there was significant progress in two of Catterick's three seasons in the FA Cup – defeated semi-finalists in 1959/60, and quarter-finalists in 1960/61.

I've no doubt I saw Harry Catterick's team play – unfortunately I cannot recollect it. I was atop Dad's shoulders at the age of three watching Wednesday take on all comers from the Spion Kop.

Talking years later with Dad, Uncle Ray and Uncle Tony – Wednesdayites to their core – each of them had said the appointment of Catterick at the beginning of the 1958/59 season had not set supporters alight with expectation.

Three full seasons later they – and all the club's supporters – could see the substantial achievements Catterick had made and the great progress the club had made: Second Division champions, fifth in the top flight and then runners-up in 1960/61.

The future beckoned and looked very promising – Wednesday most definitely on the up, and for the first time since the 1930s, winning trophies a real possibility.

Keith Farnsworth observed in *Wednesday!*, 'Catterick's success was largely achieved with the players who had been on the club's books at the time of his arrival. His strength as a manager was his ability to command the respect of his players and his capacity to extend themselves and play to their full potential. He was a hard taskmaster and a tough disciplinarian, direct and determined, a man whose no-nonsense attitude left no one in doubt about what would happen if he didn't get what he wanted. He also refused to accept any interference in what he regarded as his domain.'

No question players were developed by Catterick – Ron Springett, Peter Swan and Tony Kay gained their first international caps in the manager's time at Sheffield 6. Future captain Don Megson had arrived at the club as a left-winger – it was Catterick who persuaded him that left-back was the better position for him to make a career, and his 442 appearances for Wednesday bear clear testament to that.

Farnsworth went on to point out that Catterick made a key decision in appointing Tommy Eggleston as trainer-coach in 1958. It enabled the pair to be 'a formidable partnership' – a partnership that laid the ground for the success over the next three years.

Peter Swan observed in *Setting The Record Straight*, 'Catterick was a hard man and I liked that type of manager because he'd give you a good bollocking when you needed it. He was quite a big guy who spoke with a lot of authority, so you wouldn't mess about … when you'd had a good game, he would congratulate you, saying something like, "Brilliant, you've done a good job today."'

Training facilities at this time were basic – changing at Hillsborough and then walking to the training ground at Middlewood Road.

Swan confirmed that training consisted mainly of running laps round the pitch, followed by sprinting and then a game would finish the training session off. Very little was done with the ball.

Catterick was clearly thorough in his preparation and requirements – he'd talk to players individually and explain what he wanted them to do and let them know about the opposition and individual players they were facing. Tactics and set pieces came to the fore – a particular formation they adopted had Swan as part of a 'swivel formation' at the back with Tom McAnearney and Tony Kay providing cover if one of them was attacking down one side; the other would stay back, more or less in the centre of the pitch – the defence was therefore not caught flat. It meant the team were more flexible – under Eric Taylor they were essentially square at the back.

Peter Eustace, the midfielder and future Wednesday manager, was an apprentice during Catterick's time at Hillsborough. He said in Keith Farnsworth's *Wednesday Every Day of the Week*, 'Harry Catterick never really spoke to me, but I recall that, after Derek Dooley had asked him to take a look at the juniors and he'd watched us play for about ten minutes, he always gave me a sweet whenever he passed in the corridor. He didn't say a word, but just put his hand in his pocket and offered me a sweet – and, as I took it to mean he must be pleased with me, it was a gesture which made me feel good!'

Don Megson's view, told to the *Star* in 1977, 'Harry Catterick was a man completely without frills and this was the character of our football of the time. We were skilful, hard and forceful and we soon found that he had the personality to command discipline. You were under no illusions as to what he wanted from you, as far as we were concerned, we had a job to do on Saturday and nothing else mattered. Under Eric Taylor we had the tag "The Yo-Yo team" and Harry's mindset was, "That isn't going to happen to me."'

Catterick was very keen to sign the centre-forward Joe Baker from Hibernian – a £50,000 offer was rejected by the Edinburgh club, the board refused to increase Wednesday's offer. Catterick's contention was that Baker would have enabled the jigsaw to be completed and Wednesday would win the league championship in 1961/62. We'll never know.

Behind the scenes, Peter Swan felt the relationship between Eric Taylor and Harry Catterick was not good – players evidently only had the benefit of hearsay but it was clear to them the relationship was not as it should be.

It was more than not good – Taylor's focus was on the ground and the facilities at Hillsborough – and in *Harry Catterick: The Untold Story of a Football Great*, Rob Sawyer reflected an incident one winter's morning where there were no satisfactory training facilities: the only alternative that Catterick could see was to have a single-file circuit within the North Stand. Taylor apparently sent a note to Catterick informing him that the training session had to stop because it would damage the stand and create dust. Catterick had no time for such an instruction and carried on.

The matter was reported by Taylor to the chairman – the upshot according to Catterick was 'that Eric no longer spoke to me but sent typewritten messages across a 12-foot corridor from his office to mine. I would sometimes receive as many as seven or eight notes, headed as "Internal Communications" each day. I found the situation ludicrous.'

All the players were shocked by Catterick's departure, announced after the game against Leicester City on 10 April 1961 – they all liked and respected him. He called the players in to talk with them individually.

Eric Taylor was back in temporary charge after Catterick departed – but he retained Catterick's style of play, not the direct style of play employed when he had previously been in charge.

Catterick reflected after he had left the club, 'The ambitions of Mr Taylor and I just did not mix. Mr Taylor's number one aim was the improvement of Hillsborough as a soccer stadium. My number one aim was the improvement of the team. It was as simple as that. When an unstoppable force meets the immoveable object, something has to give. My departure followed a very stormy scene with Eric Taylor and Dr Stephen. I had been promised an increase in salary and improved contract terms that failed to materialise.'

In a separate observation, Catterick said, 'Eric had built a brick wall around himself – I tried to knock it down and didn't succeed in moving one brick.'

Supporters had seen a golden chance for success thrown away by the club as Catterick departed. They put it down to the board – and particularly Eric Taylor – who they perceived failed to back Catterick's ambition on the playing side with the necessary financial support.

In the *Star Green 'Un* on 15 April, Fred Walters observed, 'It has been evident that something like this would inevitably happen sooner or later.' He went on to comment, 'When Harry

Catterick came to Hillsborough, he got the players to play the only effective style possible, which is based on two hard-working wing-halves and two energetic inside-forwards. This leads to a style of play whereby you have seven men in defence, when necessary, and seven men in attack nearly all the time. This, more than anything, has been the contributing factor to these three very successful playing seasons.'

Catterick joined Everton in April 1961, taking over from the departed Johnny Carey. He was a great success at Everton – winning the First Division in 1962/63 and 1969/70 and, rubbing salt into Wednesday's wounds, the FA Cup in 1965/66. Additionally, he persuaded Wednesday captain and England international Tony Kay to join him on Merseyside.

He moved to a non-executive role at the club in April 1973 before taking up the manager's position at Preston North End in August 1975, staying for two seasons before he left in May 1977.

Catterick subsequently worked as a scout for Southampton during Lawrie McMenemy's time in charge at The Dell.

He passed away at Goodison Park after suffering a heart attack following a game in March 1985.

Born:	26 November 1919, Darlington
Died:	9 March 1985
Appointed:	14 August 1958
Departed:	8 April 1961
First game:	3 September 1958: Stoke City (h), Second Division, won 4-1
Last game:	8 April 1961: Leicester City (h), First Division, drew 2-2
Best league season:	1960/61 First Division, second

Record	P	W	D	L	F	A	Win%
League	119	67	29	23	257	143	56.3%
FA Cup	12	7	2	3	20	10	58.3%
Total	**131**	**74**	**31**	**26**	**277**	**153**	**56.4%**

Note – Catterick did not take charge of the team until 1 September 1958

7

Vic Buckingham

THE FORMER Tottenham Hotspur defender was appointed after the popular Harry Catterick's departure – with the latter's success it was always going to be a challenge for the genial Buckingham.

Unlike both his predecessor and indeed successor Alan Brown, Buckingham has been described as flamboyant – not an adjective readily ascribed to Wednesday managers down the years. Perhaps the nearest equivalent is Ron Atkinson.

In *The Book of Football Obituaries*, Ivan Ponting wrote, 'Vic Buckingham was something of a football romantic. The teams he managed reflected his own natural elegance and flamboyant personality – they were entertaining and aesthetically pleasing … even if they did not achieve consistent success.'

He'd played for his one league club, Tottenham Hotspur, before and after the Second World War.

Buckingham's managerial career began at the London-based amateur club Pegasus, followed by stints at Bradford Park Avenue and West Bromwich Albion – winning the FA Cup with the Midlands club in 1954. He moved abroad to manage Ajax Amsterdam in 1959.

Looking to return to this country, he had verbally agreed to join Plymouth Argyle, then in the Second Division, before being given the green light by that club to join First Division Wednesday in May 1961. Having worked abroad, he applied some of the ideas he'd picked up on the continent – in training a focus on working with the ball. His style of play was different – he wanted the centre-half to play the ball out, the centre-forward to lay it off. He tried to change the style of play almost overnight and in Peter Swan's opinion that was 'asking too much'.

Buckingham had a more relaxed style of management – he did not give players a good bollocking, and in Swan's view he 'couldn't do that'.

One of the manager's quirky mannerisms was to flick the brim of his trilby hat each time he put it on.

And when the team played in London, more often than not one of Buckingham's theatrical friends came into the dressing room – the manager greeting them with a kiss whether they were male or female. Evidently it caused some of the players to question Buckingham's sexuality – albeit they quickly concluded it was simply the way he was.

Among others, the team met stars of the time including Leslie Crowther and Roger Moore.

It seems quite incongruous in early 1960s Sheffield to have such a manager at Wednesday, a club whose supporters were predominantly working class with many employed in the thriving steel mills and factories of the time.

At the start of his first season, 1961/62, Wednesday were among the title favourites having finished runners-up to the double-winning Tottenham Hotspur team the previous campaign.

It didn't happen that way – Wednesday never in contention for the title but they finished a creditable sixth in the top flight. Add to that they reached the quarter-finals in their first campaign in European competition – narrowly losing to Barcelona over two legs in the Inter-Cities Fairs Cup.

Towards the end of that season, in April 1962 the team had a poor run – three defeats in four games – and the manager reacted by implementing training sessions morning and afternoon. Players were not impressed and complained to Eric Taylor that they were being overtrained and were tired for the games on Saturday.

Genial and charming he may have been, but Buckingham was determined and did not shy away from taking his players to task and being critical when required.

He had a fall-out with goalkeeper Ron Springett. The manager had tried to break the terms of the England international's contract and insist he move to Sheffield rather than continue to train in London. Taylor prevailed and Wednesday would not renege on the contractual term.

His second season produced a further sixth-placed finish in the First Division and defeat in the early rounds of the Inter-Cities Fairs Cup and FA Cup. Harry Catterick's Everton won the First Division title.

Towards the end of that season, reports emerged of disharmony between the manager and Jack Mansell who undertook the coaching – evidently the two were not talking.

In his final season, 1963/64, Wednesday again finished a creditable sixth in the table for the third year running.

Under Buckingham, progress in the FA Cup was elusive – exiting at the third-round stage twice and once in the fourth round.

Buckingham left the club two days before the end of the campaign having been informed his contract would not be renewed.

Strong rumours emerged that things were not going well behind the scenes and there was a concern that discipline was lax in the dressing room.

The *Star Green 'Un* reported on 11 April, 'The air around Hillsborough's lofty portals had been filled all week with speculation about the future of the Owls' team boss and in that respect the announcement of his dismissal came as no surprise,' Under the headline 'Such A Complex And Proud Character', Tony Hardisty said that Buckingham was 'outwardly calm at dismissal'.

He went on, 'I have always found the utmost difficulty in deciding just what is going on behind those clear blue eyes for certainly the Owls boss is as proud and complex a character as you will meet in this fascinating game ... in the three years he has been in Sheffield there have not been a handful of men who have really understood him.

'Sheffield Wednesday supporters are starved of success … They pillory the players, of course, but most of all they pillory the man in the hottest seat of all, the team manager.'

Midfielder Peter Eustace recollected in *Wednesday Every Day of the Week*, 'Vic Buckingham was a completely different type from Catterick. He was an extrovert who would talk to anybody, and although I didn't always fully understand what he was saying to me, his words stuck and made a lot of sense as time passed. He would talk about football being a mental game, and describe a good team as a meeting of minds.'

Keith Farnsworth noted in *Sheffield Wednesday: A Complete Record 1867–1987*, 'Buckingham was the elegant and flamboyant Londoner who brought a touch of colour and something of the world of showbusiness to the game. After Catterick he must have seemed nonchalant and easy-going. In truth he did not lack steel in his make-up, but his philosophy was less rigid. If Catterick was the realist, Buckingham was the idealist, the romantic … [he] declined to make his players fit a preconceived format. He wanted them to use their knowledge and experience, urging them to express themselves on the field. He wanted them to entertain.'

On occasion he started a pre-match team talk with the words, 'How shall we play it today, boys?'

Peter Swan, the England international centre-half, made captain by Buckingham after Tony's Kay's departure to Everton, had a good relationship with the manager and said in *Peter Swan: Setting The Record Straight*, 'I was impressed with the fact that Buckingham valued and respected my opinions as captain. He would invite me into his office in the build-up to a game and ask me what I thought about the opposition and discuss tactics. That would never have happened with his predecessors, Eric Taylor or Harry Catterick. They simply told you what they wanted and wouldn't ask you to contribute any ideas.'

Reflecting on the betting scandal which emerged after Buckingham's departure, Ivan Ponting noted in *The Book of*

Football Obituaries, 'When the full facts emerged, Buckingham was mortified that any players of his could be caught up in such dishonesty.'

After Wednesday, Buckingham's next managerial appointment was back at Ajax followed by stints at Fulham, Ethnikos in Greece, Barcelona, Sevilla and back to Ethnikos. His final role as a manager was in Kuwait in the 1990s.

Buckingham's trophy wins were at other clubs – the FA Cup at West Bromwich Albion and domestic trophies at Ajax and Barcelona.

Perhaps his greatest achievement may have been at Ajax – nurturing the talents of a young Johan Cruyff, no question one of the greatest players of all time, and introducing him to first-team football, and in time he aided his transfer to Barcelona.

Born: 23 October 1915, London
Died: 26 January 1995
Appointed: 8 May 1961
Departed: 9 April 1964
First game: 19 August 1961: West Bromwich Albion (a), First Division, won 2-0
Last game: 8 April 1964: Stoke City (h), First Division, won 2-0
Best league season: 1961/62, 1962/63, 1963/64 First Division, sixth

Record	P	W	D	L	F	A	Win%
League	124	57	26	41	229	186	45.9%
FA Cup	8	3	2	3	8	9	37.5%
Fairs Cup	10	5	0	5	25	18	50.0%
Total	**142**	**65**	**28**	**49**	**262**	**213**	**45.7%**

8

Alan Brown

INITIAL SPECULATION on the man to fill the Hillsborough hot-seat after Buckingham focussed on Blackburn Rovers manager Jack Marshall.

Reporting in the *Star Green 'Un*, Tony Hardisty commented on 27 June 1964, 'At any rate he [the new manager] will be a far different personality to Mr Buckingham; more of a realist and more resilient and forthright in his approach to the cut-throat job of guiding a First Division outfit ... more than once I have heard a whisper that Blackburn's Jack Marshall might land the Hillsborough plum and he would seem the kind of man to fill the bill.'

Weeks later, Alan Winston Brown was confirmed as team manager. He was born in Northumberland and played for Huddersfield Town as a centre-half before the Second World War, during the war years working as a physical training instructor in Sheffield, and put in charge of a group of 'Bevin Boys' – boys conscripted to work in the coal mine as part of their compulsory national service.

Additionally, he worked as a coach for the Sheffield and Hallamshire FA.

After the war, at the age of 32 he was snapped up by Burnley and made captain of the Clarets and became a key component of what became known as the 'Iron Curtain' defence. Jimmy Logie, the renowned Arsenal forward who opposed Brown many times, regarded him as 'a frightening individual'.

Ex-Wednesday player Ian Porterfield, who played for Brown at Sunderland, recollected, 'He was as tough as nails. You didn't mess with him.'

Ivan Ponting wrote in *The Book of Football Obituaries*, 'It is difficult to imagine any football manager being harder or straighter than Alan Brown. No club in his charge ever lifted a major trophy, yet he remained a hugely respected if somewhat idiosyncratic member of his profession, his name a byword for truth, frankness and rigid discipline.'

Brown retired from playing at the age of 35 after finishing his career at Notts County.

After a stint at Sheffield 6 as a coach, starting in January 1951, he returned to Turf Moor as Burnley's manager in 1954, taking the reins at Roker Park as Sunderland's manager in 1957.

He guided his boyhood club to promotion to the top flight at the end of the 1963/64 season. Sunderland's directors allegedly reneged on a promise to pay Brown a bonus for his success, and he left Roker.

Hillsborough and Sheffield Wednesday beckoned – in the wake of the illegal betting scandal which had seen David 'Bronco' Layne, Peter Swan and Tony Kay all banned from the game for life.

The *Daily Express* reported on 8 July, 'Alan Brown, the strong man of Sunderland, yesterday tore up the remaining three years of his contract and joined Sheffield Wednesday ... to lead wavering, scandal-hit, bribe-shaken Wednesday.'

Brown said, 'The real job at Roker Park has already been done ... I am attracted to Sheffield Wednesday who are in difficult times.'

Eric Taylor, general manager of Wednesday, said, 'Obviously we have offered a lucrative contract. It is for more than three years.' Taylor promised big signings to come   Jim McCalliog at £37,500, the British record for a teenager in October 1965, and striker John Ritchie for £70,000 in September 1966 the standouts.

On the managerial position the newspaper continued, 'It also carries the rather whimsical title of "labour and productions manager". Under that heading Brown will control the team, tactics, coaching, scouting and buying.'

In the *Star Green 'Un* on 11 July, the new manager said, 'I have a great many friends there [at Wednesday] and I can tell you they are a wonderful club to serve. They have had their share of knocks in recent days but they are a club with grand traditions and a reputation throughout the game for treating their servants very fairly.'

He went on, 'I believe firmly in a high standard of physical fitness, but if my players are prepared to work as I want them to work then we shall get along just fine … Players have no need to fear me – despite the fact that I am tough as teak!'

Brown's application for the post was one of 60, cut down to a shortlist of nine. Eric Taylor stated, 'I am certain the club has made a first-class appointment. He will help to make us one of the outstanding clubs in the country.'

In November 2012, *FourFourTwo* magazine reported, 'The puritanical Brown was seen as the man to cleanse Hillsborough. He was evangelical about his work, quite literally. At Sunderland, he became a member of the Moral Rearmament League, an international organisation which stood for honesty, purity, unselfishness and love.

'To say that Brown went on a moral crusade at Wednesday would be an understatement, and he instructed his players to be whiter than white. "I tell all my lads under the age of 21 that they must never let me see them with a cigarette," he told [*Guardian* and *Observer* journalist] Arthur Hopcraft. "I advise against drink as well – boys may see it and think it's the right thing to do."'

Following the betting scandal revelations, Peter Swan claimed that Brown told him to go home and pray for forgiveness.

The opening paragraph of the *FourFourTwo* article captured key elements of the man – 'Religious zealot, trained in the art of hand-to-hand combat and a pioneer whose training methods and tactical innovations would later influence the likes of Don Revie, Malcolm Allison, Arsène Wenger and José Mourinho. Alan "Bomber" Brown wasn't your average manager.'

Captain Don Megson had these words about the manager, in *Don Megson: A Life In Football*, 'If you wanted to get yourself out of Hillsborough during the mid-1960s, then challenging Alan Brown was the quickest way to find the exit. For four years, he ruled over Hillsborough with an iron fist – it was his way or the highway … Everything about Alan was about power, discipline and moral fortitude.'

Megson recounted that there had been big fall-outs with established first-team players Peter Johnson and Tom McAnearney. Johnson became peripheral to the manager's plans and McAnearney lost the captaincy.

Additionally, McAnearney said that a coaching job promised by Brown never materialised and that despite being at the club over 14 years he was not given a testimonial. He added in *Wednesday Every Day of the Week*, 'I never spoke to Brown again after I left. He was a stubborn man. Once he has made up his mind, there was no changing his opinion – even if he knew he was wrong.'

Wednesday's left-back Norman Curtis, who was coached by Brown, commented in the same book, 'Alan was a hard taskmaster, and he was not a man you could kid. But he was often very kind and sympathetic, sometimes when you didn't expect it.'

Don Megson acknowledged that Brown was 'not an ogre' – highlighting his reaction to David Ford's broken leg at Werder Bremen, helping the player on to and off the aeroplane and driving him home. 'If you were with Alan, he was with you all the way.'

Consistent with the times, there was a low-key introduction for the manager in the home programme for the first game of 1964/65, against Blackburn Rovers, 'It is not proposed to dwell on off-the-park matters since then [the last home game of 1963/64], save to say that we believe this club is now embarking on a new era.

'We have a new manager in Mr Alan Brown … he is happy to return to Sheffield Wednesday and we in turn are happy to have him back, this time of course as team manager.'

Brown's first season in charge was unremarkable, finishing eighth in the First Division and exiting the FA Cup in the third round.

An interesting article appeared in the *Star Green 'Un* in September 1965 – questions put to the Wednesday manager by Tony Hardisty.

'What do you consider the most important element in a manager-player relationship?'

'That's an easy one. The players should have absolute confidence in the integrity of their manager. The mainstay of such a relationship lies with the manager, who on no account should divulge to a soul even the smallest word given in confidence without the permission of the player ... there can be no advance of ideas without such a relationship. It is very, very important.'

'You have told me that the principles of Moral Rearmament have played an important part in your life in recent years. Just how big a part do these principles affect your professional life?'

'There is really only one course of action to take – begin with yourself and set the best possible example. But I do not discuss my own personal beliefs with the players. I would only wish that they might take the best of what they see in my own conduct and try to forgive my own weaknesses.'

'What annoys you (apart from pressmen)?'

'Dirty play. There is not a lot of it, really, but when I see it, it annoys me intensely.'

In 1965/66 the league campaign was disappointing – finishing 17th in the table – but it was more than made up for by the FA Cup. Undoubtedly the highlight of Brown's tenure at Hillsborough was the run the team had to reach the FA Cup Final in May 1966.

Drawn away from home in each round, they won those games at the first time of asking. Leading 2-0 at Wembley in the final early in the second half and BBC TV commentator Kenneth Wolstenholme, at least, thought the FA Cup was coming to Sheffield. It was not to be – three goals by Everton without reply meant the trophy was Merseyside-bound.

Brown commented to the *Sunday Express* the following day, 'This is the best final I have ever seen. We had as much control of the play as our rivals throughout. That last goal? These unfortunate incidents always seem to happen in cup finals. But we will be back here again.'

The *FourFourTwo* article reflected, 'Brown reacted angrily to suggestions from the media that his side were simply too tense, and froze when victory was within their grasp. The implication was that Brown was unable to "relax" his players sufficiently. Brown told a Sheffield journalist, "Don't you dare come to me and make such ridiculous suggestions."'

The Wembley defeat would be the nearest Brown came to winning silverware in his managerial career.

Peter Eustace, who played in the final, was clear that the credit for reaching Wembley belonged to Alan Brown, speaking in *Wednesday Every Day of the Week*, 'We did it on the back of his knowledge of football and psychology.'

Separately, well before the FA Cup Final there had been a great furore about the allocation of tickets to the players for that game – it was reported they would be getting 12 each, well below the number most clubs allocated to their players when they reached the showpiece.

It gave rise to possible strike action by the Wednesday players – an apparent refusal to play in the FA Cup Final! Brown had confronted his players after the away game at Blackburn Rovers, 'I will play the reserves in the cup final. None of you are playing.'

Brown organised a press conference and displayed his displeasure, 'What am I running a football team or a ticket agency?'

On 1 May the *Sunday Mirror* had praised the manager, 'Thank heaven soccer still has men of courage. I salute manager Alan Brown of Sheffield Wednesday, the man who has had the guts to clamp down openly on a football racket.'

The threat of a player revolt dissipated – given the chance to play in an FA Cup Final there was only one outcome, captain Don Megson the last man standing of the potential rebels. 'Alan was a fair man though. A few days later, he'd told us he'd arranged for us to get 12 tickets as members of the team and 12 tickets in our family's name. We ended up getting 24 tickets. Alan would never break, not even if his life depended on it,' he said in *Don Megson: A Life in Football*.

The 1966/67 season promised much after the previous campaign's finale but progress was limited – with the acquisition of target man John Ritchie the team changed their style of play, finishing 11th in the table.

Progress in the FA Cup saw Wednesday reach the quarter-final and a last-minute defeat away at Chelsea. It was the nearest Alan Brown came to fulfilling his statement that the club would be back at Wembley.

Meanwhile, striker John Hickton had been sold to Middlesbrough – as Don Megson put it in *A Life in Football*, 'It was the biggest clanger Alan Brown and Wednesday ever made.'

I'd seen Hickton score a hat-trick in a 4-0 Boxing Day win over Arsenal in 1965 – the first 4-0 Boxing Day win I'd seen at Hillsborough – and he looked a quality player. He carried on his goalscoring form on Teesside – netting over 150 goals.

A good start to the league campaign in 1967/68 petered out as the new year approached.

Brown's last game in charge was in the First Division at home to Sunderland, a 1-0 defeat.

A game I recollect for all the wrong reasons. Frankly dire. Two teams, with one little better than the other. The quality of football so poor that I remember a comment from a wag on the Spion Kop, 'If this is First Division football, I'm going to report it under the [recently introduced] Trade Descriptions Act.'

In fairness the programme for Wednesday's next home game acknowledged the poor performance – the first words, 'A fortnight ago this afternoon we played Sunderland on this ground. We played badly, very badly. The players know it and you know it. We are all agreed.'

As for the change in manager the programme reported, 'Following their meeting last Thursday the board of directors of Sheffield Wednesday announced that Mr Alan Brown had asked to be released from his engagement as team manager and that it had been agreed to accede to this request forthwith. In the interim the duties of team manager will be the responsibility of Mr Jack Marshall.'

As far as Don Megson was concerned, Brown's departure came as a complete shock – albeit he had been reported in several newspapers as having been mulling over for some time a return as manager to former club Sunderland. The sacking of Ian McColl gave him the opportunity to do just that on a reported salary of £12,000 a year.

Peter Eustace said in *Wednesday Every Day of the Week*, 'Everybody was devastated when he left. It was a bitter blow, and people will never know how much it affected the club and the players.'

Jim McCalliog had similar views, telling the same book, 'That was a major turning point in Wednesday's history, because something went out of the club the day he left, and things fell into a decline which it took many years to halt.'

In the *Star Green 'Un* on the Saturday after his resignation the front-page headline, 'THIS HAD BEEN BREWING FOR WEEKS – BROWN'.

The sports paper included a piece by Tony Hardisty, reporter attached to Wednesday, highlighted as 'exclusive', 'Brown left his steak lunch with the Sunderland team in the Roker Hotel to tell me, "No one will ever persuade me to tell the full story of why I left. But I will tell you this: my conscience is perfectly clear. I acted entirely properly all the way through. This was no sudden decision, you know. I made it known some weeks ago to the Hillsborough board that I would leave eventually."

'But why, I asked him – why leave the club you once told me could have your services for as long as they wanted them?'

'"Precisely why I won't tell you or anyone. You are wasting your time asking. But things happen, and you would like them to be cleared up to your satisfaction. I will only say that things have happened and that I gave everyone concerned the fullest opportunity to put things right."'

Hardisty asked Brown about Wednesday's future prospects, 'I do think they have the basis for a very formidable side and I do expect them to do well in the future. We did not have the success I would have liked for them but I do like to look back on our Wembley appearance which I am sure, was a great thing for the city and the players.'

The reporter also questioned whether or not there was a failure to support Brown in the transfer market, 'No. Money doesn't come into this at all. Neither on the team's side nor for myself.'

Elsewhere in that edition, Hardisty was reflecting on Brown's tenure, 'Now he has quit Sheffield Wednesday ... leaving behind bitterness and consternation in the Hillsborough boardroom and on the terraces. Wednesday have had a bad run of late. Confidence is at a low ebb. The public disenchanted. Alan Brown could give you a hard time when the mood took him. I don't hold that against him, it was part of his make-up...

'He came [to Hillsborough] at a very difficult time when the bribery scandal had sickened so many. In a very short space of time he gave the club back its self-respect ... I have personally had more battles with him than I care to tell you about. But for all that, it is hard not to admire – even grudgingly – a character whose mulish stubbornness and pride were awesome – if self-destroying qualities.

'Few Wednesdayites will be shedding tears tonight ... But I do believe that the time will come when Hillsborough fans will look back on the Alan Brown era and say, "He gave the club a foundation, a backbone."'

Lawrie McMenemy regarded Alan Brown as his mentor. While McMenemy was manager at non-league Bishop Auckland, Brown invited him to join the coaching staff at Hillsborough. The new coach laudatory in his praise. 'For devotees of Alan Brown's teachings the sadness is that in the modern game he will be remembered best only by those insiders he influenced ... when you have spent a year or two working with such a pre-eminent master it is the equivalent of reading for a degree at Oxford or Cambridge. Alan Brown deserves his own place as a pathfinder for the English game,' he wrote in *My Autobiography: A Lifetime's Obsession*.

McMenemy went on, 'Alan had one of the strongest personalities I have known. I would go as far as to say the strongest.'

He reflected on his time at Hillsborough and highlighted that Brown and Eric Taylor 'didn't always agree'; indeed there were 'many occasions when we knew they had clashed'.

The manager insisted all his staff undertook coaching courses – primarily at the FA's headquarters at Lilleshall.

By all accounts Brown's focus on training underlined his progressive thinking – he was ahead of his time as he took time out to talk to the players, analyse and assess movements in a game, all focussed on producing an effective and winning team pattern of play.

To underline the progressive thinking, Brown had his own version of 'total football' before the term became associated with the Dutch team of the early 1970s. Positionally, central defenders were the most static outfield players in Brown's fluid and flowing approach – other outfield players expected to fill the place of a man who had moved and changed his position. Innovation a key element of the manager's approach.

Another man who regarded Brown as his mentor was Brian Clough, who had played under him at Sunderland in the early 1960s. 'I'd have been nothing in management without him. He taught me the values of discipline and the need to control exactly what was happening at a club. That was down to Alan Brown. He was my mentor,' the *FourFourTwo* article from November 2012 quoted Clough saying.

McMenemy underlined in *Wednesday Every Day of the Week*, 'Alan Brown was very big on discipline. It was part of everything he did, cleanliness, dress, on the field, in your lifestyle, in your eating habits.'

Peter Eustace observed in the same book, 'Ordinary players became good ones and good players very good under Alan, who had the knack of boosting your self-belief and at times making you feel wonderful.'

Wilf Smith, Wednesday's right-back in Brown's team of the 1960s, added, 'For me, Brown was great. He could be a strange man sometimes, but I would never say a word against him, and it's doubtful whether anybody in that 1966 team had anything but respect and admiration for the man. He didn't always do what you hoped, but what he did was invariably for your benefit.'

Former Wednesday caretaker Ron Ward also recollected, 'Alan Brown was probably the most difficult of all the managers I worked with. If Alan said black was white, then black was white – no argument! Yet, if he was a funny beggar at times, I must give him his due and say that if he promised to do something for you, he would move Heaven and Earth to do it.'

For relaxation – switching off from the pressures of club management – Brown spent hours with his budgies and canaries in the large aviary he had in the garden at his Bents Road home.

Having left Wednesday, Brown stayed for four years in his second spell at Roker Park – sacked in late 1972 with the club close to the bottom of the Second Division. Months later new manager Bob Stokoe took Sunderland to the FA Cup Final and a famous victory against hot favourites Leeds United.

Brown subsequently had a short one-season spell with Hamarkameratene in Norway, his time there ending in 1974.

Having announced his retirement and moved to Cornwall he was tempted back to the role of chief coach at Plymouth Argyle – finally retiring in 1977.

After Brown's passing, *The Independent*'s obituary on 12 July 1996 stated, 'He will be remembered as a man who believed that rules, both for football and life, were sacrosanct. For example, he always refused to sanction material inducements to parents of promising youngsters, at a time when that practice was widespread, even if it meant losing a possible future star. His contempt for the moral bankruptcy that spawned the recent "bung" scandals must have been total. His career never attained the dizziest heights, but his personal standards did. Emphatically, Alan Brown was not for turning.'

Born: 26 August 1914, Consett
Died: 9 March 1996
Appointed: 1 August 1964
Departed: 8 February 1968
First game: 22 August 1964: Blackburn Rovers (h), First
                     Division, won 1-0
Last game: 3 February 1968: Sunderland (h), First
                     Division, lost 1-0
Best league season: 1964/65 First Division, eighth

Record	P	W	D	L	F	A	Win%
League	153	53	39	61	208	209	34.6%
FA Cup	13	9	1	3	28	15	69.2%
League Cup	5	2	1	2	9	7	40.0%
Total	**171**	**64**	**41**	**66**	**245**	**231**	**37.4%**

9

Jack Marshall

LANCASTRIAN JOHN Gilmore Marshall had 12 years – interrupted by the Second World War – at Burnley as a full-back before injury ended his playing career. He was encouraged to take up coaching and physiotherapy, taking his first coaching role at Bury in 1949, before moving to a similar role at Stoke City, and then to Sheffield 6 as chief scout and physiotherapist in January 1955. He combined his role at Hillsborough with that of trainer for the England national team.

Maintaining the Wednesday connection, he left Hillsborough in 1958 to become manager at Rochdale after Harry Catterick had left that post to take on the managerial position at Hillsborough.

He left Spotland in 1960 to take the reins at First Division Blackburn Rovers – staying there until February 1967 following relegation from the top flight the previous season.

Alan Brown brought Marshall back to Hillsborough as assistant manager in March 1967, less than a year before his own departure from the club.

Known as 'Jolly Jack' throughout the game, Marshall was evidently a likeable individual.

A feature on him written by Wednesday reporter Tony Hardisty in the *Star Green'Un* on 4 November 1967 said, 'Jolly Jack, Laughing Jack, Jack of all trades Jack … The easy some say perpetual smile has given wrinkles to what must have been a pleasant, likeable face at birth.'

The article moved on to football with Marshall commenting, 'There is no doubt in my mind that these players are the very best I have dealt with. They are a constant credit to the club and supporters … I have never dealt with finer, more dedicated, more honest professionals.'

Marshall considered the future bright for Wednesday with the youth, team spirit and work rate in the camp. Hardisty concluded his article, 'Work rate. Ponder that. Ponder too on the kind of men who infuse that all important spirit in the dressing room. Men like Jack Marshall. Aide extraordinary.'

With Alan Brown's surprise departure, Marshall was handed the role initially on a temporary basis on 11 February 1968; within 72 hours he accepted it on a permanent basis, though apparently somewhat reluctantly.

For supporters at the time Marshall's appointment was not one to set the pulses racing – it seemed what it was, a so-called safe pair of hands promoted from within.

In the home programme dated 23 March, the club made reference to the 'team manager', stating, 'The above position – vacant as a result of the departure of Mr Alan Brown – was offered to and accepted by John [Jack] G. Marshall on Monday, 11 March. He, the players and all "The Owls" stand for rely on your support. Thank you.'

Inheriting a relatively young team from Brown, the new manager ensured that Wednesday ended that season without being drawn into a relegation battle.

Captain Don Megson commented in *A Life In Football*, 'Jack had a reasonable reputation as a manager, but as I had been 100 per cent devoted to Alan Brown, who'd been an all-encompassing figure. I honestly didn't rate our team, and without the organisation drilled into us by Alan, I didn't think we'd be able to keep our performance levels. Jack didn't have the strength of character to maintain the discipline and harmony that was needed.'

Reportedly, at Marshall's first team talk centre-half Vic Mobley requested to play the ball out from the back – his previous instruction under Brown had been to get the ball to

David Ford as quickly as possible; Marshall was receptive to Mobley's request. And the manager wanted Johnny Fantham to play on the wing instead of up front in the middle. As Megson observed, Brown had only just left the club and it became clear the players were starting to fragment.

After Brown's departure Wednesday won three games – one in the FA Cup and two in the league, both away. The club finished 19th in the table.

In the last home programme of the season, a telling comment, 'But there is no point glossing over the facts. You supporters know we are not good enough. We know it, too. So, the ball is in our court once more.'

For the record the programme continued to reference the board of directors and the general manager and secretary, Eric Taylor, in its directory – no mention of the team manager! That would be rectified at the start of the 1968/69 season.

At the beginning of that campaign Marshall had a spell in hospital having his appendix removed. That season proved to be a challenging one for Wednesday and the manager – several players submitting transfer requests.

A dismal 3-1 defeat in the League Cup at Fourth Division Exeter City continued the club's inauspicious start in that competition.

While Marshall was hospitalised, Wednesday were involved in one of the games of the season at Hillsborough – a nine-goal thriller against Manchester United, Charlton, Law, Best and all. Behind on three occasions, Wednesday went on to win an epic encounter 5-4.

And during that season Wednesday achieved one of their most notable postwar wins in the FA Cup – at Elland Road in a third-round replay following a 1-1 draw at Hillsborough. Hosts Leeds United – who would go on to lift their first league championship that season – were clear favourites but on the night, Wednesday were in command and they emerged comfortable 3-1 winners.

Shortly after that win, local and national newspapers featured Marshall and next-door neighbour Lawrie McMenemy – then manager at Doncaster Rovers – seemingly in good cheer and talking with each other over the garden fence at their homes in Moorcroft Road, Sheffield.

Any good cheer would soon evaporate, Wednesday losing at Second Division Birmingham City in the next round of the FA Cup.

In the first two months of 1969 Marshall was reported to have been on several scouting missions for players – including to Scotland and Northern Ireland – with targets referenced in the *Star Green'Un* which included Dave Wagstaffe (Wolverhampton Wanderers), Jimmy Greenhoff (Birmingham City) and Danny Hegan (Ipswich Town). All to no avail as there were no incoming players.

A 5-0 home defeat by Arsenal at the beginning of March was the beginning of the end of Marshall's tenure at Hillsborough.

After learning that the club had decided not to renew his contract upon its expiry at the end of June 1969, the manager took matters into his own hands and resigned on 18 March.

The club's first programme after Marshall's departure made these observations, 'Followers of Sheffield Wednesday will need little bringing up to date with the events of the club in the past week or so. Much water has flowed down the Don since we were here to play West Bromwich and it is a topic that has been well aired.

'Suffice now for us to record that chief coach Mr Tom McAnearney is now in charge of team duties at Hillsborough and we are sure that every one of you has nothing but good wishes for this popular Wednesdayite and his staff in the task they are facing.'

The chairman, Dr Andrew Stephen, responded to questions put to him in the *Star Green'Un* on 22 March, 'I think it is a fair assumption that we shall appoint what is commonly called a "tracksuit" man ... There is no panic to make an appointment. It may be next week, next month or in the summer.'

Following the resignation there was an 'avalanche' of letters for the 'Tell It To Tony' feature (readers' letters to Tony Pritchett) in the *Green'Un* under the headline 'The Wednesday Slump Fans

Have Their Say'. A full page dedicated solely to Wednesday. The letters would not have made comfortable reading for Jack Marshall.

The feature letter and recipient of three Guineas (£3 3s 0d; £3.15) was from Frank Dobson from Ashdell Road, Sheffield, who started his correspondence, 'I have often thought of adding to the plethora of abuse at Wednesday in your column,' but instead he focused on the team's results since the start of the year. He presented the First Division table based on results in 1969 – Wednesday were bottom of the pile, a mere five points from their 12 games (two points for a win at that time).

Peter Hancock of Vickers Road, Sheffield, the recipient of two Guineas for his letter, observed, 'All Wednesdayites are utterly sick and tired of seeing Wednesday beaten almost every week.'

Local journalist Keith Farnsworth commented in *Sheffield Wednesday: A Complete Record 1867–1987*, 'Marshall gave the manager's job all he had got, but he had to have a spell in hospital in early 1968/69 and, with the post-Brown disenchantment growing among certain players, he always seemed to be fighting a losing battle.'

Scottish international midfielder Jim McCalliog acknowledged that Marshall was a nice man to get along with, but he did not find his appointment an inspiring one.

With Tom McAnearney in temporary charge until the end of the season, the *Star*'s Wednesday reporter commented, 'Who takes over? My money's on Tommy.'

His interim time in charge did not go to plan – 11 First Division games played to the season's end, without a win. Wednesday finished 15th in the table.

Supporters were distinctly unhappy with the interregnum between permanent managers, their feeling that the club was being allowed to drift.

Marshall returned to Bury as manager prior to the start of the 1969/70 season but was dismissed for financial reasons after seven games.

His final role in football saw him return to Blackburn Rovers as physiotherapist in 1970 and he stayed in that role until retirement in 1979.

Born: 29 May 1917, Bolton
Died: 1 January 1998
Appointed: 11 February 1968
Departed: 18 March 1969
First game: 17 February 1968: Swindon Town (h), FA Cup fourth round, won 2-1
Last game: 8 March 1969: Coventry City (a), First Division, lost 3-0

Record	P	W	D	L	F	A	Win%
League	46	12	16	18	46	60	26.0%
FA Cup	7	2	3	2	11	11	28.5%
League Cup	1	0	0	1	1	3	0%
Total	**54**	**14**	**19**	**21**	**58**	**74**	**25.9%**

10

Danny Williams

AS SUMMER 1969 moved into July, no appointment had been made at Sheffield 6 – the *Star Green 'Un* highlighted the favourites for the position: Jimmy Scoular (Cardiff City), Jimmy Adamson (Burnley) and Bill McGarry (Wolverhampton Wanderers).

The following week, Danny Williams was appointed as the club's manager. Wednesday reporter Tony Pritchett commented, 'When you come to think of it, Danny Williams was an obvious candidate for the Sheffield Wednesday job ... even though he was not among the 170 hopefuls who answered the Owls' advertisement back in March.'

Born in Thrybergh, near Rotherham, Danny Williams was a one-club man during a playing career that commenced in 1943 – he made a record 620 appearances (including those in wartime football) for Rotherham United, primarily as an inside-forward.

In the early years his footballing career was combined with working as a miner at Silverwood Colliery – working down the pit from 1943 to 1952.

He served the Millers as trainer and coach before becoming manager in 1962. He left the club in February 1965 after a disagreement over selling players, and having turned his back on football moved to Bournemouth.

Persuaded to return to club management by Swindon Town in the summer of 1965, he enjoyed great success – winning the League Cup in 1969 as a Third Division club, defeating top-flight Arsenal at Wembley, and that same season he led Swindon to promotion to the Second Division for the first time. For good measure they added the Anglo-Italian League Cup to the trophy cabinet that season, beating Roma 5-2 on aggregate in the final.

No doubt the underdogs' exploits at Wembley and promotion had caught the attention of the Wednesday board of directors.

The general reaction to Williams's appointment was a positive one. The first Wednesday home programme of the 1969/70 season had an article entitled 'Welcome Home Danny' – a brief biographical summary of his time in the game followed by, 'Now Williams is at Hillsborough, his appointment being the spectacular and popular climax to Wednesday's long search for the right man ...We look forward to Danny settling in and striking up a blend with his coaching staff. The players, we are sure, will respond to their new boss's infectious enthusiasm and humour.'

The next edition had the 'Danny Williams Page' – a regular feature of that season's programmes and the first time a Wednesday manager had used the medium to communicate with supporters. He commented, 'I know it is going to be a demanding season for us all ... I'm sure that you want Wednesday to play attacking football and get a lot of goals. That's the way I like to play it, but as perhaps you know as well as I do, we hardly have the staff for this at the moment.'

Keith Farnsworth later wrote in *Sheffield Wednesday: A Complete Record 1867–1987*, 'He seemed the ideal man for the vacancy at Hillsborough and his appointment was hailed as an inspired choice. Unfortunately, his 18 months with Wednesday proved disastrous. He took over a team in decline, troubled by internal strife and fading spirit, and soon discovered that he had inherited an awesome task.

'Danny was one of football's genuine characters, a likeable happy-go-lucky fellow. But the situation at Wednesday was very different from that at Swindon, and, exposed as he was, he lacked the support, ingenuity and tact to halt the slide.'

Farnsworth went on to assess Williams's dealings in the transfer market – parting with 13 players and acquiring nine, selling better players than he bought.

He noted that Williams once said his only good players were David Ford, Peter Eustace and Wilf Smith – all players he sold. The author went on, 'In any event, his comment did not help the cause, but it was typical of the man's simple honesty – and perhaps underlined his lack of awareness that psychology is a vital commodity in big-time soccer.'

At that time Wednesday's finances were not in good shape and that influenced the decision to sell first-team regulars Jim McCalliog and John Ritchie (at a reported knockdown price of £25,000 back to Stoke City) before the start of the 1969/70 season, followed by midfielder Peter Eustace in January 1970.

Williams's first season started off badly – the team clearly struggling – by mid-November Williams observed in the *Green 'Un*, 'There are so many bad sides in the First Division that 30 plus points could do it … I told our supporters' club in midweek that I thought that we would get out of trouble and I am sure we can.'

Not so: that season proved to be calamitous – relegation from the First Division after a last game of the season chance to retain their First Division status at Hillsborough went disastrously awry – a 2-1 home defeat to a Manchester City team who had their focus on the forthcoming European Cup Winners' Cup Final. Wednesday finished bottom of the table on 25 points.

In the programme for this crucial game the manager observed, 'I'm a great believer in fate. "Whatever will be, will be" is my motto and if fate decrees that our efforts be met with success, then I'm sure we shall go on to build a better Wednesday.'

Those sentiments about fate seemed odd to me at the time and certainly very odd now. A passive acceptance. Having been at that game it was not so much fate but the way Wednesday played and underperformed on the night that led to defeat and relegation.

Add to that humiliation in the domestic cups – defeat at home to Fourth Division Scunthorpe United in the FA Cup and defeat at Dean Court to Third Division Bournemouth in the League Cup.

My only interaction with the manager was through the pages of the *Green 'Un* – an 'Ask Danny' feature, after relegation had been confirmed, in May 1970.

'Why wasn't Graham Pugh given his chance and what happened to the Norman Piper [Portsmouth] deal which seemed on the cards for so long?'

'I did persist with Graham for a long time but he had had a lot of injury. He really has worked hard for me and I have helped. But a succession of illness and injuries has worked against him.

'As for Piper, I admit we looked at him a lot. But they wanted a lot more than I thought he was worth – about twice as much actually and I decided that the money involved was not worthwhile. This must be a manager's judgement and I made it.'

Williams made some interesting observations in the same feature to other readers' questions including, 'I reckon if we could have had this present team at the start of the season, we might not have set the First Division on fire, but I'm sure we wouldn't have been relegated.'

Having watched the team throughout that season I think at the very least Williams was being optimistic. For much of the campaign Wednesday were locked in a relegation battle with performances – and more particularly results – at the wrong end of poor.

To a question about why Williams insisted on a man-for-man defence rather than zonal marking, he responded, 'When I came here, we were obsessed with 4-3-3 and I sat there week after week just waiting to be hit ... just waiting to lose. I judged it was time for a change and I stand by man-for-man. My view is that if a man is not good enough to mark his opponent efficiently, he's no business being in the First Division.'

With Wednesday preparing for the new season after relegation, the *Coventry Evening Telegraph* noted on 11 July 1970, 'The coming season will be important to Danny Williams, the Sheffield Wednesday manager. Last season was his first in charge at Hillsborough, and the blame for

Wednesday's relegation could not be laid at his feet ... He has laid his plans well and has made two big captures this summer in wing-half Sammy Todd [Burnley] and John Sissons [West Ham United]. Wednesday look like playing a big part in the promotion race.'

Why Williams was absolved of the responsibility for relegation is not referenced. For me, as the manager he had to take that responsibility.

In his first programme notes for the Second Division campaign he finished his column with, 'Nothing but 100 per cent will do. That's what I promise you. I hope you'll support us still.' That last sentence struck me as having an air of desperation.

Williams had cause to be concerned – the average attendance at Hillsborough nosedived from 26,619 for the last season in the top flight to 16,051 for the first in the Second Division. That reduction of over 10,000 in home support is the largest fall in consecutive seasons in Wednesday's history.

And on the field Wednesday did not make a good fist of it – they never looked like being in the promotion picture and the contributions of Todd and Sissons failed to live up to expectations.

A 5-1 home defeat to Luton Town on 10 October prompted many supporters on the Spion Kop to sit down in protest during the game. That particular result had further ramifications after ex-player Peter Eustace gave an interview to BBC Radio Sheffield five days later and said, 'I find myself asking if it would have happened 18 months ago and I don't think it would. I think the blame has to be put not on the people playing on Saturday afternoons but on others. There are people at Sheffield Wednesday doing things that would not be done at any other club in England.'

Eustace's comments drew the ire of general manager Eric Taylor, who was reported as being 'dumbfounded' by the remarks, and replied, 'We cannot allow people to give opinions about our club which cannot be related to fact. I feel sure the matter will be taken up with the Football League and West Ham United [who Eustace had signed for earlier in 1970].'

As well as the poor league form, Wednesday exited the two domestic cup competitions at the first time of asking. They were 13th in the table when Williams was sacked in January 1971.

His departure came as no surprise. Perhaps more surprisingly, supporters chanted 'Taylor out, Taylor out' as their go-to protest. And that would not be the last time or indeed the last manager for whom such chants were heard. A clear concern on the terraces about the perceived influence of Eric Taylor at the club.

Following his departure, Tony Pritchett wrote in the *Star*, 'Nothing that Danny Williams did in those 18 eventful months of his reign earned him as much respect as the manner of his going. The dignity and discretion with which Mr Williams spoke on the day the axe fell was in curious contrast with many of the impulsive outbursts which marked the eventful term of office as team manager at Hillsborough.

'His mood seemed to be not of anger or humiliation but of fatalism and genuine regret that he had not done better for his beloved Wednesday … he had a lifelong devotion to the Owls. It was this feeling more than the money which tempted him to leave Swindon.

'From that first astonishing TV interview [after the opening-day 4-1 defeat at Manchester City] when he claimed he had "only six good players", Danny was seldom out of the headlines.

'The reporters loved him. After the match quotes, before the match predictions, tips about signings, background information, Danny helped us all…

'Danny had regrets but no recriminations, sorrow but no anger. He accepted that he had to carry the can for the run of bad results … "I don't want to say anything that will hurt Wednesday. They deserve more than that."

'Nonetheless, there was disagreement between Wednesday and Williams over the compensation package for his dismissal.

'He had more than three years left on his contract when he was dismissed and it reportedly took two years before he accepted £10,000.'

Pritchett finished his piece, 'He came to Hillsborough when the fortunes of the club were almost at rock bottom. Although he could not arrest the decline, he worked like a horse trying and the fact that he failed does not mean that elsewhere, where the pressures are lighter, he won't bubble to the top again.'

A week later, Pritchett reflected on the now ex-manager, and referred to the 'explosive first few weeks of Danny's reign' and his 'outspoken way … Danny's time in the hot-seat was marked by the chasing of countless hares … remember Scullion, Dougan, Campbell, Boyle, Byrom, Hunt and the rest'.

Williams later commented in the *Green 'Un* on his time at Hillsborough, 'I was not given enough time at Wednesday. I hold nothing against Wednesday, although it was like a bomb exploding inside me when I was told to go.' He described his spell at Sheffield 6 as 'miserable'.

His next managerial position after leaving Hillsborough was at nearby Third Division Mansfield Town, appointed in November 1971, staying three years before returning to Third Division Swindon Town as manager in 1974. Four years in that role before moving to the general manager position at the County Ground in 1978. A brief return as caretaker manager of the team in the 1980/81 season before he retired in 1985.

Williams passed away in February 2019.

Born:	20 November 1924, Rotherham
Died:	3 February 2019
Appointed:	17 July 1969
Departed:	25 January 1971
First game:	9 August 1969: Manchester City (a), First Division, lost 4-1
Last game:	16 January 1971: Orient (h), Second Division, won 2-1

Best League Season: 1969/70 First Division, 22nd (relegated)

Record	P	W	D	L	F	A	Win%
League	67	16	16	35	71	114	23.8%
FA Cup	3	1	0	2	4	7	33.3%
League Cup	4	0	2	2	3	5	0%
Total	**74**	**17**	**18**	**39**	**78**	**126**	**22.9%**

11

Derek Dooley

IF THERE is one man – and there is only one man – who towers above Sheffield football and has the affection, admiration and respect of supporters of both Sheffield clubs, it is Derek Dooley. He bridges the divide in the city. The only man ever able to do so.

As a player he lived and breathed Wednesday, the only club he played for. His impact on the field phenomenal – 46 goals in 30 games during 1951/52, it remains a club record, and a career tally of 62 goals in 61 league games.

Dooley's world came crashing down on Valentine's Day 1953 at Preston North End's Deepdale – he ran hard into a challenge, colliding with the home goalkeeper George Thomson. He was stretchered from the pitch having broken his leg.

But that was Dooley – fearless, utterly fearless.

In the Preston Royal Infirmary that evening he showed initial signs of recovery but there were complications and by Tuesday doctors identified that gangrene had set in to a wound and there was no option – they had to amputate Dooley's leg.

Years later I had the opportunity to talk with Tommy Docherty, the accomplished Scottish international and manager, who had played for the home team that day. His comment, 'He should never have gone for the ball, he had no chance of getting it.'

Wednesday paid Dooley to the end of his contract in June 1953; the Professional Footballers' Association provided him with £200. The local *Telegraph* and *Star* newspapers set up a Shilling Fund for him which raised £2,700 – enabling him and his wife, Sylvia, to purchase a house in Norton for £2,100, a house he lived in all his life.

A testimonial was held for him at Hillsborough in March 1955 – a crowd of 55,000 attended providing receipts of £7,500.

Jobs as a journalist and at a local bakery followed. He appeared on ITV television's *This Is Your Life* with host Eamonn Andrews.

In 1962 he was appointed to run the newly created Wednesday Development Fund – a job that paid less than the one he had in the bakery, but enabled him to become directly involved with football and his club again. He was a success in his new role as the fund grew from strength to strength.

After the dismissal of Danny Williams from the manager's position, Dooley was undoubtedly a shock appointment to replace him in January 1971. And he was the first ex-Wednesday player to be appointed to manage the club.

The first programme after his appointment introduced the new manager, 'Derek, the lion-hearted player, who was perhaps the greatest Wednesdayite of them all, accepted the position of team manager at the club … if Derek Dooley is the number one admirer of Sheffield Wednesday, then the club is the number one admirer of the man.'

In his autobiography, Dooley later recollected, 'To say I was flabbergasted and amazed by the unexpected turn of events would be putting it mildly.'

Dooley had been invited to the boardroom one Friday morning to a meeting with secretary and general manager Eric Taylor and chairman Dr Andrew Stephen. Taylor uttered the words that left Dooley speechless, 'What would you think if we offered you the job as manager?'

As Dooley commented in his autobiography, 'It probably sounds like something out of schoolboy fiction when I say the prospect of managing the club I'd supported and played for was like a dream come true, but I cannot explain my feelings in any other way. It was as if some fantasy from my boyhood had suddenly become reality.'

A dream invitation for Dooley – he still wanted time to consider the role and the implications and to talk with Sylvia. As he observed, 'It was a case of Sylvia knowing exactly what my reaction to the offer would be and she agreed it was a golden opportunity I could not dream of rejecting.'

There was some concern the club were taking advantage of Dooley's status as a Hillsborough legend to stem the substantial criticism that was coming their way at Wednesday's demise. Dooley did not share that view.

In the *Star Green'Un* after the appointment, Tony Pritchett commented, 'Outside his family nothing means more to Dooley than Sheffield Wednesday. Don't we all owe a man like this our respect and support?

'So, let's give Derek a chance. Let's stop the kicking and see how it goes ... and I'd like to see the militant Shareholders' Association set an example. Their quarrel is with the board. But the board are now 100 per cent behind Dooley so let's leave them to it.'

Dooley's record as manager was an improvement on his immediate predecessors and indeed successors – but in his three years in charge there was not the sustained success expected and yearned for by the supporters.

A disappointing 15th in the table at the end of 1970/71. The following season – Dooley's first full campaign in charge – saw little improvement, finishing 14th in the Second Division. Defeats in the early stages of both domestic cup competitions added to the disappointment.

Supporters' frustrations at the time were not aimed at Dooley but again at Eric Taylor. On many occasions the 'Taylor out, Taylor out' chant heard from the Spion Kop. Not once did I hear such a chant directed at Dooley.

In the early months of 1972/73 Wednesday went to the top of the table and hopes were raised – only to be dashed as results fell away. A tenth-placed finish in the league together with a better than average season in the FA Cup – losing in the fifth round at home to First Division Chelsea, and defeat at the third-round stage in the League Cup.

At the start of that season Dooley had been instrumental in Wednesday handing out contracts to the previously banned Peter Swan and David Layne, albeit their return opposed initially by chairman Andrew Stephen and some of the directors. Clearly well past their prime, Swan made 13 appearances, Layne not playing for the first team.

Swan's assessment in *Setting The Record Straight*, 'Derek Dooley was brilliant and I thought the players should have kicked their own grannies for him because of what he was doing for them ... Derek was a good manager, but for me he wasn't hard enough with the players.'

Mercurial winger and crowd favourite Willie Henderson, bought from Glasgow Rangers in September 1972, appreciated the manager, saying in *Our Lowest Ebb?: A New History of Sheffield Wednesday's Darkest Times – 1973–76*, 'He was great for me ... He did talk tactics with the team, and plans for taking on the opposition, but he did not interfere with what I thought was my natural game.'.

Alan Brown, by then managing Sunderland, had these words of praise for Dooley in the programme for the game between the two clubs at Roker Park in September 1970, 'I was fortunate to be his coach and I never fail to recount his story of terrific personal effort to succeed and his absolute trust in his coaching staff. He was without doubt the finest man to step on a piece of green grass.'

Alan Driscoll, writing in the Huddersfield Town programme for the game against Wednesday in November 1972, observed that Dooley was not a manager who shouted the odds; he was 'quiet-mannered, pipe-smoking and he expounds cooly and soundly on any subject relating to soccer'.

The early weeks of the 1972/73 season saw a mystery virus hit the club – results fell away, a downward slide in the table, attendances falling. Chairman Sir Andrew Stephen and vice-chairman Keith Gardiner quit the board in early December 1973.

Matt Sheppard, the new chairman, was appointed along with new directors. He commented, 'I'm confident about the future ... We are going to climb up that ladder.'

Ian Vickers, reporting in the *Green 'Un* on 8 December, stated, 'The new chairman of Sheffield Wednesday smokes cigars and his Rover car has a number plate which contains the letters MS followed by three numbers. But Matt Sheppard says he prefers to remain in the background.'

At this point Dooley felt that the team had started to turn the corner. Not so the board of directors and for his part Dooley felt that his allies on the board – notably Sir Andrew Stephen – were no longer there to support him.

Wednesday were 20th in the Second Division and had been summarily knocked out of the League Cup at Queens Park Rangers, losing 8-2.

No matter; Dooley's departure from Hillsborough was appallingly timed – he wasn't expecting it, neither were the supporters. It was Christmas Eve 1973. Journalists and printers at the local newspaper had been enjoying an early finish at a local hostelry until they were called back to work on a new late edition – 'Dooley Sacked' emblazoned across the front page.

Dooley was devastated and he recollected going to see the players downstairs after his unscheduled meeting in the boardroom. Evidently, he was able to utter only two sentences before he broke down and left. He vowed never to return to Hillsborough.

For his part, Matt Sheppard stated, 'We took the decision to replace Derek Dooley because we felt that decision was in the best interests of the club. The decision having been made, it was necessary to act upon it immediately – and it was particularly unfortunate that the announcement should coincide with Christmas Eve.' It was much more than unfortunate.

Keith Farnsworth reflected in *Sheffield Wednesday: A Complete Record 1867–1987*, 'Dooley made a number of excellent signings, putting his faith in such men as [Dave] Clements, [Brian] Joicey, [John] Holsgrove, [Ken] Knighton and [Willie] Henderson. If he had been given the job sooner, and if the climate had been happier, he might have survived longer and achieved more ... in the final analysis, even idols are human whose fates are in the hands of others.'

Looking back at his time in charge, maybe Dooley was too genial a man to be an effective man-manager.

While I never met Derek Dooley, I recollect an incident on the way back home from the opening fixture of the season at Swindon Town in 1973/74, the supporters' coach substantially delayed leaving Swindon after a window had been smashed by a local throwing a brick at it.

We arrived at the motorway services for a break just as the Wednesday team coach was leaving – except we noticed it was not smoothly driving out of the service station. It started and moved forward 50 yards, stopped, started again – and moved forward a further 50 yards.

Dooley was in the front seat talking to the driver, while about 100 yards behind the coach were two Wednesday players trying to catch up with the vehicle, one of whom was Dave Clements, the Irish international. It seemed the players were running to catch the coach as it moved away; the coach accelerated, the players slowed, the coach slowed, the players speeded up and so on for a good half-minute. This spectacle unfolding as the supporters' coach wended its way into the service station.

It was not a good look. On the supporters' coach we were not impressed. The team had been well beaten, and then these apparent shenanigans.

After leaving Hillsborough, Dooley went on to join the club across the city the following year – initially as commercial manager – and he stayed in different positions, including that of chairman, at the Lane for the next 32 years. He was successful in all his roles there.

The praise for Dooley's work at Bramall Lane was unstinting – Dave Bassett, the manager who worked with Dooley as his chairman for eight years, stated in his autobiography, *Settling the Score*, 'I have nothing but the highest regard for him. I met him when I first joined the club and had a wonderful eight years with him. He was a football man and every club should have a Derek Dooley on the board ... he is a very honourable man, honest as the day is long and lives for the game, a loyal servant to football and his clubs.'

Dooley returned to Hillsborough for the first time since his sacking to attend the First Division derby in March 1992 – presented to the crowd, all four sides of the ground, three blue and white, one red and white, rose to him as one. The applause was deafening. And knowing how he had departed the club almost 20 years previously I certainly recollect welling up as I looked on and shed tears. It was that emotional.

For his part, Dooley recollected the occasion in his autobiography, 'Happily from every corner of the stadium the Unitedites and Wednesdayites roared their approval and a moment I had faced with trepidation and reluctance proved to be one I knew I would always remember with pleasure.'

Derek Dooley passed away in March 2008. In *The Independent*, Ivan Ponting provided a fulsome tribute, 'Professional football has thrown up few more inspirational tales of triumph over adversity than that of Derek Dooley ... in 2003 Dooley became a Freeman of his home city, received an OBE for his services to football, and fans on both sides of the Sheffield divide were gratified but hardly surprised. To them he had long been regarded as little short of royalty.'

A major road has been named after him in the city – Derek Dooley Parkway; at Hillsborough he has a lounge, Dooley's, named after him and the Derek Dooley Wall of Fame. At Bramall Lane there is a statue of him in the centre of the car park outside the main entrance.

Probably not best suited to football club management, there is no question that Derek Dooley reflects all that is good about football, all that is good about Sheffield. He was universally liked and respected at both city clubs. He bestrode the partisan divide as a colossus.

Born:	13 December 1929, Sheffield
Died:	5 March 2008
Appointed:	25 January 1971
Departed:	24 December 1973
First game:	30 January 1971: Swindon Town (h), Second Division, drew 2-2
Last game:	22 December 1973: Crystal Palace (a), Second Division, drew 0-0
Best league season:	1972/73 Second Division, tenth

Record	P	W	D	L	F	A	Win%
League	122	39	31	52	150	168	31.9%
FA Cup	7	2	2	3	9	13	28.5%
League Cup	6	3	2	3	11	19	50.0%
Total	**137**	**44**	**35**	**58**	**170**	**200**	**32.1%**

12

Steve Burtenshaw

FIVE WEEKS between the departure of Derek Dooley and the appointment of his successor – Gerry Young in charge of the team in that period (seven games, one win, five draws, one loss).

Supporters were hoping for and anticipating an experienced big-name manager who would take the club back to the First Division. Names mentioned at the time included Brian Clough – then at Third Division Brighton & Hove Albion – ex-Wednesday captain Don Megson and Colin Addison among others. None of the above made their way to Sheffield 6.

Looking back, perhaps the advertisement for the role should have given the clue to the next managerial appointment, 'Applicants must be in the 35-45 age group with previous experience of team management desirable but not essential.'

Why team management experience was seen as desirable but not essential is a good question – only the board could answer that one. To supporters that approach was flawed – badly flawed.

The club received 70 applications and they apparently approached Ron Atkinson in his first managerial role at Kettering Town, but he was not interested, citing a lack of experience.

It came as a surprise when Steve Burtenshaw emerged as the successful candidate and was appointed.

He'd been recommended by Yorkshireman Bill Nicholson, the Tottenham Hotspur manager, and received endorsement from Scottish international Frank McLintock who had worked with him during his time as captain of Queens Park Rangers.

Burtenshaw had served his national service in West Germany before returning to embark on a 17-year playing career with his only club, Brighton. He moved to Highbury as a coach in 1967, and was in that role during the Gunners' double-winning season of 1970/71. His seven years at Arsenal were followed by a brief spell as chief coach at Queens Park Rangers.

Like Dooley, the new man had no managerial experience.

Burtenshaw's first match in charge at Hillsborough was notable for being Wednesday's first game played on a Sunday – a 3-1 victory against Bristol City. Thereafter victories were few and far between – a total of 14 in his time in charge.

Weeks later, the Hull City manager, Terry Neill, acknowledged, 'I doubt whether there is any club in the country who have had the misfortunes of injury and virus problems that the Owls have had.'

For Burtenshaw, his first full season as manager ended with a last-gasp win against Bolton Wanderers at Hillsborough to retain Second Division status. The tension in the ground for that game was tangible, the pressure huge, the relief when Ken Knighton scored the only goal in the 84th minute overwhelming.

Wednesday finished 19th in the table having been knocked out of both domestic cup competitions at the first time of asking.

Chairman Matt Sheppard quoted in *The Sun*, 'The club will never again come this close to the Third Division.'

In the following Saturday's *Star Green'Un*, new Wednesday reporter Ian Vickers commented, 'Wednesday will surely look back on the disappointing season and not allow themselves to be trapped in the same position ever again ... Under Burtenshaw Wednesday have taken 15 points from 16 games. He's a man used to success but after Wednesday completed their 11th hour escape, he said the pressure was far greater at the bottom ... he looks certain to have a good future in management ... he's frequently talking about "good habits". We wait, and hope that Wednesday will get into winning habits next season and keep to them.'

One notable addition to the playing staff early in the new season was the midfield player Colin Harvey, purchased from Everton for a reported £60,000.

No one thought – least of all the supporters – that things could get any worse for the club. They could and they did, much worse.

For fans it appeared next to nothing had been learned from the previous seasons, and 1974/75 resulted in the humiliation of the club being relegated to the third tier for the first time in its history. Not only relegated – that was confirmed on 1 April after defeat at Nottingham Forest with five games still to play – but a season that produced only five league wins, and only two league goals from 29 December 1974 to the end – 17 games. After winning at Southampton at the end of December those 17 games produced three draws and 14 defeats.

In more than half the season's league games the team failed to score – 22 games, Wednesday's joint-worst on record, with 1919/20.

Wednesday amassed a meagre 21 points all season, 11 points adrift of Cardiff City in 23rd place, the cries of 'All we are saying is give us a goal' from supporters a regular refrain.

Defeat at the first time of asking in both domestic cup competitions underlined the woes at Sheffield 6. The mood among supporters at its lowest ebb as the club slid into the Third Division.

In the programme after relegation had been confirmed, Burtenshaw had this assessment, 'We have got to pull our socks up and reshape the playing staff … We must look for a better-balanced side next season and we must consider reinforcing our present squad.' Following the worst season in the club's history these were not the words to inspire.

Such were the times and dire straits the club was in that the *Sheffield Star* launched a 'Save Our Owls' campaign in January 1975.

Supporters were more than disillusioned and disenchanted – Wednesday appeared to be in freefall – and there was little confidence in Burtenshaw arresting the decline. Add to that the club's finances were in a very poor state.

The first season in the Third Division started badly – indeed many supporters wondered why Burtenshaw was still at the helm.

It was inevitable the manager would pay the price for the team's failure at the start of the season: with Wednesday 16th in the Third Division, he left the club after eight league games – four of them defeats and an early exit from the League Cup to lowly Fourth Division Darlington.

Chairman Bert McGee stated, 'Results, lack of success and our determination to succeed is why the decision was taken.'

Captain John Holsgrove later commented, 'Very few [players] were getting on with the manager … it was clear the club was not right for him,' while striker Brian Joicey stated that the manager 'did not know what was required for a Wednesday team', quoted in *Our Lowest Ebb?: A New History of Sheffield Wednesday's Darkest Times – 1973–76*.

Forward David Sunley was not impressed with the manager. Quoted in *A Quarter of Wednesday: A New History of Sheffield Wednesday 1970–1995*, he said, 'He was a typical Cockney. He'd say one thing to your face and behind your back he'd say another. In the end he lost the respect of a lot of players … as a person through his man-management, a lot of players did not have respect for him. When he was sacked the dressing-room was bubbling. It seems awful to say it but it was a relief.'

Sunley's fellow striker Brian Joicey was succinct, adding in the same book, 'Whoever appointed Steve Burtenshaw had a hole in his head.' He went on to say, 'Wednesday needed a strong manager, they did not appoint one and it showed. He had plenty of good coaching ideas but no man-management.'

If there is a worthwhile legacy resulting from Burtenshaw's tenure at the club it was the creation of Middlewood Rovers, Wednesday's nursery team, which kept associated schoolboys together for a year before they signed as apprentices – future first-team players in the Middlewood team while Burtenshaw was at the helm at Sheffield 6 included David Grant, Peter Shirtliff, Mark Smith, Mel Sterland and Charlie Williamson.

After Burtenshaw's departure, chairman Bert McGhee said in the programme, 'I won't criticise Steve Burtenshaw in any way, shape or form for he did a lot of good for Wednesday. But with the lack of success, we had to take action and with Gerry Young being chief coach he must bear some of the responsibility too. Steve took it like the man he is.'

In his book, *Our Lowest Ebb?: A New History of Sheffield Wednesday's Darkest Times – 1973–76*, author John Dyson noted that Burtenshaw initially agreed to meet with him and talk about his time in charge, but was told that 'on reflection, he found thinking of his time at Hillsborough too upsetting and a little depressing'. Sadly, I think many supporters would include the word depressing in their description of Burtenshaw's tenure.

Born:	23 November 1935, Portslade
Died:	17 February, 2022
Appointed:	28 January 1974
Departed:	1 October 1975
First game:	2 February 1974: Fulham (a), Second Division, lost 4-1
Last game:	27 September 1975: Crystal Palace (a), Third Division, drew 1-1
Best league season:	1974/75 Second Division, 22nd (relegated)

Record	P	W	D	L	F	A	Win%
League	66	13	16	37	66	105	19.6%
FA Cup	1	0	0	1	2	3	0%
League Cup	4	1	1	2	2	3	25.0%
Total	**71**	**14**	**17**	**40**	**70**	**111**	**19.7%**

13

Len Ashurst

JIM MCANEARNEY, the reserve team manager, took on the caretaker manager role after Burtenshaw's departure – two games in charge: one 1-1 draw and one 2-0 win. He was retained on the backroom staff of the new manager – until the financial issues affecting the club began to bite and he was made redundant in 1976.

Referring to the next managerial appointment, chairman Bert McGee stated, 'I want a winning kind of manager ... I have not met him yet, so I cannot say who he will be.'

Prior to the appointment of Len Ashurst, Johnny King, then manager at Tranmere Rovers, had been over to Hillsborough a couple of times and interviewed. King considered the role was virtually his if he wanted it.

Bill Shankly, the legendary manager of Liverpool, who had retired suddenly – in many people's eyes prematurely – at the end of the 1973/74 season, had pointed King to the position at Hillsborough, 'I've been asked who's the best young manager in the game and my finger stops at you son. Go and have a look at Sheffield Wednesday.'

King had done just that and decided the job was not for him. 'Taking on such a big club was just too much.' King said to Shankly, 'I don't think it's for me.' In response, Shankly made his views clear, 'Jesus Christ son, they might be like a rocket that's bound for the moon and nobody to fly it.' Shankly clearly not best pleased.

King made this assessment in *Shanks: The Authorised Biography of Bill Shankly*, 'I still think he [Shankly] wanted me to take it so that he could work alongside me.'

What might have been!

Len Ashurst had a successful playing career with Sunderland – the left-back, described as a 'hard full-back', appearing 468 times for the Black Cats, a record for an outfield player at the club. As a player he had been managed by Alan Brown on Wearside.

He finished his playing career at nearby Fourth Division Hartlepool United in 1973 having taken on responsibilities of player-manager two years earlier.

In his three years in charge he improved the club's league position season on season. His progress in the north-east had alerted Gillingham who appointed him as their manager in 1974.

Little more than a year later and Bert McGee saw in Ashurst the profile required to lead Wednesday, with the club continuing to freefall – the manager's experience working to a tight budget allied with his man-management skills no doubt to the fore.

Ashurst was alerted to the vacant role by Len Shackleton, the legendary Sunderland and England player of the 1950s – the latter having made representations on his behalf.

A meeting in Sheffield with the club's hierarchy, and Ashurst was offered and accepted the position.

The new manager held the view that you only get the opportunity to manage one big club in your career – in his case Wednesday would be the first of two (the other being Sunderland).

Introducing Ashurst in the club programme, McGee wrote, 'We have at the helm now a man for the future with a club of the future. We are all impressed by his honesty, purpose and dedication ... we have the men [Ashurst and assistant Tony Toms] who can help us realise those dreams after far too long in the doldrums.'

For his part Ashurst observed, 'I am glad to be back among northern folk, where they call a spade a spade and expect to give a fair day's work for a fair day's pay ... Everyone will know there will be a new breath of wind blowing through the place, even a whirlwind if necessary.'

He noted the task ahead at Hillsborough was 'formidable and onerous'.

For the players, Ashurst's arrival was undoubtedly a culture shock. He underlined his thinking. 'Sheffield Wednesday is a slumbering giant. But it will be shaken apart. Things will be done at Wednesday that were done at Hartlepool. I'm thinking of cleanliness, discipline, a few things I'm told have been missing. I want hungry fighters ... I've told the whole of the Wednesday staff that Wednesday has, in my eyes, been down in the dumps too long. If they are not ashamed of this, they shouldn't be here. The club's position is disgusting,' he was quoted in *A Quarter of Wednesday: A New History of Sheffield Wednesday 1970–1995*.

Ashurst arrived after an acrimonious departure from Gillingham – and he recollected that the first letter he opened in his time at Hillsborough was a writ issued by the Kent club for walking out on his contract, the matter only resolved over a year later with a reported payment of £5,000 by Wednesday.

To underline the financially straitened times, in the home programme against Gillingham there was an appeal for digs for Ashurst and for trainer Tony Toms.

Playing fortunes were at a low ebb and continued in that vein for some time. After a 2-0 home defeat to Swindon Town had left the team third from bottom, Toms suggested they take the players away for one of his overnight 'bonding sessions' camping on the Yorkshire Moors. Ashurst missed the session because he was not feeling well.

Overnight camping on the moors led to national publicity for the club and more importantly a win on the Saturday, 2-0 against Chester City.

Weeks later and Wednesday were still in deep trouble in the table, Ashurst was 'stressed out' and in time confined to his sick bed with pneumonia.

Johnny King held the view that having taken the job, Ashurst 'had a nervous breakdown as a result'. During his absence, Toms took caretaker charge – four games undefeated in that period.

The league was a hard slog in 1975/76 and again the team made no impression in the two domestic cup competitions.

Through the new year Wednesday struggled for results – it came to a last-day showdown in April 1976, Wednesday v Southend United. The winner would retain Third Division status – the loser destined for relegation, Wednesday in real danger of dropping into the Fourth Division for the first time in their history – in what would have been relegation in two successive seasons. Everything on that game.

A nervous tension filled Hillsborough – Wednesday winners, 2-1 and a 20th-placed finish.

That close-season, Ashurst made major changes to the playing personnel – the one he particularly highlighted was goalkeeper Chris Turner, promoting him to the first team to replace Peter Fox, who moved to Stoke City. Ashurst regarded it as his 'most important decision', giving Turner his debut on the opening day of the 1976/77 season.

Interestingly, the manager recounted a negotiation with the Burnley chairman, Bob Lord, over the transfer of Paul Bradshaw from Turf Moor. Ashurst reflected that he learned a great deal from the negotiations, and was pleased he'd achieved a reduction in the proposed fee of £25,000 to the unusual figure of £19,444.

Ashurst's only full season in charge – 1976/77 – saw Wednesday show a marked improvement by finishing eighth in the table coupled with a decent run in the League Cup to the fourth round. Clear progression in terms of performance and results. The manager's confidence to the fore, he commented in his last programme notes of the season, '1976/77 has been a season of progress for Sheffield Wednesday, and it has led me to the conclusion that we can hit the target next season – **and that target can be nothing less than promotion!**' That last half-sentence in bold text. Stark and clear.

It was not to be. In the following campaign Wednesday failed to register a single victory in their first ten league games. A 2-1 defeat at Preston North End on 4 October 1977, and a slump to the foot of the Third Division table, signalled the end of Ashurst's time at Sheffield 6.

Ashurst speculated that his future may have been sealed at the previous Tuesday night home game against Plymouth Argyle when an injury-time equaliser by the away team prompted the unfurling of a banner – 20ft long – in the North Stand opposite the directors' box which read 'ASHURST OUT – McCREADIE IN' (mentioning Eddie McCreadie, an ex-Chelsea and Scottish international player).

The club programme after the manager's departure observed, 'If the timing of the announcement on Wednesday morning was a surprise to many supporters, they must believe that the board acted with the best interests of the club at heart.' It referred to 'stern measures' – Ashurst's dismissal – having been taken.

There was an acknowledgement that the manager 'gave 100 per cent and more in a whole hearted battle to take Sheffield Wednesday back to the top of the tree. He demanded the same from his players, and was not the sort of man to shirk his part of the bargain.'

Years later Ashurst said he was told by chairman Bert McGee that he had laid the foundations for the club's success in future seasons.

He considered his biggest legacy may have been that he recommended Jack Charlton as his successor and not Eddie McCreadie.

He felt the first six months of his Hillsborough reign were the most difficult of his career. Indeed, the chapter in his autobiography on his time with the club is entitled 'Fire Fighting at Hillsborough'.

While on-field results were not of the level required, he made important player acquisitions – including goalkeeper Bob Bolder – later sold to Liverpool for a sizeable fee – Jeff Johnson, Dave Rushbury and Ian Porterfield. Add to that the former manager of cross-city rivals United – John Harris – joined as chief scout and stayed to make a significant contribution to the club through to 1986.

Alan Biggs, the Sheffield-based broadcaster and sports journalist, reflected in the former Sheffield nostalgia magazine *My Kind of Town* that Ashurst 'would play practical jokes on me whenever I went to Hillsborough to interview him. He would have a chair that would dismantle the second you sat on it.

'At post-match press conferences, he would try to embarrass me and play to the gallery. The radio stations would get their interviews first and then it was time for the printed press. He was quite a fearsome character … I remember leading with the first question after one game, asking him about the match and how he felt about the result and, deadpan, he responded with, "All I have to say to you Alan is – your flies are undone."

'I did the worst thing possible and looked and of course everyone fell about laughing!'

Ashurst made his family home at Eccleshall in Sheffield while he was manager at Hillsborough.

Having left Wednesday, he managed Newport County, Cardiff City, Sunderland, Al-Wakrah (Qatar), Cardiff City, Pahang (Malaysia), and Weymouth.

After finishing his managerial career, he joined the Football Association – focussed on the academy system that had been introduced – and he became a Premier League match delegate responsible for assessing match officials.

He was inducted into the League Managers' Association Hall of Fame in 2014.

Born: 10 March 1939, Liverpool
Died: 25 September 2021
Appointed: 16 October 1975
Departed: 5 October 1977
First game: 18 October 1975: Cardiff City (a), Third
                  Division, lost 2-0
Last game: 4 October 1977: Preston North End (a),
                  Third Division, lost 2-1
Best league season: 1976/77 Third Division, 8th

Record	P	W	D	L	F	A	Win%
League	92	31	27	34	101	112	33.6%
FA Cup	5	3	0	2	8	4	60.0%
League Cup	9	6	2	1	21	10	66.6%
Total	**106**	**40**	**29**	**37**	**130**	**126**	**37.7%**

14

Jack Charlton

EX-PLAYER AND captain Ken Knighton was brought in to take temporary charge in the wake of Ashurst's departure.

But it soon became clear who Wednesday had in mind as the permanent successor – Jack Charlton.

A stellar playing career – World Cup winner with his brother Bobby as England triumphed at Wembley in 1966 – Charlton acknowledged that if Wednesday's centre-half Peter Swan had been available for England (he had been banned in 1964 as a result of the betting scandal) he may never have had the chance to star for his country.

Charlton amassed a total of 35 caps for England and made a record number of appearances for his one club – Leeds United – 629, and 96 goals (holding ninth place in that club's all-time scoring list – an achievement in itself given his position of centre-half).

His first foray into management at Middlesbrough – appointed in August 1973, he was an instant success. Promotion to the First Division in his first season and 15 points ahead of the second-placed club in the days when it was two points for a win. In that season Wednesday on the receiving end of a rampant Boro – losing 8-0 at Ayresome Park.

In 1974 Charlton received the OBE and the Manager of the Year award – the first time it had been presented to a manager outside the top flight.

He stayed with the Teesside club for four seasons – achieving a highest-placed finish of seventh in the First Division. He left of his own accord, determining to spend time with family and enjoying his leisure pursuits – principally fishing.

Wednesday director Roy Whitehead had made a call to Charlton in October 1977 saying the club wanted him to be their manager. Charlton was not interested in taking the conversation any further given that Len Ashurst was in post.

Ashurst departed and with Wednesday rock bottom of the Third Division, Charlton accepted two tickets to watch the home game against Chesterfield – his presence in the North Stand spotted by supporters. Putting two and two together, they pleaded with Jack to take the now vacant managerial position.

A lacklustre performance by the Owls – in Charlton's words 'they were bloody awful!' – albeit with a 1-0 win. Jack took a walk round the ground to the South Stand and a meeting with the directors – and by 6.45pm he was introduced as the next manager of Sheffield Wednesday.

He reflected that it may have been the fact Wednesday could only move in one direction that attracted him to the job.

In his first programme notes he ascribed responsibility for performance to the players and himself, adding, 'I also expect the fans to accept their share of the responsibility and give the team the backing they deserve.'

Journalist Alan Biggs recalled as a young radio reporter being 'pretty much in awe of him'. He observed in *My Kind of Town*, 'He certainly wasn't orthodox, he took people as they were. I don't suppose there were many tactics involved; he'd get the best players he could and just mucked in with them.

'There was something that resembled a social club at Hillsborough with bar, dartboard and a snooker table and that is where I'd go on a Friday to interview Jack about the following day's game. He'd always be playing darts or snooker when I went in.'

Charlton recollected in *Jack Charlton: The Autobiography*, 'Before long I discovered there had been a lot of aggravation at the highest level at the club. Fortunately, there was a change of personnel in the boardroom and I was able to get on with the job of finding a coach and organising the players.'

Maurice Setters joined as coach, and from Charlton's recollection he was on about £4,000 per annum – a low salary for the time.

Discussions between Setters and Charlton set the way forward – Wednesday had to up their work rate. Add to that the manager determined that initially at least the approach had to be simplified – throw the ball into the box and play from there.

Charlton had laid the ground with the directors – that first season was focussed simply on staying in the division (Wednesday finished 14th). This was followed by the same 14th-placed finish the following year.

In that first season Charlton learned that Setters and Tony Toms had been in the dressing room with the reserves after a 3-0 defeat to Everton when Bert McGee came in to castigate them. Charlton was less than pleased – he needed to lay the law down with the chairman.

In his autobiography he recalled marching into a board meeting and asked for a word with McGee outside. As he put it – with the help of a few expletives – he made his views clear, 'You've been down to abuse my staff about results. Don't do it again. If you have any comments to make about the team talk to me … Any information relating to the workings of this club stays within these gates or you can stuff your job.'

McGee was evidently shaken by the manager's words. As far as Charlton was concerned, the chairman had to be told there and then or the opportunity would be lost.

Charlton stabilised and consolidated in those first two seasons, followed by a memorable encounter with First Division Arsenal in the FA Cup, the tie settled at the fifth time of asking in the Londoners' favour.

Add to that the manager had changed the spine of the team – big goalkeeper, Bob Bolder, elevated to the first team, solid centre-half, Mike Pickering, made captain after signing from Southampton in October 1978, and big centre-forward,

Andy McCulloch signed from Brentford for the start of the 1979/80 season.

That season saw a more attacking style of play – spearheaded by the acquisition of winger Terry Curran from First Division Southampton. He formed a very effective strike partnership with Andy McCulloch. Curran's flair and skill quickly made him a fans' favourite. And in that 1979/80 season promotion was secured to the Second Division.

For supporters, five long seasons in the Third Division came to an end. Undoubtedly, Jack Charlton was the man who resurrected Wednesday from the abyss.

And that promotion campaign brought the famous 4-0 win for Wednesday against United in the Sheffield derby on 26 December 1979 – a game remembered as the 'Boxing Day Massacre'.

That result presaged a period of decline for the club across the city.

Wednesday back in the Second Division and a suggestion from the Bramall Lane club that an annual Steel City Cup game between the two rivals could be established. Charlton's words in response to the point, 'They might need the prestige of playing us but we don't need the prestige of playing them.'

Tommy Tynan – a crowd favourite and top scorer in Charlton's first season – was one player who did not see eye-to-eye with Big Jack. Tynan commented in *Tommy: A Life at the Soccer Factory* of the 1977/78 season, 'I scored 21 goals and was player of the year, and he was still trying to rule my life … because he was trying to tell me I shouldn't be going out with Elaine. I don't think he liked the idea of her working in a nightclub. I just told him, "She's my girlfriend, I'm going out with her."'

The other disagreement came over the playing style at the start of the 1978/79 season; Charlton said Tynan had to play up front on his own – four games in and substituted four times. Tynan was clear that the system wasn't working, 'I went into his office and told him I couldn't play the way he was asking me to play, that I needed someone big up front with me. He was playing five across the midfield and I told him that I needed a big target man if he was going to use that sort of system. I told him I couldn't carry on the way things were going and he said, "Either you play this way or not at all." I said, "I'll go on the [transfer] list."'

Much to the dismay of supporters, Tynan left the club and joined Lincoln City.

Ian 'Spider' Mellor – the first goal hero of the derby day 'Boxing Day Massacre' recalled his transfer to Sheffield 6, for £40,000 from Chester City in July 1979.

The plan was to meet the manager at Hillsborough to discuss the transfer and terms – it went out of the window. Jack wanted to pursue one of his great passions – fishing. They met at the Ladybower Inn in the Peak District.

Mellor recollected in *Spider: I Wish You All You Wish Yourself*, 'Jack was still wearing his wellies and cap ... He took his fishing rod into the lounge bar. The pub was busy, though that didn't stop Jack talking so loudly in his broad Northumberland accent that regulars and day-trippers overheard our conversation.

'In fact, the whole pub shut up once Jack started to outline my wages and bonus structure. He didn't care about the other drinkers. What sort of football manager does that? In my view he was being ignorant and inconsiderate. But that was Jack, an eccentric whose individual style made him an interesting and unpredictable character.'

Terry Curran commented in *Regrets of a Maverick*, 'Jack's lack of finesse on the training ground didn't win him too many brownie points with us. But I was more concerned about his tactics. Jack was the ultimate route-one merchant ... Jack would also have happily blown the final whistle the second Wednesday took the lead. He constantly preached about keeping clean sheets and winning football matches 1-0.'

In his own autobiography, Charlton pointed out that a small minority of Wednesday supporters were involved in hooliganism at away grounds – most notably the riot in 1980 at Oldham Athletic's Boundary Park where visiting fans ran on to the pitch and hurled objects following Terry Curran's sending-off with home player Simon Stainrod for an alleged altercation – play held up for half an hour and further consequences for the club with the Football Association.

Curran recollected, 'Big Jack came out on to the pitch to try to restore order and nearly copped it himself. I remember seeing him crying in the dressing room because he was so ashamed of what happened. It was the first time I'd ever seen a grown man reduced to tears and it upset me even more.'

In the club programme following the riot at Oldham, Charlton said, 'There is no condoning the actions of the lunatics who have disgraced our club ...We want honest, loyal football lovers supporting Wednesday not lunatics who use football to air their grievances against society.

'My message to those hooligans is, "If you want to get rid of me – go out and do what you did at Oldham again." Then I'll leave and go to a club where I can make some real progress. Over the next two years we will be taking serious steps to sort out the savage element in this club.'

The potential prospect of Charlton leaving sent a shudder down the spine of the supporters. He stayed.

Three seasons in the Second Division and Wednesday finished tenth, fourth and sixth over that period. They narrowly missed out on promotion in 1981/82 – ironically the season three points for a win was introduced. If it had remained at two points for a win Wednesday would have been promoted.

In his last programme notes for the 1981/82 season, Charlton said, 'Sadly and most disappointingly we have missed out on the promotion. I know how sickened you all are and everyone here at Hillsborough, directors and coaching, playing, office and ground staffs all share the view.'

He went on to confirm he intended to stay on as manager for another season, and added, 'If we do not then get promotion it will be right for me to leave the club on what I believe will be amicable terms.'

The following season Wednesday finished a disappointing sixth in the table. In the FA Cup they reached the semi-final – losing 2-1 to Brighton & Hove Albion at Highbury. Many supporters – me included – thought Wednesday had a good chance of making it to the final.

It was not to be.

Striker John Pearson recollected the dressing room after the game, quoted in *Back In The Big Time: Sheffield Wednesday's Return to Division One 1984–86*, 'The changing room was very quiet and down. Jack was emotional, in tears. But it wasn't for himself, it was for the club and the players. I remember being impressed that a World Cup winner would care so much.'

Charlton had made the decision to leave the Hillsborough hot-seat before the FA Cup semi-final and handed his resignation letter in to chairman Bert McGee. In response, he received a letter offering him new improved terms and conditions for the following season from McGee, together with individual visits to his home from each of the directors asking him to stay.

To no avail – Charlton's mind was made up. He was disappointed that he had failed to achieve his ambition of taking Wednesday from the Third Division to the top flight but for him it was time to move on.

An important change that took place during Jack Charlton's tenure was the day midweek games were played – for decades they had been on Wednesday evenings (across the city at Bramall Lane it was Tuesday evening). Charlton changed it to Tuesdays at Sheffield 6 – his clear and simple rationale that it provided the maximum time for players to recover between Saturday and midweek games.

After Charlton passed away in 2020, Brian Glanville's obituary of him in *The Guardian* said, 'Surprisingly, he took over at Sheffield Wednesday, a great club struggling in the Third Division. Passionate, dictatorial, unorthodox and considerate by turns, taking players to stay with his parents in Ashington for training, Charlton saved Wednesday from humiliating relegation, turned the team round with long-ball methods, and reached an FA Cup semi-final in 1983 three years after gaining promotion to the Second Division. But he resigned that year, saying people were not smiling at him in Sheffield any more.'

He briefly returned to Middlesbrough as caretaker manager at the end of the 1983/84 season before taking his next permanent managerial role back in his native north-east as manager of Newcastle United for the start of 1984/85.

It is worth highlighting that more than half of Charlton's games as a club manager took place while he was in charge at Hillsborough.

Undoubtedly, the role for which he is best known in management was during his time in charge of the Republic of Ireland.

Before Charlton's arrival the national team had not qualified for any major tournament finals – that changed, reaching two World Cups – most notably reaching the quarter-final at Italia 90 – and a European Championship.

During Italia 90 the Irish team and management staff had an audience with the Pope in Rome – the Pope acknowledging Charlton, 'I know who you are: you're the Boss.'

Charlton was awarded the highest honour by that country – honorary Irish citizenship. His statue stands at Cork Airport.

I met Jack Charlton once at a joyous 35th-anniversary celebration dinner of the 'Boxing Day Massacre' at Hillsborough: film of the match, player reminiscences, meeting the heroes. I approached Jack and asked him one question: nothing to do with Wednesday, 'Jack, who was in your little black book?'

A look of acknowledgement from the ex-Wednesday manager, maybe a question he wasn't expecting, certainly not at this event, and then a long pause, almost uncomfortably so, before he responded. 'Tommy Smith,' and off he went.

Tommy Smith, the hard-man Liverpool captain of the time chimed with me – he and Charlton must have had more than the odd flare-up and altercation. And the other? My guess would have been one of the Chelsea players – Ron Harris or Peter Osgood maybe.

Forty-plus years earlier and that information would have caused a media frenzy.

As background – in October 1970 Charlton appeared on a Tyne Tees Television programme talking about his career and his approach to the game. Geoffrey Green in *The Times* observed, 'Charlton himself emerges as the man he is, warm, forthright, articulate and honest.'

The broadcaster Fred Dineage asked the questions.

'You have had your fair share of cuts and bruises. What is the worst thing that has happened to you?'

'I cannot mention names but I have a little book with two names in it and if I get the chance to do them I will … they know who they are.'

Hue and cry in the media – the Football Association charged Charlton with having made remarks likely to bring the game into disrepute. The FA suspended him from international duty. Ultimately Jack was only asked to make an apology for his comments. 'I apologise that, through me, the press were given an opportunity to knock football.' Jack Charlton 1 the press 0.

At that social event Jack was very open, warm and engaging with supporters, comfortable having his photograph taken and signing autographs.

Born:	8 May 1935, Ashington
Died:	10 July 2020
Appointed:	8 October 1977
Departed:	27 May 1983
First game:	12 October 1977: Exeter City (a), Third Division, lost 2-1
Last game:	14 May 1983: Crystal Palace (h), Second Division, won 2-1
Best league season:	1981/82 Second Division, fourth

Record	P	W	D	L	F	A	Win%
League	253	101	79	73	345	288	39.9%
FA Cup	22	9	5	8	26	24	40.9%
League Cup	23	8	9	6	36	29	34.7%
Total	**298**	**118**	**93**	**87**	**407**	**341**	**39.5%**

15

Howard Wilkinson

WITH CHARLTON'S departure there was inevitable speculation focussed on his successor– names highlighted in the media included Lawrie McMenemy, Norman Hunter, Emlyn Hughes, George Kerr and John Bond.

But it was a born and bred Wednesdayite who was appointed – Howard Wilkinson.

Born in the Netherthorpe district of Sheffield, he attended Abbeydale Grammar School. He won England youth honours while at school, joining Wednesday in June 1962. Over four years he made 22 first-team appearances, scoring three goals, playing as a winger.

He transferred to Brighton & Hove Albion in 1966, and the move proved ideal for his future career into coaching – he enrolled on a coaching course run by his Seagulls colleague Steve Burtenshaw (one of Wilkinson's predecessors as manager at Sheffield 6).

Leaving Brighton, he returned to Sheffield in 1971 to study for a degree in physical education, combining these studies with being player-coach and later player-manager at non-league Boston United.

He had a spell teaching back at his Abbeydale school and became the Football Association's regional coach based in Sheffield. Subsequent managerial stints came at non-league Mossley and the England non-league team before he took the same role for the England under-21s.

In 1980 he joined Third Division Notts County as coach to manager Jimmy Sirrel, subsequently taking the team manager position in July 1982 with the club in the top flight.

With the departure of Jack Charlton, many supporters were hoping for a so-called 'big name' – for some therefore Wilkinson was a surprise choice. Add to that he had stepped down a division to take the manager's role at his boyhood club. The second ex-Wednesday player to take the position at Hillsborough.

Years later, Wilkinson acknowledged he was very much an unknown quantity at the time of his appointment, 'One of the headlines when I got the job was 'Howard who?''

In the first programme of the season an athletic-looking manager – pictured topless – opened with the words, 'Putting pen to paper for the first time as manager of Sheffield Wednesday caused, I am sure, even the celebrated names of the past to pause, take a deep breath and reflect. Imagine then my feelings as I embark on a season in charge of the club I supported as a boy, played for and continued to support long after my departure. This club inspires that sort of feeling …Returning therefore was a little like coming home.'

He soon demonstrated that his appointment was an inspired choice: promotion in his first season in charge – Wednesday back in the First Division after 14 seasons' absence, the longest the club had been out of the top flight.

Imre Varadi, the striker signed from Newcastle United in July 1983, was impressed with the manager in the discussions leading to his transfer to Sheffield 6. 'In every sentence he said to me it was not about "if" we're going to get promotion, it was "when" we were going to get promotion. He was so determined with the way that he spoke to me, the way that he sold the club,' Varadi told the *All Wednesday* podcast.

During that first season under Wilkinson's direction, it felt like there was something really building for Wednesday on the pitch.

Undefeated well into November, there was a growing momentum to the league campaign – Wednesday went down to their first defeat at Crystal Palace on 26 November, and at the end of the game the home club's players looked as though they'd won the league and cup final rolled into one. Evidently they celebrated with a drink of champagne!

Wilkinson's reaction to the defeat underlined that Wednesday would immediately bounce back and build an unstoppable train destined for promotion.

That 15-game unbeaten run from the start of the season established a new club record.

Excellent progression in the league was coupled with strong showings in the two cups – going out at the quarter-final stage in the FA Cup and League Cup, after defeats in replays at First Division Liverpool and Southampton respectively.

Wednesday finished runners-up to Chelsea in the table on goal difference having achieved 88 points – perhaps their 11 games in the cup competitions had sapped some energy for their league endeavours.

At the end of that promotion season two important first-team players – Gary Megson and Gary Bannister – had not signed new contracts. Wilkinson responded immediately – they were exiled from the squad and eventually joined Nottingham Forest and Queens Park Rangers respectively.

Key players who served Wednesday well were signed by Wilkinson; they included Martin Hodge, Lawrie Madden, Imre Varadi, Lee Chapman, Brian Marwood, Nigel Worthington and Nigel Pearson among others.

An excellent eighth-placed finish in that first season back in the top flight followed by an improved fifth place, dropping back to 13th and 11th in the next two seasons.

In the club programme following the 1-1 draw at home to Arsenal in February 1987, a reflection from the manager, 'Football is a team game and it is the collective strength of a team that matters. When 11 individuals commit themselves to the cause, bad luck, coincidence, reasons and excuses fly out the window. Last week's performance bore the true Sheffield Wednesday trademark … it gave our supporters immense pleasure and pride, and our players a feeling of a job well done, because they were true to themselves and did their best. There's never been anything wrong with that and throughout time it's earned a lot of ordinary people a small place in history.'

In the knockout competitions Wednesday's best season under Wilkinson came in 1985/86 – knocked out of the FA Cup at the semi-final stage, 2-1 by Everton after extra time. Heart-wrenching. Players and supporters in tears.

Looking at training under Wilkinson, central defender Lawrie Madden commented in *Back In The Big Time: Sheffield Wednesday's Return to Division One 1984–86*, 'It was tough. There was lots of running, but we bought into it. Results helped – we were winning! Also, many of the players, myself included, had a point to prove. We perhaps hadn't quite made it elsewhere, so were hungry and motivated for success … He was also big on motivational speeches in the dressing room. Alongside Micky Lyons, who was the heart and soul of the team, we'd get really psyched up for matches.'

In the same book, captain Lyons remembered the training, 'Howard got us to be the fittest team in the league! Every Monday in training we would be running. He'd have us running up and down hills for an hour or more non-stop. He ran our bollocks off! I loved it though.'

One key aspect that comes through from the players' observations is the strong camaraderie and team spirit that was engendered in Wilkinson's groups.

In July 1985 Garry Thompson, the striker from West Bromwich Albion, signed for a club record £450,000. He was impressed with the first meeting with Wilkinson in Sheffield, writing in his autobiography *Don't Believe a Word*, 'Howard Wilkinson's wife greeted us in the car park and immediately whisked Louise [Thompson's partner] away to view houses which would take up the entire afternoon … Howard was warm and friendly … the money sounded good but that was not the bit that attracted me. One minute I'd got Ben [Thompson's son] next to me; and the next he was gone. Then I could see him out in the distance, playing on the pitch with Howard Wilkinson, shooting into the net with Howard celebrating each and every goal with him.'

Thompson acknowledged, 'Wilkinson was ahead of the game in many respects. We'd play 11-a-side and he would break down patterns of play, work with the defence and midfield separate, work on set plays. Everything we did in 1985, folk were doing ten to 15 years later.'

Not everyone Wilkinson signed felt so positively about the manager – Mark Chamberlain signed from Stoke City in September 1985 and he reflected in *Match of My Life Stoke City*, 'I actually didn't want to go [to Wednesday], but Stoke said that I had to as the club desperately needed the money ... In the very first practice game we played together, I was losing my full-back and Mel [Sterland] shouted "Spin" and belted a long ball down the wing for me to chase ... he kept doing this all session and afterwards I said to him, "What are you doing? Just give me the ball short."

'"I can't do that," he said. "I have to shout 'spin' and belt the ball down the line into the space for you. It's your job to get it!"'

Chamberlain did not enjoy Wilkinson's style of play. His 40 starts and 48 substitute appearances in nearly three seasons with the club perhaps reflected that he, and Wednesday, were not best suited.

Dick Chester, Wednesday's club secretary in the period 1984 to 1986, gave some interesting insights in *Football – An Insider's Job*, '[Wilkinson] was very much under the cosh when it came to convincing the chairman for incoming player transfers. [Chairman] Bert McGee in true Yorkshire fashion always wanted a pound and a penny for every pound spent. His usual response was along the lines of, "Ah well, Howard, we'll give this one the green light if you must have him, but you know you will always do better growing your own cucumbers."'

Underlining the tight grip on money, Chester stated that Wilkinson spent a net £250,000 on transfers in the period he was at the club – a paltry sum compared to other top clubs – and testimony to his abilities as a coach and manager that he was able to take Wednesday so far forward.

Chester clearly enjoyed the working relationship with Wilkinson, calling him 'the best manager I had the pleasure of working with'. And he'd worked with many in his time at Sheffield United and Lincoln City.

He said that Wilkinson had 'a thoroughly professional staff supporting him from grassroots development to the first team' – highlighting among others Alan Smith, the club physiotherapist, who later went on to provide the same services to the England national team.

Chester commented, 'I was present many times in Howard's office with Alan and listened to what were in those days revolutionary discussions relating to correct intake of food, calories, their benefits both in terms of health, training and playing, the constant need to control those correct levels to enhance bodily strengths and shape, speed of movement and how these could overcome that of opposing teams.'

Mel Sterland, who played for Wilkinson at Hillsborough and later at Elland Road, when Leeds United won the First Division championship in 1991/92, succinctly observed in the Leeds v Sheffield Wednesday matchday programme on 19 January 2025, 'What a manager. Detailed, he got everything spot on.'

Separately, he commented, 'At Sheffield Wednesday when Howard was manager, we knew we were going to win games – you could see the fear, nobody wanted to come and play at Hillsborough especially the way we played at 100 miles an hour.'

Imre Varadi said during the *Mel & Imre Show* on YouTube, hosted by Alan Biggs, in February 2025, 'Howard Wilkinson built a team, a winning team, and what people don't realise back then, with his coaching ability he played three centre-halves with two wing-backs … he was one of the first managers to do that and he doesn't get enough credit for doing that.'

In the media – particularly the London-based press – Wednesday, and Wilkinson, were criticised for playing the so-called long-ball game. The style of play Wednesday adopted suited the players of the time and was successful.

Early in the 1988/89 season Wilkinson considered that without further resources he could not take the club any further.

He was receptive to overtures from Elland Road to take charge of Leeds once it became clear Wednesday would not provide the additional financial resources for players he considered necessary for further progress.

Wednesday's pay structure at the time prevented the signing of several big-name players after fees had been agreed with their clubs – for example Mark Wright (Southampton) and Chris Fairclough (Nottingham Forest) who went on to sign for Derby County and Tottenham Hotspur respectively.

The approach to pay scales and big transfers changed at Hillsborough in the years following Wilkinson's tenure as a result of changes in the boardroom. Future managers benefitted, starting with Ron Atkinson.

The manager found it difficult to leave his boyhood club – a final meeting with his players led to his emotions getting the better of him and he made for the boot room where the tears flowed. He had built a strong bond with his players and coaching staff, and considered he could have stayed at the club for a long time – if it had not been for the approach taken by the directors.

Wilkinson had 18 months left on his contract when he left, chairman Bert McGee commenting on his departure, 'We are sorry to lose him because he served the club well for five years. His record will always show how wrong his critics were.'

It was reported that the clubs had agreed a compensation fee of £75,000.

Looking back years later, Wilkinson commented, 'The whole thing about that group [the squad] was that to a man they were all at one time or another, in a game or a competition, they were all big characters. You had to be a big character to be in the team because the demands were unbelievable that I put on them. There was a great sense of being in a team, the group was a very, very strong group.'

Joining Second Division Leeds in November 1988, Wilkinson made them an effective unit and quickly gained promotion to the top flight, winning the First Division in 1991/92 – the last English manager to win England's top flight.

He left Elland Road in 1996, moving on to work for the England national team setup and becoming caretaker manager in 1999 and 2000 as well as managing the England under-21s between 1999 and 2001.

Then a brief return to club management with Sunderland in 2002 before a final managerial stint at Shanghai Shenhua in 2004.

Working as chairman of the League Managers' Association added to the breadth of Wilkinson's career.

Crucially, for Wednesday, Wilkinson was there when most needed in the dark days of 2010 and 2011 when at one point it looked as though the club may go into administration. Initially he returned as 'technical adviser' to then chairman Lee Strafford and chief executive Nick Parker, before becoming chairman prior to the acquisition by new owner and chairman Milan Mandarić.

Wilkinson won the Bell's Whisky Manager of the Month award in January 1985.

He was awarded the OBE in 2024 for services to football.

Born: 13 November 1943
Appointed: 24 June 1983
Departed: 10 October 1988
First game: 27 August 1983: Swansea City (a), Second Division, won 1-0
Last game: 1 October 1988: Aston Villa (h), First Division, won 1-0
Best league season: 1985/86 First Division, fifth

Record	P	W	D	L	F	A	Win%
League	214	95	56	63	309	264	44.3%
FA Cup	25	12	8	5	46	34	48.0%
League Cup	24	12	5	7	48	33	50.0%
Full Members' Cup	3	1	0	2	2	2	33.3%
Total	**266**	**120**	**69**	**77**	**405**	**333**	**45.1%**

16

Peter Eustace

FOLLOWING HOWARD Wilkinson's departure, chairman Bert McGee commented, 'Every change must be regarded as an opportunity and a challenge.'

Assistant manager Peter Eustace was put in charge of the team on a caretaker basis after apparently declining the opportunity to join Wilkinson at Elland Road.

He wasted no time in putting himself forward for the role, 'I think I could do a good job for them. I understand the feelings of the club and its make-up and that is very important.'

Wednesday would be advertising the job and it was reported they already had a list of candidates – including Steve Coppell at Crystal Palace, Lou Macari at Swindon Town, Wednesdayite Jim Smith at Queens Park Rangers, Ray Harford at Luton Town and Graham Turner at Wolverhampton Wanderers; the chairman told Eustace to apply for the job in writing.

In the event he was confirmed as the permanent manager after two games in temporary charge – the third Wednesday manager to have played for and managed the club.

Eustace was unconcerned that he was apparently not the first choice. He took the role with the team seventh in the First Division, making Frank Barlow from Barnsley his assistant.

As a player Eustace was signed as an apprentice to Wednesday in 1961 following impressive displays with his local club Stocksbridge Works. He worked as an apprentice mechanical engineer at the local steelworks –

recommended by fellow employee and former Wednesday player Frank Slynn.

Initially a wing-half, he progressed to a more attacking and creative midfield role. From 1965/66 Eustace was an automatic choice in the midfield and had several call-ups for the full England squad without making an international appearance.

During his time in charge, Danny Williams had said that Eustace was the club's best player but within months he was sold to West Ham United in January 1970 for a reported club record fee of £100,000 – his first game for his new club back at Hillsborough!

The move to London did not work out as planned and two years later he was loaned to Rotherham United. Prior to the start of the 1972/73 season he signed for Wednesday albeit his return did not match his first spell at Hillsborough – totalling 281 appearances and 26 goals in his combined spells at Sheffield 6.

For the 1975/76 season he moved on to Peterborough United where he finished his playing career. Three years working for his father-in-law's building company in Stocksbridge followed.

In 1979 he was recruited by former team-mate Ken Knighton as coach at Sunderland, culminating in promotion back to the top flight for the Black Cats.

Howard Wilkinson brought him back to Hillsborough as his assistant manager for the start of the successful 1983/84 season.

For his first game after his appointment was announced he said, 'I'm determined to prove that the board has made the right choice … Howard did an excellent job here, he taught me a lot and set the kind of example which has left me well equipped to cope with the challenge I now face.'

Eustace's time as manager was not a success. He lasted 109 days and 21 games in charge – the shortest period on record at the time.

Some supporters were concerned that a more high-profile name had not been appointed – the benefit of Eustace's appointment was continuity.

But there it ended – his approach had a strong emphasis at away games on defence which was not appreciated by many supporters. I recollect a match at The Den in December 1988 where it appeared Wednesday's approach was to achieve a draw – what looked like nine or ten men behind the ball for much of the game. A 0-0 draw looked a certainty until the home team scored in the last minute.

No doubt there was thinking and method behind the approach taken but it was not attractive to watch and more particularly the necessary results were not coming in for Wednesday.

Added to the issues with the football and the lack of success on the field, there were several public spats with players. It led to Wednesday reporter Paul Thompson commenting in the *Star Green 'Un* on 7 January 1989, 'We are not used to seeing so much Hillsborough dirty linen being washed in public.'

At the beginning of the new year, midfielder Gary Megson had fallen out with the manager. 'I do like Sheffield Wednesday but I don't like the way it's being run at the moment. It's no secret that the manager and I don't get on,' he told the *Star* on 3 January. Within days Megson had been transferred to Manchester City.

On the eve of the game with Liverpool at Hillsborough that same month the *Liverpool Echo* observed, 'Sheffield Wednesday boss Peter Eustace is beginning to feel the heat at Hillsborough. Four successive league defeats and only one win in 12 outings means that Wednesday can ill afford to slip up at home to Liverpool tomorrow … Eustace has had to deal with three transfer requests in recent weeks, emphasising the discontent within the ranks.' Mel Sterland, Kevin Pressman and Alan Harper the players with the transfer requests.

In the event the Liverpool game finished a 2-2 draw. But the end was not long in coming – three more league games and a defeat in the FA Cup brought Eustace's tenure to an end. It came as no surprise. Wednesday had slipped down to 18th in the table by the time of his departure.

In his final game before dismissal, Eustace opened his column in the club programme, 'Fellow Wednesdayites, we're passing through a difficult phase at present, and I know how our supporters feel about things because I share exactly those same feelings of concern and frustration and I feel them deeply.'

A 2-0 defeat at home to Manchester United at Hillsborough was the manager's last game in charge.

In the following week's club programme, captain Mel Sterland wrote, 'Peter Eustace and I had our differences but those were sorted out and it was a bit sad to see him leave the club. I wouldn't wish that on anybody and I'd like to wish him all the best in the future.'

In the *Star Green 'Un*, Paul Thompson, under the headline 'Eustace The Brave', stated the team's 'collapse [was] not all his fault'. He observed, 'In the circumstances the job of managing Wednesday who remember went through rocky spells even under Wilkinson – turned out to be too complex and demanding for a managerial novice, even one who had worked as Wilkinson's number two … if Peter made a mistake, it was in taking on the job in the first place.'

Thompson went on to ask the question, 'The disturbing thing is that if close observers of the club, including some players, could see at the time that it was probably the wrong appointment, why could not the board see it as well?'

Eustace had reportedly signed a contract until 1991 and compensation would be due for early termination.

Following his departure from Hillsborough he was appointed to the coaching staff at Leyton Orient before leaving to join Charlton Athletic as reserve team manager in November 1989.

Frank Clark recruited him as his assistant manager back at Leyton Orient. Once Clark took the managing director role at the club Eustace was promoted to team manager in 1991. He remained in charge for three years before departing in April 1994.

He held further roles as a scout with West Ham United and for a brief period back at Wednesday when Chris Turner was manager. He was made redundant in July 2003 when the club were taking cost-cutting measures.

He had a brief period working with Harry Redknapp at Portsmouth, leaving in May 2008, and subsequently ran a public house in Derbyshire.

Born: 31 July 1944, Sheffield
Appointed: 28 October 1988
Departed: 15 February 1989
First game: 29 October 1988: Charlton Athletic (a),
                 First Division, lost 2-1
Last game: 11 February 1989: Manchester United (h),
                 First Division, lost 2-0

Record	P	W	D	L	F	A	Win%
League	17	2	7	8	12	27	11.7%
FA Cup	2	1	0	1	6	3	50.0%
League Cup	1	1	0	0	3	1	100%
Full Members' Cup	1	0	0	1	0	1	0.0%
Total	**21**	**4**	**7**	**10**	**21**	**32**	**19.0%**

Record includes two games as caretaker manager

17

Ron Atkinson

ATKINSON'S ARRIVAL at Sheffield 6 in February 1989 felt like a breath of fresh air – in contrast to his predecessor he was naturally outgoing, a seasoned and successful manager and his style of football was easy on the eye.

His appointment came as a surprise – a very pleasant one at that. He was manager at Atlético Madrid where there had been a difference of view with the president, Jesús Gil. Atkinson's nickname for Gil was 'Mad Max'. It was Gil who appointed Atkinson in October 1988 – 96 days later, much to the manager's astonishment he was sacked. During his tenure he had taken the club from near the bottom of the league to third place.

Interestingly, Atkinson stated there was interest from Seville, Valencia and Las Palmas to continue his career in Spain after the Atlético Madrid sacking – but by that time he had committed himself to Wednesday.

Atkinson's background was as a midfield player – a one-club man with Oxford United. He moved into management with Kettering Town in 1971, before spells at Cambridge United, West Bromwich Albion, Manchester United – where he was in charge for six years and twice won the FA Cup – before a return to West Bromwich Albion and then moving to Atlético Madrid.

In his first notes in the club programme, the new manager said, 'It's fair to say that I had hoped to stay in Spain a bit longer than I did but the chairman's weekend call brought me to Sheffield Wednesday – and I'm delighted to be here. This is a big club, so big in fact that twice in the earlier stages of my managerial career, 14 or 15 years ago, I turned down the chance to come here because at that time I didn't feel I had sufficient experience.'

His aim in the short term was to try to ensure that Wednesday retained their top-flight status.

As the review of the season in the club programme observed, Atkinson 'soon raised morale, set fresh standards in team play and made swift moves into the transfer market' – including midfielder Carlton Palmer and striker Steve Whitton.

Atkinson quickly steadied the ship – albeit Wednesday's status as a First Division club was not confirmed until they had defeated Middlesbrough in the penultimate game of the season, a 15th-placed finish in the table reward for Atkinson's fine work.

He had been working without a contract since he joined in February and there was real concern that other clubs – home and abroad – would come in for him. He agreed a contract for a year, stating in the *Star*, 'The biggest single factor affecting my decision was that I enjoy it here. It's a smashing club, the players have responded brilliantly to what I have asked them to do and the board have allowed me to get on with the job. On top of that, the support is magnificent.'

At the start of the new season Atkinson commented, 'I believe we can achieve a great deal and continue that climb in the right direction which we began at the tail end of last season.'

That 1989/90 campaign – Atkinson's first full season in charge – seemed to be one of consolidation for the most part. On the last day of March, before the game against Tottenham Hotspur, Wednesday were 13th in the table on 40 points. Six games left – Wednesday lost four of the next five – leading to a critical last day, in danger of relegation but definitely in the box seat, three points ahead of Luton Town and a better goal difference.

The unthinkable happened – Wednesday lost at home to Nottingham Forest, the Hatters won at Derby County. Wednesday relegated. They were not – as many observers had reflected – 'too good to go down'. It was Atkinson's first relegation as a manager.

At that point Atkinson offered his resignation to chairman Dave Richards – Richards was having none of it and offered the manager a two-year extension to his contract which was accepted.

Coincidentally, the end-of-season dinner with the supporters' club was scheduled for the evening after the final game – players and fans together. The fans clapped the team as they entered the room that evening, something Atkinson never expected. 'The one thing I will always remember about Sheffield Wednesday are the fans. Howard Wilkinson had done very well at Hillsborough in a very functional way. My style was rather different. I wanted Wednesday to play with a bit of flair, and the fans, I think, appreciated that,' he wrote in his autobiography, *The Manager.*

Atkinson vowed to the supporters present that night that they would put it right next season.

As a matter of professional pride and personal belief he wanted to get the club back to the top flight at the first time of asking – and he wanted the players to stay together and commit to that. Some were out of contract – but such was the belief in their manager and each other that they stayed together.

At that time Graham Taylor had just been appointed England manager and there was a vacancy at Villa Park – it came to light later that Atkinson had been sounded out regarding his interest in the position. He decided to remain at Hillsborough.

Wednesday promoted at the first time of asking after the 1990/91 season, finishing in third position – and the team playing with a verve, style, panache and authority that many had not seen before. A style that was free flowing, attacking and one that was winning football. The team exuded a *joie de vivre*, a camaraderie and a will to win that was at its zenith under Atkinson.

Supporters buoyed and enthused by the quality of football – 'Big Ron's Barmy Army' a regular refrain throughout his time at Sheffield 6.

Many memorable games that season in the league – perhaps the standout at the Goldstone Ground against Brighton & Hove Albion in October 1990. Wednesday's football that night stylish, rhythmic, almost hypnotic in its captivating brilliance – the opposition chasing the proverbial shadows. Wednesday playing in their yellow and blue away strip. Wednesdayites behind the goal chanting 'Brazil, Brazil, Brazil' as they greeted every pass and move by the away team; 4-0 Wednesday and it could have been double that score.

Atkinson's view was that if the team had not been involved in the League Cup that season, they would have been promoted as champions.

But what an involvement with the League Cup – the manager's prowess and shrewdness perhaps encapsulated on that Sunday afternoon in April 1991 under the twin towers at Wembley Stadium: the Football League Cup Final against one of his previous clubs, Manchester United. Second Division underdogs Wednesday defeated Alex Ferguson's United 1-0. The last club outside of the top flight to win either the League Cup or FA Cup and it was Ferguson's first defeat in a major cup final.

Thoroughly deserved on the day, the manager's tactics for the game spot on – nullifying the threat down the Red Devils' left flank of their 'teenage sensation' Lee Sharpe and stretching their defenders across the backline creating space for the Wednesday midfield to surge forward.

And the preparation for the final spot on – the times when to work hard in the days leading up to the game and the times to relax. And perhaps his masterstroke on the coach journey to the stadium – inviting his friend, the Liverpool comedian Stan Boardman, aboard to tell jokes and let the players relax and take their mind off the upcoming game. It worked to perfection.

Wednesday's first major trophy for 56 years and a day at Wembley that supporters would never forget – John Sheridan's magnificent strike from outside the box beating the flailing arms of Manchester United keeper Les Sealey to record the only goal of the game.

Among others, Atkinson brought into the club the Swedish international full-back Roland Nilsson – 'a Rolls-Royce of a player' – John Sheridan and Dalian Atkinson.

The manager praised Nigel Pearson as the best captain he ever had – pointing out that he kept the players in line in the dressing room.

Many of the Ron Atkinson team of the early 1990s went into management – Pearson, Nilsson, Sheridan, Viv Anderson, Chris Turner and Trevor Francis (returned to management).

He brought the England international Viv Anderson to Hillsborough from Manchester United in January 1991 – in his autobiography *First Among Unequals*, Anderson observed, 'Larger than life, Atkinson's personality ruled supreme over the playing side of the club. The board were anonymous ... He was an open person who spoke his mind and was very good with words.'

Many of the players have stated that Atkinson was the best manager they'd played for. I recollect talking with David Hirst in 2003 who talked very positively about 'Big Ron', someone he regarded as a 'man's manager'.

Hirst also commented in *A Quarter of Wednesday: A New History of Sheffield Wednesday 1970–1995*, 'He liked a laugh, but he liked to win. In training he did what he felt – some days he would just walk around Hillsborough Park. He didn't treat everyone the same ... sometimes he would tell a player to take the day off.'

Atkinson brought the recently sacked Queens Park Rangers player-manager Trevor Francis to Hillsborough as a player in March 1990. Francis's view in *One In A Million: The Autobiography*, 'Playing under Ron was like a breath of fresh air. He was great, a player's type of manager. No one who has played for Ron has a bad word to say about him because he was just great to play for.'

John Sheridan certainly considered Atkinson the best manager he'd played for, and commented in *A Proper Player: The Career of John Sheridan*, 'I thought he was a great manager. I got on really well with him and all the lads got on well with him. He knew how to treat players, that was his strength. Training was enjoyable all week. Even if you were playing five-a-side it had to be played the right way. And he'd let you have a pint if you wanted a pint if it was done the right way.

'In my view if Ron had stayed at Wednesday another three or four years, we would definitely have won more major honours. There was no messing about with Ron, he knew how to treat players and get the best out of them.'

Sheridan was involved in an incident with Atkinson which brought the team closer together. A pre-season tour of Italy in 1990, the squad were staying at an old mansion in Acqui Terme in northern Italy. Sheridan one of three players to break a curfew – it led to an altercation between manager and player.

Chris Turner remembered the incident on the pre-season tour of Italy very well – Sheridan breaking the curfew and Atkinson then letting the players decide whether or not the miscreant midfielder stayed at the club. Sheridan back at the hotel – Ron asked for a show of hands among the players, 'Who wants him to leave?' No hands raised. Atkinson made it clear 'that's your decision' and it undoubtedly brought the players even closer together – a band of brothers, one for all and all for one.

The goalkeeper was clear that Atkinson never intended Sheridan to leave the club – it was first-class man-management. Although Turner commented, 'It would have been interesting if all the hands went up!'

Atkinson said in *The Manager*, 'That meeting [with the players] played its part in getting Sheffield Wednesday to promotion and to Wembley in the same season. I'd given them some responsibility and a stake in the coming season. They paid me back.'

He reflected on his departure from the club in May 1991. It presented him with the biggest dilemma he'd faced in his professional career – to stay at Hillsborough or move to Villa Park, to Aston Villa the club he regarded as 'my club'; the club he had supported since boyhood.

He'd achieved the most successful season in Wednesday's modern history, promotion back to the top flight and winning the League Cup. And he felt that Wednesday had in place the foundations to become one of the country's best teams.

Atkinson acknowledged in *Big Ron: A Different Ball Game* that he 'would be surrendering arguably the most satisfying job I have ever had ... It was a case of heart ruling head in many ways.'

He'd planned to let the Wednesday directors know of Villa's approach after the team's open-top bus parade around the city centre. It did not work out that way – the media had got hold of the story that he planned to leave Hillsborough for Villa Park after a conversation with Atkinson's accountant and Villa's legal representatives had been overheard.

This was messy. Very messy. Wednesdayites in their hundreds made for Hillsborough to let Atkinson know he was very much wanted as their manager – no question everyone wanted him to stay and build on what had been achieved, the board keen that he stay. Atkinson relented and agreed to remain, much to the relief and jubilation of the supporters.

Stay – but not for long. Aston Villa representatives went to his home, upped their financial offer 'considerably' – to a reported £250,000 a year for three years (though this was not the deciding factor according to Atkinson) and he reaccepted the job at Villa Park.

The change of heart went down very badly with many Wednesday supporters, the word 'Judas' readily bandied about. The *Star Green 'Un* ran a centre-page spread of readers' reactions to Atkinson's departure. My views on the way the manager had acted were negative and I made my contribution to the torrent of outpourings – the vast majority of which were critical of the now departed manager.

Under the heading, 'The Ron Way To Do It' I wrote, 'In the heat and emotion generated by the extraordinary events at Hillsborough it is perhaps difficult to remain objective. Within a matter of days Ron Atkinson has moved from being seen as a people's hero, a kind of demigod to the faithful at Sheffield 6 to being branded a "Judas" full of deceit and exemplifying self-interest to the full.

'In the cold light of day Atkinson's achievements at Hillsborough may well be overshadowed by the manner of his departure, but it would be quite wrong to dismiss those achievements. Without question Ron Atkinson produced a team of style and authority, full of pride, skill and commitment which played a quality and coherence of football unsurpassed by a Sheffield Wednesday team in the last 30 years.

'Promotion to the First Division and that magnificent day at Wembley are a fine testimony to Atkinson's skills as a football manager. One must pay tribute to those skills.

'Nonetheless the whole affair of his leaving the club was squalid and shabby. For one who sought loyalty from the players and supporters his actions were the height of hypocrisy.'

After his tenure at Villa Park ended in November 1994, within months he was appointed manager at Coventry City in February 1995 – moving to the role of director of football in November 1996.

As his managerial career progressed Atkinson made more appearances as a football pundit on television.

In *The Daily Telegraph Chronicle of Football*, a section entitled 'The Cult of the Manager' had this description of Ron Atkinson, 'He did as much as anyone to make the modern football manager a cult figure, the image, voice and spirit of his club, and also a sort of tribal leader whose views on football and life are worthy of public notice.

'This celebrity was largely media-created ... Atkinson succeeded because he was shrewd and experienced and also sported a tan, sunglasses and a jangle of gold jewellery and appeared on television a lot.'

Born:	18 March 1939, Liverpool
Appointed:	15 February 1989
Departed:	6 June 1991
First game:	18 February 1989: Southampton (h), First Division, drew 1-1
Last game:	11 May 1991: Oldham Athletic (a), Second Division, lost 3-2
Best league season:	1989/90 First Division, 18th (relegated); 1990/91 Second Division, third (promoted), 1990/91 League Cup winners

Record	P	W	D	L	F	A	Win%
League	123	47	35	41	160	152	38.2%
FA Cup	9	3	3	3	12	15	33.3%
League Cup	13	9	3	1	24	7	69.2%
Full Members' Cup	3	1	1	1	7	9	33.3%
Total	**148**	**60**	**42**	**46**	**203**	**183**	**40.5%**

Above statistics for Atkinson's two spells as manager

18

Trevor Francis

FRANCIS WAS the first player to be transferred for a £1m fee in this country in February 1979 – moving from Birmingham City, his first club, to Nottingham Forest. As a player he won 52 England caps together with achieving club honours at Nottingham Forest including winning the European Cup in 1978/79 and 1979/80.

He went on to play for Detroit Express, Manchester City, Sampdoria, Atalanta, Glasgow Rangers, Queens Park Rangers, Wollongong City (Australia) and Wednesday.

Veteran player Francis was the heir apparent after Ron Atkinson's departure – indeed the former manager recommended him for the position.

Francis had cut his teeth as a player-manager at former club Queens Park Rangers before leaving Loftus Road to join Atkinson at Hillsborough as a player.

His managerial start in the capital was not particularly successful – he received negative headlines when QPR player Martin Allen left the team hotel in Newcastle after receiving a call on the night before the game informing him that his wife had gone into labour, and he wanted to be at the birth. Francis fined Allen for leaving the hotel without permission.

The move to Hillsborough to join Wednesday as a player in February 1990, one that Francis thoroughly enjoyed.

Once Atkinson's departure had finally been confirmed, chairman Dave Richards was keen to maintain continuity –

Atkinson's assistant manager, Richie Barker, was approached about the job, but was not interested despite having managerial experience.

Barker recollected saying to Richards, *A Quarter of Wednesday: A New History of Sheffield Wednesday 1970–1995*, 'Trevor had been bought purely and simply as a player, but the job seemed right for him. It was a stable ship. He had a good bunch of responsible players and a team full of self-motivation.'

None of the players were surprised by Francis's appointment as manager. He became the club's first player-manager and the fourth to have played for and managed the club. He retired as a player in April 1994.

In his first notes for the club programme, Francis stated, 'While I'm a different sort of person from Ron, my aim is for things to remain much the same as they were. Continuity is very important, and, happily, the backroom staff so vital to last season's success, remains unchanged.'

On the subject of playing style, he said in *One In A Million* that he had wanted 'a very expansive team playing 4-4-2, with plenty of width to our game'. With Chris Waddle in the forward line there had to be width! Waddle (from Marseille) and goalkeeper Chris Woods (from Glasgow Rangers) two big signings made by Francis in the summer.

By all accounts Francis brought some Italian-style approaches and tactics, as he had done at QPR. The team became more disciplined and roles on the pitch more prescribed, the players' diets came into focus and altered to follow a more Italian approach, including eating pasta.

There was a more defensive approach under Francis – aiming to keep clean sheets rather than attack-minded football where the focus had been on scoring more goals than the opposition.

That 1991/92 season was an excellent one for Wednesday – finishing third in the First Division, their highest league placing for over 30 years, and qualifying for European football, albeit the following season progress in the UEFA Cup was short-lived, knocked out in the second round.

During that season Francis took decisive action regarding star striker David Hirst – Alex Ferguson, manager at Manchester United, had made a formal bid of £4m for the England international. With the backing of the board Francis rebuffed the overtures from the club across the Pennines – much to their manager's chagrin, and much to Wednesday supporters' delight.

January 1992, Wednesday, Eric Cantona – the combination of the club and the Frenchman and what it all meant. For some he was the one that got away – the French international, the maverick. Wednesday looked at him in training, he played in a six-a-side tournament for the club and then apparently Wednesday wanted to offer him a trial. That story has gained traction over time.

Francis's view was quite simple – Cantona's agent, Dennis Roach, had asked Francis to do him a favour and let the Frenchman train with Wednesday for a few days. There was no question of Wednesday ever signing Cantona – that was simply a myth. In any event such a move would have been far too expensive for the club.

Meanwhile, Cantona signed for Yorkshire rivals Leeds United – helping that club to the Football League championship in 1991/92, before he moved to Old Trafford the following season and enjoyed great success with Manchester United.

The highlights of Francis's tenure at Hillsborough were the four games at Wembley in April and May 1993 – FA Cup semi-final against United; League Cup Final against Arsenal followed by the FA Cup Final between the same two clubs (the first time the finalists for those two competitions had been the same clubs in the same season) and the FA Cup Final replay.

Only one of those games won – and that one possibly the greatest derby of them all: a record attendance of 75,364, 2-1 after extra time. Wednesdayites on the highest of highs.

In the run-up to that game Francis appeared on good and friendly terms with his opposite number at Bramall Lane, Dave Bassett. For the passionate Wednesdayite, blue and white to the very core, such bonhomie was hard to understand. No doubt the same feelings for those of a red and white persuasion.

Interesting to reflect on Francis's assessment in his programme notes for the game against Southampton in April 1993, after appearances in both cup finals had been confirmed and sitting fifth in the table, 'We are making excellent progress as we seek the ultimate goal of confirming Sheffield Wednesday as a major force in football ... I think it is fair to say that Wednesday have arrived ... we created high standards which we know we have to maintain. Our aim has to be to succeed over a long period because you only become a genuine force in football by being consistently successful.'

The 1992/93 season was to be Francis's high-water mark as Wednesday manager.

In his excellent book, *A Quarter of Wednesday: A New History of Sheffield Wednesday 1970–1995*, author Daniel Gordon contended that Francis had poor communications skills with the media and with supporters – albeit he acknowledged that most people following Ron Atkinson would struggle to compare with the latter's communication skills.

Gordon highlighted that Francis did not have a good relationship with several players, that he was a little aloof – one of the less critical quotes from the book, 'As a manager, communication was to be his undoing. Francis was unable to command the respect of the majority of his squad, even though the players had initially shown solidarity on the pitch. As the *Star's* Wednesday reporter Paul Thompson wrote, "This did not matter so much in the good times. But in times when results were bad, Francis did not have the goodwill of the players to fall back on."'

England midfielder Carlton Palmer certainly had his issues with Francis – ultimately leading to his leaving the club and joining Leeds. This, despite having a meeting with chairman Dave Richards, stating his keenness to stay at Sheffield 6 and signing a five-year contract with the club.

The Devonian's time in charge was generally very positive for Wednesday – with First Division finishes of third, seventh, and seventh before the 1994/95 season.

That season proved to be Francis's last – one when some of his tactics, substitutions and judgement came under particular scrutiny and criticism by supporters albeit the team finished 13th in the Premier League.

Very damaging for Francis was the news story that broke in the *News of the World* in September 1994 – highlighting dressing room discontent, with a damning assessment of the management style of Francis, including his man-management. Tactics were apparently an issue and the article claimed several players would be looking for a move if Francis remained at the helm.

The issues had also been highlighted on the previous night's edition of *Match of the Day*. It did not augur well.

There was an immediate 'Find The Mole' who leaked the story. Whether it was an individual or several, the source(s) have never been found. But players of the time have reflected it could have been one of a number.

A disappointing season with a 7-1 home defeat to Nottingham Forest in April 1995 presaging Francis's departure from Hillsborough.

In his programme notes for the last game of the campaign, against Ipswich Town, Francis observed, 'It may not have been the best of seasons, but I hope we can bow out with style and dignity – and so face the future with a smile which says we may not have succeeded as often as we wished but our pride and faith in our abilities remain intact.'

Francis evidently knew the sack was coming and arranged a farewell drink with journalists and some staff before the axe fell.

The timing of the announcement of Francis's departure was on the eve of the FA Cup Final – the biggest domestic game of the season at the time – and all eyes would have been on that forthcoming spectacle. The club statement read, 'The board of Sheffield Wednesday Football Club have today by mutual agreement with their manager Trevor Francis terminated the remaining period of his contract. The board would like to place on record its sincere thanks and sincere appreciation of the services provided by Mr Francis in the last four years and wish him every success in the future. The vacancy for a new manager will be advertised immediately and there will be no other statement from the club.'

Indeed, the timing of that announcement left Francis 'hugely disappointed'. He told the *Star*, 'It could have been done in a better way than it was. Having played for the club and then had four years as manager, it could have ended in better circumstances. But it was their decision. I didn't agree with it.

'I think it was the wrong decision to sack me. I would have liked to have been given the chance to change things a little and make changes to the team.'

With the supporters, I think the tide had turned and they were looking for a change.

Interesting to note in Francis's autobiography, he focussed on his time at the club up to 1993 and there is no reference to the circumstances of his departure.

In fairness to Francis, he signed magnificent players for the club and apparently had the opportunity to purchase Alan Shearer from Southampton, at a cost of £3m – which Dave Richards and the board considered too expensive.

Francis was the first Owls boss to win a Manager of the Month award in the Premier League era, in December 1993.

Having left Sheffield 6 he was appointed manager at the club where he first made his name as a player – Birmingham City – in April 1996. He later went on to manage Crystal Palace as well as working for Sky TV as a co-commentator and pundit for 21 years.

Asked by the Gary James's Football Archive website which club meant the most to him over his entire career, Francis responded, 'Who do I have the greatest feeling for? Well, it has to be Birmingham because of the time I was there as a young player and as a manager. You always have a special feeling for your first club, but that's not to say I don't have great memories of the other clubs I played for.'

He passed away in Marbella, Spain, in July 2023. In an obituary *The Guardian* observed, 'A universally popular figure, he was admired for his easygoing nature and humble approachability.'

Born:	18 April 1954, Plymouth
Died:	24 July 2023
Appointed:	18 July 1991
Departed:	20 May 1995
First game:	17 August 1991: Aston Villa (h), First Division, lost 3-2
Last game:	14 May 1995: Ipswich Town (h), Premier League, won 4-1
Best league season:	1991/92 First Division, third

Record	P	W	D	L	F	A	Win%
League	168	65	54	49	242	211	38.6%
FA Cup	17	8	6	3	24	17	47.0%
League Cup	25	13	7	5	44	26	52.0%
UEFA Cup	4	2	1	1	13	7	50.0%
Full Members' Cup	2	1	0	1	3	3	50.0%
Total	**216**	**89**	**68**	**59**	**326**	**264**	**41.2%**

19

David Pleat

NAMES HIGHLIGHTED in the media as possible replacements for Trevor Francis included former England manager Bobby Robson, Danny Wilson and possibly current player Chris Waddle stepping up in a similar way to Francis.

In the event it was none of the speculative names mentioned but David Pleat – then in charge of second-tier Luton Town. And that was a surprise. Appointing a manager who had last managed in the top tier four years earlier.

Nottingham-born Pleat started his playing career as a winger with Nottingham Forest in 1962, and went on to play for Luton, Shrewsbury Town, Exeter City and Peterborough United. A total of 185 appearances for those five clubs, scoring 27 goals. His playing career ended in the 1970/71 season.

Commencing his managerial career at non-league Nuneaton Borough in 1971, he moved to Luton as a coach working under manager Harry Haslam. He was appointed manager in January 1978 when Haslam took the reins at Bramall Lane. Pleat took the Hatters to promotion to the First Division – winning the second tier by a record number of points in 1981/82. They retained their First Division status in each of the seasons Pleat was at the helm.

Tottenham Hotspur came calling and appointed him as their manager in May 1986. In 1986/87 Spurs finished third in the top flight and runners-up in the FA Cup Final to Coventry City – playing an attacking brand of football with an unusual formation often referred to as the 'Christmas Tree', with one striker at its tip.

Following unsubstantiated claims in a newspaper – made as a result of a sting – Pleat resigned from his role at Tottenham Hotspur in October 1987. Pleat consistently denied those claims, describing them as a 'farrago of inventions'.

He quickly regained employment at second-tier Leicester City later that season followed by a return for a second spell as manager of Luton in June 1991. Relegation from the First Division followed in his first season at Kenilworth Road and he remained in charge until he was appointed Wednesday's manager in June 1995.

He was voted Luton's greatest-ever manager in a poll run in 2019.

Pleat was contacted about the role at Hillsborough by Graham Mackrell, Wednesday's secretary – a man he'd known well at Kenilworth Road when the latter was Luton's chief executive. Indeed, it was Pleat who had recommended Mackrell to Wednesday for the secretary position at Hillsborough.

It was the lure of a return to the Premier League which attracted Pleat to Sheffield 6.

David Kohler, the owner and managing director of the Hatters, was not best pleased with Pleat's departure and following a tribunal hearing received full compensation, reported at £150,000.

The new manager stated he felt 'proud and privileged to manage Sheffield Wednesday', adding that he had 'been most impressed by the professionalism of the club in general, the "feel" for football of the supporters and the importance of a democratic boardroom so that all decisions are taken in the best interests of the club'.

In time his view of the board at Hillsborough – chairman Dave Richards, Keith Addy, Graham Thorpe, Geoff Hulley and Joe Ashton – had evolved. In his autobiography, *Just One More Goal*, he said they were 'dyed-in-the-wool Sheffield Wednesday fans. In retrospect what the club needed was someone who was less attached to Wednesday but more of an independent-thinking entrepreneur.'

To support him at Hillsborough he brought in Danny Bergara as first-team coach; he'd worked with Bergara at Luton. He kept Frank Barlow and Albert Phelan on his backroom staff and he was asked by the board to retain Richie Barker – who had worked for Ron Atkinson and Trevor Francis – as a consultant. 'He would act as a conduit between the training ground and the boardroom. This arrangement did not work. I never really integrated Richie into my inner sanctum,' Pleat admitted.

Interesting to note that at the start of his tenure there were 41 professional players on the books.

Pleat moved on several big-name players quickly – including John Sheridan, Mark Bright, Chris Woods and Chris Waddle in 1996, followed by legendary striker David Hirst in 1997. No question the Wednesday team was ageing and some of those players had seen their best playing days but for many Wednesdayites it seemed too many and too quickly.

In a June 2020 interview with the *Star*, more than 20 years after he'd left the club, Pleat commented, 'I'd taken over a team of fading stars. Waddle, Sheridan, Hirst. These were very good players but were now in their twilight.'

Author Elliot Huntley observed in *A Proper Player: The Career of John Sheridan*, 'From the moment David Pleat was appointed, it was clear he intended to run things his way. His blueprint for success, however, was labyrinthine and recondite. Of course, no one can ever really be sure what his masterplan entailed but it seemed, at least to the untrained eye, to involve the systematic freezing out of his experienced and established stars.'

John Sheridan was one of those stars – reduced to reserve-team football at Wednesday, though clearly still good enough for the Republic of Ireland international team! The midfielder said in *A Proper Player*, 'That's what Pleaty wanted, players who wouldn't answer back.' Sheridan went on, 'It was the things that Pleat used to say to me in the reserves that pissed me off. "I love the way you get the young lads playing," he'd say, and then every Saturday he'd leave me out.'

Looking back in that 2020 *Star* article, Pleat acknowledged, 'Maybe in particular I could have built the team around Sheridan more in that first season. I could have got closer to him and tried to integrate him more. Maybe I should have done, but it was difficult.'

Wednesday ended a disappointing 15th in the Premier League in Pleat's first season in charge – their worst finish since the return to the top flight in 1991/92. Indeed, on the last day of the season – away at West Ham United – Wednesday remained in danger of relegation if results had gone against them.

Other leading players were let go – including Andy Sinton, and Chris Bart-Williams. It's worth noting that none of the big names who departed Sheffield 6 during Pleat's reign went on to have great success.

On player incomings he was responsible for the signings of the two Italian stars, Benito Carbone and Paolo Di Canio, and there's no question they lit up the play for Wednesday in his time in charge. And, for me, without doubt Carbone is the most skilful player I've seen wear the blue and white stripes.

After an initial excellent start to the 1996/97 Premier League campaign – Wednesday top of the table in October 1996 – the team fell away somewhat as the season progressed but still finished a creditable seventh.

At the end, Pleat noted it had been 'a very positive season' and added, 'We have adjusted the staff to a group who respect each other and play determinedly for the club.'

Progress in the cups was moderate under Pleat – a best showing of the fifth round in FA Cup and League Cup, and Wednesday's only entry into the UEFA Intertoto Cup saw the club bow out after the group stage.

A poor start to 1997/98 culminated in a 6-1 defeat to Manchester United at Old Trafford, leaving Wednesday at the foot of the Premier League table, and led to Pleat's departure in November 1997 – Alex Ferguson's warm words of support after the game having no impact on the board's decision to part ways.

The club issued a press release, 'Ultimate responsibility for the team's performance rests with the team manager, and the board were unable and unwilling to allow the situation to drift further.'

It went on to reflect on his time in charge, 'Pleat spent his first season halting the deterioration which began under the previous regime ... in retrospect, the Pleat era will perhaps be remembered best as one of transition.'

Dave Richards described Pleat as a 'good guy', adding that football management was 'highly paid, highly dangerous.'

In the *Star Green 'Un*, Wednesday reporter Paul Thompson pointed out, 'Pleat's exit surprised no one except perhaps for its timing.'

David Pleat received the Premier League's Manager of the Month award for August 1996.

The Wednesday job was the last permanent manager's role that Pleat undertook. He returned to Tottenham Hotspur in 1998, appointed as director of football by chairman Alan Sugar. He went on to be caretaker manager at Spurs on three occasions.

He left that club in 2004 and had advisory roles at Portsmouth, West Bromwich Albion and Nottingham Forest before returning to Tottenham in 2010 in a recruitment scouting role. He continued in a role of recruitment consultant for the club before leaving in 2024.

As well as his work with various clubs he has worked for the Premier League as an analyst for youth games and advising on academies.

He has served on FA panels responsible for discipline, transfer tribunals and permits for overseas players as well as being a long-serving member of the League Managers' Association board.

In demand as a co-commentator in radio and television he has worked for the BBC and ITV.

Additionally, he has written a column for *The Guardian*.

Born: 15 January 1945, Nottingham
Appointed: 14 June 1995
Departed: 2 November 1997
First game: 19 August 1995: Liverpool (a), Premier
                   League, lost 1-0
Last game: 1 November 1997: Manchester United (a),
                   Premier League, lost 6-1
Best league season: 1996/97 Premier League, seventh

Record	P	W	D	L	F	A	Win%
League	89	26	28	35	116	147	29.2%
FA Cup	5	3	0	2	10	5	60.0%
League Cup	8	3	2	3	14	12	37.5%
Intertoto Cup	4	2	1	1	7	5	50.0%
Total	**106**	**34**	**31**	**41**	**147**	**169**	**32.0%**

20

Ron Atkinson Returns

FOLLOWING DAVID Pleat's departure, Peter Shreeves took on the role of caretaker manager in November 1997, overseeing one game in charge (a 5-0 win over Bolton Wanderers) – Shreeves had joined the club as a coach in June 1996.

Wednesday were in deep trouble in the Premier League – only nine points taken from the opening 13 games under Pleat.

It was reported that chairman Dave Richards had earmarked former manager Howard Wilkinson for the role but the latter was only four months into a four-year contract with the FA and apparently unable to gain his release.

Cue the return of another former manager – Ron Atkinson.

Having left Sheffield 6 in May 1991, 'Big Ron' had three years at Aston Villa – winning the League Cup in 1994 (by doing so he became the first manager to win trophies with three different clubs) – and a season and a half at Coventry City.

Since his departure from Highfield Road, he'd undertaken work in television together with enjoying the opportunity to relax after 25 years in football management.

'Life in the old dog yet!' was the *Star Green Un*'s welcome headline, noting, 'He has done a short-term rescue act before, and he is capable of doing it again. His charisma can lift a club and supporters … and because of his aura and record is the type of manager who can attract players.'

There was not universal acceptance of the return of Atkinson among Wednesday supporters. I'd written to the *Green 'Un* – the

'In Off The Post' feature on 22 November 1997 – and under the headline 'Decision is too hasty' I said, 'Rarely in the history of the game can there have been such an appointment of a club's manager that has stirred the passions and emotions in quite the way that Ron Atkinson's return to Sheffield 6 has done.

'The assessment and reaction to Big Ron's appointment is primarily at two levels – the first is based on emotion and reflects the manner of Atkinson's departure from Hillsborough … but perhaps the most important assessment of the appointment is at the more objective level – the credentials of Atkinson for the manager's role.

'And in this regard it is difficult to understand the board's apparent assessment that he is the right man for the job. Undoubtedly in the autumn of his career and with his best managerial days behind him, Ron has been out of football management for the better part of a year, his services apparently not sought by other clubs … it is difficult to alter the impression that Ron's appointment has been made in haste by a club accepting and underlining that it is in crisis.'

I was not alone – other correspondents made reference to Atkinson being 'too old for the job, his image is a joke and he will not inspire the current team', and 'the decision to re-employ Ron Atkinson has filled me with anger and disgust' and so it went on.

I'm pleased to readily acknowledge that events would show that I – and the other correspondents – were wholly and totally wrong!

In his autobiography, Atkinson confirmed he'd had an approach from representatives of the Northern Ireland FA to lead the national team into the European Championship qualifiers – a role on a part-time basis and one that interested him.

Enter Dave Richards – keen to sign Atkinson on a three-year deal. The ex-manager evidently saw things differently – for him to come in as a 'fireman' initially to address the pressing issue of avoiding relegation, and then assessing how things stood. An initial deal to the end of the 1997/98 season was agreed.

Atkinson was concerned that the adverse reaction from supporters when he departed six years earlier may rear its head again – the chairman assuring him that a recent local radio phone-in had him as the overwhelming choice for the job. Richards could not have been a reader of the *Green 'Un* where the opposite reaction was the case.

BBC News Online reported, 'Atkinson, one of the most colourful characters in the game, arrived in a blaze of publicity … he swept into the club in his Mercedes and immediately vowed to save Wednesday from the drop, a feat that looked beyond them at the time.'

The returning manager commented, 'There are very few clubs who could have tempted me back, and of course, this was one of them … I am completely convinced that Wednesday have the potential to break into the very top bracket … and there's not one single reason why Sheffield Wednesday haven't got the ability to be an absolute giant.' Bold words indeed.

The first game at home to Arsenal – the reaction from the substantial majority of the crowd was enthusiastically positive. A deserved win against that season's eventual champions helped persuade the doubters and cement the popularity of his appointment among his supporters.

Atkinson turned the fortunes of the club around and Wednesday avoided relegation, finishing the season in 16th place on 44 points. The club programme referred to the manager's return as 'The Second Coming'.

Add to that he brought in players of the calibre of the Swedish international Niclas Alexandersson and the Brazilian centre-back Emerson Thome.

Wednesday had the skilful Italians Benito Carbone and Paolo Di Canio in their ranks – the latter Atkinson referred to as 'the volcano' and said 'he should have been born with a four-minute warning'. Evidently, Di Canio presented challenges to the manager. None more so than after the away game at Bolton Wanderers – where Wednesday played poorly and lost 3-2. Di Canio described a physical assault with punches flying between manager and player as emotions ran high in the dressing room afterwards – the two having to be separated by coaching staff and players.

Coming towards the end of that season, Atkinson was looking forward to another campaign at the helm at Hillsborough – and had talked with Richards about working with Wednesday's ex-player and captain, Nigel Pearson, with a view to the latter succeeding him in due course.

But thinking had changed in the boardroom – Atkinson highlighted the result of the last game of the season at Crystal Palace, a late goal for the home team resulting in defeat for the Owls, and more particularly the result meant Wednesday finished 16th rather than 13th in the table. That significantly impacted the prize money for the club – Wednesday received £800,000 rather than £1.3m.

And it was this drop in income which Atkinson cited as being at the root of his departure at the end of the 1997/98 season – never mind the £6m-plus the club would have lost if they'd been relegated! This was in addition to the £10m loss Wednesday would soon post in their accounts.

A statement said, 'The board have given extensive consideration to future appointments and the development of the club's resources in line with the other Premier League sides. It is the intention to restructure the team management with a long-term development.'

The decision to part company with Atkinson came as a great surprise to supporters and the substantial majority had a very different perspective to the board – the manager had saved the team from relegation, hardly the time to dispense with his services.

Atkinson stated that Wednesday had made him an offer which was much less than his existing wage agreement – the chairman referring to the financial difficulties of the club – and it was an offer he couldn't accept. He was less than impressed with the way he had been treated.

Atkinson's last management job came at Nottingham Forest, appointed in January 1999; it was not a success. Forest relegated, and Atkinson confirmed he was retiring from football management.

He continued working as a football pundit for ITV; his time in that role came to an end abruptly in April 2004 after he made an inappropriate comment on air.

He briefly returned to the club where he had his first start in club management – non-league Kettering Town – as director of football in January 2007. He left in April 2007.

Since that time Atkinson has appeared occasionally on television and undertaken after-dinner speaking engagements.

Appointed:	14 November 1997
Departed:	30 June 1998
First game:	22 November 1997: Arsenal (h), Premier League, won 2-0
Last game:	10 May 1998: Crystal Palace (a), Premier League, lost 1-0
Best league season:	1997/98 Premier League, 16th

21

Danny Wilson

ATKINSON'S DEPARTURE focussed Wednesday's attention on who would be next.

Howard Wilkinson's name came into the frame along with several others including Dave Bassett, Nigel Pearson, Martin O'Neill and Nigel Spackman. Initially, 'Former Wednesday star Danny Wilson has ruled himself out, insisting he will be staying as Barnsley manager,' said BBC News Online on 17 May.

I think if Mr Bassett's name had gained any traction there would have been a reaction among supporters.

At least three leading managers were contacted about the role – Philippe Troussier, the manager of South Africa at the World Cup in France, Gérard Houllier, then technical director of the French Football Federation, and Walter Smith, the very successful boss at Glasgow Rangers.

Of the three it appears Houllier came close to coming to Sheffield 6 – terms apparently agreed except for an outstanding matter on payment to be received in the event that Houllier was sacked. Negotiations on that point dragged on to the extent that Houllier took a different route and became joint manager of Liverpool with Roy Evans.

Smith then came even closer to being appointed – the club claiming a three-year deal had been agreed with the Scot with a press conference planned for the new manager. However, a late offer from Everton 'lured him away' to Goodison Park, the club evidently disappointed by Smith's 'late change of mind'.

Chairman Dave Richards turned his attention to ex-Wednesday player Danny Wilson, manager at Barnsley, who had steered that club to the Premier League, only to be relegated after one season. No matter that Wilson had apparently 'ruled himself out' weeks earlier.

Negotiations took place on the compensation fee – reported at £500,000. All this much to the chagrin of Barnsley supporters.

Wilson's playing career started with hometown club Wigan Athletic before taking in spells at Bury, Chesterfield, Nottingham Forest, Scunthorpe United (on loan), Brighton & Hove Albion, Luton Town, Wednesday and Barnsley. He gained 24 caps for his national team, Northern Ireland.

Honours won included the League Cup, with Luton in 1988 and with Wednesday three years later.

Wilson joined Barnsley as a player in 1993, then moved into management, initially as player-manager, before concentrating solely on management from 1995/96.

Among Wednesdayites his appointment was received generally positively. Buoyed by the goodwill resulting from his success as a player at Hillsborough and his success at neighbours Barnsley, any lack of pedigree in the managerial world was put to one side.

Additions to the squad included Dutchman Wim Jonk, Argentinian Juan Cobián, and Northern Ireland midfielder Danny Sonner.

The manager had a good first season – finishing in 12th position – an improvement on 1997/98.

After the season's conclusion the club advertised 'An Evening with Mick Miller and Danny Wilson' at Hillsborough, priced £30.95. Why the Wednesday manager was referenced after the comedian was not mentioned.

But the campaign had been overshadowed by the Paolo Di Canio affair – the player sent off and subsequently suspended for 11 games having pushed over referee Paul Alcock in the home game against Arsenal. The Italian never played for Wednesday again and was subsequently transferred to West Ham United for a knock-down fee reported at £1.5m.

It was the following season that proved disastrous for Wednesday – not helped by poor dealings in the transfer market. Simon Donnelly and Phil O'Donnell, purchased from Celtic before the season began, played far fewer games than anticipated because of injuries.

Signed in the close-season, strikers Gilles De Bilde from PSV Eindhoven and Gerald Sibon from Ajax fell short of expectations.

Interesting to note that as manager Wilson did not know the pay agreements the players had – contract negotiations the domain of the club secretary and chairman. And Wilson preferred it that way.

The first nine games in the Premier League that season – one draw and eight defeats. And in that run of games, I recollect the 8-0 rout at St James' Park which was as abject a display as I can remember from any Sheffield Wednesday team I've watched – the team seemed to raise the white flag very early on in the game and the score could easily have been double figures.

With the benefit of hindsight if Wilson was going to be replaced in that ill-fated season it ought to have been after that game.

In October he acknowledged, 'What we know is that this is going to be a long season for us, but I have every confidence we will get out of trouble.' That confidence was misplaced.

Wednesday's first win came after ten games – the omens were far from good. In fairness, Wilson had to sell several of the club's better players to help address serious financial issues with the bank – including Benito Carbone and Emerson Thome both at knock-down transfer fees reported at £850,000 and £2.7m respectively, to Aston Villa and Chelsea. And moreover, with no reinvestment back into the playing squad.

Wilson commented in his autobiography, *I Get Knocked Down: But I Get Up Again*, 'My job was becoming very, very difficult. I had results going against me, the chairman criticising the team, and our best players being sold without me being consulted. The squad were completely demoralised, and my job was to motivate them.'

For me, and I think many supporters, it was the sale of these quality players that signalled that Wednesday – with no replacements – were starting to consider that relegation may be inevitable.

As the season progressed matters had reached such depths that in January 2000 four Labour MPs – Clive Betts, Bill Michie, Joe Ashton and David Blunkett – had publicly called for Wilson's dismissal. Ashton had been a Wednesday director for a decade; Blunkett a cabinet minister in Tony Blair's government of that time.

Blunkett was quoted, 'In my opinion, it would be best for the club if Danny Wilson was to leave.'

While the MPs may have been reflecting the growing concerns of some Wednesday supporters, it was hardly appropriate for senior politicians – albeit Wednesdayites of many years' standing – to publicly call for a manager's dismissal.

Indeed, Alastair Campbell, Blair's official spokesman, called Wilson to apologise. 'Danny, I'd like to apologise to you for everything that's happened. I'm not apologising on behalf of the four MPs but because of them. It will not happen again,' Wilson recounted in *I Get Knocked Down: But I Get Up Again.*

Wilson commented, 'I knew they were out of order. To this day, I do not forgive any of them. They stepped out of line and tried to use their political power to voice their personal opinions, which was very wrong.'

To underline the financial problems and their impact – merchant bank Charterhouse Development Capital had invested £16m in the club (a 37 per cent share), and in Wednesday's last five Premier League seasons they had accumulated £30m in debt. It was not looking a good investment for Charterhouse.

The four Labour MPs met with Charterhouse. Joe Ashton wrote to chairman Dave Richards after that meeting, quoted in *The Guardian* on 20 January 2000, 'Charterhouse admitted to us that if the club were to be sold then all the debts would be lumped together. Those debts of course would be a serious deterrent to any prospective purchaser.

'It might then be thought that if Sheffield Wednesday were to be downsized from a business with £23m turnover with £18m debts in the Premier League to a First Division club of £9m with no debts it would be much easier to sell the club and regain some of the investment ... the clear impression we gained from the bank was that it now anticipates relegation and naturally regard it as their duty to protect their assets.'

It is against this backcloth that Danny Wilson had to operate as manager of the football club. Very difficult times.

Dave Richards stepped down from the chair in February 2000 – he had come under pressure from supporters for the manner in which the club was being run and the consequent impact on the field of play. Wilson observed that Richards had been very good to him and they had a very strong relationship. Supporters had a less positive view of the chairman.

Howard Culley succeeded Richards. It was Culley who went to the training ground in March 2000 in the wake of defeat at Watford, which left the team next to the bottom of the table, to let Wilson know the decision had been made to release him from his contract.

Culley had two prepared letters – the first one stated that Wilson had resigned, which the manager vehemently reacted to. He had most definitely not resigned. The other letter stated he'd been sacked. Wilson signed the second letter and questioned the club's motive for the first – it may have been to avoid paying him compensation.

Add to that Wilson was not impressed with the way the club dealt with the communication of his departure – stating he had asked for an hour so that he could talk with his family before the news broke. He reflects that despite having been promised they would wait, the club released the statement straight away.

Wilson was clearly hurt by the way he was treated at Hillsborough and stated he did not return to the ground for a long time after his dismissal.

Of the supporters, he said, 'In contrast to the club's behaviour, the supporters have been absolutely fantastic towards me ... I think they understand that we were going through a torrid time at board level when I was manager. They didn't get on my back, and even when I was sacked, I received letters of support from fans thanking me for my efforts. I cannot thank them enough for their encouragement over the years and they will always hold a very special place in my heart.'

Danny Wilson received the Premier League Manager of the Month award for January 2000.

His managerial career after Wednesday took him to Bristol City, MK Dons, Hartlepool United, Swindon Town, Sheffield United, Chesterfield and Barnsley.

His appointment at Bramall Lane drew a mixed response – his playing and managerial career with Wednesday had not gone down well with some of their supporters. Indeed, at the press conference to announce his appointment there were protests in the car park outside the Cherry Street Stand – audible on BBC Radio Sheffield who were broadcasting live from the ground.

Commenting on Wednesday supporters at the time of his Bramall Lane appointment, Wilson said, 'Surprisingly, I didn't get any stick from Wednesday fans. They actually nicknamed me "Agent Wilson", joking that they'd put me in the role to do a job on the Blades!'

Born: 1 January 1960, Wigan
Appointed: 6 July 1998
Departed: 21 March 2000
First game: 15 August 1998: West Ham United (h), Premier League, lost 1-0
Last game: 18 March 2000: Watford (a), Premier League, lost 1-0
Best league season: 1998/99 Premier League, 12th

Record	P	W	D	L	F	A	Win%
League	67	18	13	36	68	98	26.8%
FA Cup	7	3	2	2	9	6	42.8%
League Cup	6	2	2	2	8	5	33.3%
Total	**80**	**23**	**17**	**40**	**85**	**109**	**28.7%**

22

Paul Jewell

THE LAST nine games of the Premier League season – indeed of Wednesday's Premier League era – they were under the control of temporary manager and previously coach Peter Shreeves, assisted by Chris Waddle. A brief upturn in results but all to no avail – the club were relegated finishing in 19th place on 31 points.

In the media, several names came to the fore as speculation mounted on who would succeed Danny Wilson – possibly Shreeves and Waddle. For a long time the favourite appeared to be Joe Kinnear the former Wimbledon manager – but he ruled himself out – Bruce Rioch, Steve Bruce and David Moyes all mentioned.

In the event none of those were chosen. Paul Jewell was the appointment and aged 35 the youngest-ever permanent manager appointed by the club.

As BBC Online reported, 'The Hillsborough board have opted for Jewell's proven ability to mastermind a promotion campaign from the First Division.'

Jewell started his playing career at Liverpool as an apprentice. He joined Wigan Athletic in December 1984 without having made a first-team appearance for the Merseyside club. Four years at the Lancashire club before a transfer to Bradford City where a ten-year stay yielded 269 appearances for the Bantams, scoring 56 goals.

Before the end of his playing career Jewell joined the coaching staff at Valley Parade, taking on the management role after the departure of Chris Kamara in January 1998. At the end of his first full season in charge Bradford gained promotion to the Premier League.

On the face of it the appointment of Jewell was a real positive statement of intent by Wednesday. Manager at a Premier League club in Bradford who had managed to maintain their top-flight status on reportedly meagre resources; his move to the second tier was received positively by supporters.

His departure from Valley Parade did not go down well with chairman Geoffrey Richmond – Jewell resigned after the chairman called City's 17th-placed finish 'a disappointment'. He was put on gardening leave until a compensation package was agreed with Wednesday.

Given Jewell's achievements at Valley Parade, there was a feeling among supporters that he might just spark a revival and a real assault up the table and a challenge for promotion.

He was reportedly on a three-year deal at Sheffield 6.

Before the start of the season he observed, 'I definitely feel what happened last season has left a lot of apathy around the place. People's confidence has been badly affected and too many people have got used to losing.' He was full of praise for the supporters, 'I'm used to dealing with people who love their football but the fanaticism and enthusiasm of Wednesday supporters is something else.'

Jewell's time in charge was not a success.

Perhaps symptomatic of the times, I recollect the game away at Tranmere Rovers in September 2000 – the team arrived at the ground without any kit, it had been forgotten! They looked like a rag tag and bobtail outfit in their borrowed kit from their hosts – ill-fitting green garments did not aid the cause and almost inevitably they lost, 2-0.

During Jewell's tenure the club set a new record of eight consecutive defeats. Following a 4-1 loss at Wimbledon in February 2001, Wednesday languishing bottom of the First Division, the parting of the ways looked inevitable. The manager had lasted eight months.

The team were in and around the relegation zone of the Championship for much of his short tenure.

On the day of his departure, 12 February 2001, BBC Online described Wednesday as a 'crisis club'.

The Guardian reported, 'Paul Jewell has been sacked as manager of Sheffield Wednesday after just eight months in charge.

'In another day of turmoil at Wednesday, Howard Culley has also stood down as chairman of the First Division side almost a year to the day since taking over.' Geoff Hulley took over as chairman – the third such appointment in a year.

The now ex-manager spoke to BBC Radio 5 Live, 'Clearly, I'm bitterly disappointed. I think any manager near the bottom of any league of any country is going to be under pressure given the club's current position.

'But I have to say I didn't see this coming. Of course I'm aware we're bottom of the league, but we're all grown men here.

'Obviously, it's not nice getting sacked, but I don't think I have been given enough time. But people have to make decisions and the board believe what they have done is in the best interests of Sheffield Wednesday.

'You don't need too much common sense to realise that to stay in this league when I first took over was going to be an achievement in itself. And I've no need to make excuses – the facts speak for themselves. Simon Donnelly and Phil O'Donnell have hardly kicked a ball this season and Wim Jonk the same, along with Andy Hinchcliffe, while Gilles De Bilde has not pulled his weight.

"Look at the players I was forced to let go in the summer. The likes of Niclas Alexandersson, Peter Atherton, Ian Nolan, Pavel Srníček and Richard Cresswell, Danny Sonner and others.

'In contrast, I've barely been given a penny to spend. My biggest money buy was Steve Harkness for £200,000, while I had to play a load of kids from the reserve and youth teams who in normal circumstances would not be ready for first-team football.

'But a decision has been made because the board felt a change was needed. Let me just say the supporters have been fantastic and the staff have been great, although they are in a state of shock like me.'

Jewell went on, 'I have no regrets joining Sheffield Wednesday, but I am confident I will be stronger for this because I have learned a lot in the last seven months.'

Assistant manager Peter Shreeves commented, 'All the coaching staff are very disappointed on behalf of Paul Jewell. He was a young lad faced with an almost impossible mission and we all felt that he did it to the best of his ability, although unfortunately results never went for him.'

Given Jewell's record as a manager – both before and after his time at Sheffield 6 – he could be described as 'the right man at the wrong time'.

Peter Shreeves was again handed the caretaker manager role; Wednesday reportedly £18m in debt at this time.

Jewell returned to management with Wigan Athletic in June 2001. He gained promotion to the Championship in his second season in charge, followed by promotion to the Premier League at the end of the 2004/05 season – Wigan's reaching the top flight for the first time. Runners-up in the League Cup Final of 2006 and he maintained the club's Premier League status until he resigned at the end of the 2006/07 season.

His next managerial position was at Pride Park, joining Derby County in November 2007. He could not save the Rams from relegation – with a record low of 11 points in the Premier League – and resigned on New Year's Eve 2008.

He went on to take the role of manager at Championship club Ipswich Town in January 2011 before parting company by mutual consent in October 2012.

Appointed assistant manager at West Bromwich Albion in January 2018, his employment there lasted only a short time.

In December 2018 he was appointed director of football at Swindon Town leaving in July 2021.

Additionally, Jewell has worked as a TV and radio pundit.

Born: 28 September 1964, Liverpool
Appointed: 21 June 2000
Departed: 12 February 2001
First game: 13 August 2000: Wolverhampton
                 Wanderers (a), First Division, drew 1-1
Last game: 10 February 2001: Wimbledon (a), First
                 Division, lost 4-1

Record	P	W	D	L	F	A	Win%
League	31	7	5	19	33	58	22.5%
FA Cup	2	1	0	1	3	4	50.0%
League Cup	5	4	0	1	12	6	80.0%
Total	**38**	**12**	**5**	**21**	**48**	**68**	**31.5%**

23

Peter Shreeves

WITH JEWELL'S departure, new chairman Geoff Hulley turned to coach Peter Shreeves to arrest the decline – for the third time at Sheffield 6 he took on the temporary manager role.

Welshman Shreeves made his name at Reading in his playing career – his only Football League club. He left Elm Park in 1966 after seven years, followed by spells at non-league Chelmsford City and Wimbledon, Shreeves's playing career ended by a broken leg.

He took up a coaching role at Charlton Athletic in 1973 and moved to White Hart Lane to take up a coaching position with Tottenham Hotspur in 1974. He progressed through the coaching ranks before being appointed manager of the club in 1984 following the departure of Keith Burkinshaw.

Two seasons as manager of Tottenham before his departure from White Hart Lane. He moved on to coach at Queens Park Rangers, followed by a brief spell as assistant manager at Watford – combining that role with assistant manager for the Wales national team.

Shreeves returned to White Hart Lane as manager for one season after Terry Venables had moved to the role of chief executive in 1991. A spell as assistant manager at Chelsea followed before he was appointed assistant manager at Hillsborough by David Pleat in 1996. He undertook the caretaker manager role following Pleat's departure, reverting to assistant manager in Ron Atkinson's second spell in charge.

After a short spell working with Danny Wilson, he moved to Nottingham Forest as Atkinson's assistant in 1999. He returned to Hillsborough as caretaker manager following the departure of Wilson, and was retained as Paul Jewell's assistant manager and in prime position to take the reins on a temporary basis.

Referring to the team, Shreeves observed, 'We've got the piano players and the piano carriers. Unfortunately, we've got too many piano players.'

Bottom of the table on taking the job, the Welshman turned things around – eight wins from the 15 games remaining that season ensured Wednesday comfortably avoided relegation, finishing in 17th place.

Shreeves acknowledged it was 'a disappointing season from our point of view, the fans were magnificent, the players average'.

Key signings included the returning Carlton Palmer and the Norwegian Trond Egil Soltvedt, both from Southampton, and who played a major part in the change of fortunes. Shreeves made a point of highlighting that 'Carlton was magnificent in the dressing room'.

Assistant manager Terry Yorath reflected in his autobiography, *Hard Man, Hard Knocks*, that the team had only won once in the previous 11 games prior to Jewell's dismissal – describing the players as not 'battle-hardened'. They were recruited from lower divisions – 'all we could afford but at least they were prepared to work'. He was particularly complimentary about Soltvedt – a 'key signing on a free transfer' – adding, 'And we made him captain because he was a good pro. He was completely different to the other foreigners. His work ethic was brilliant.'

Wednesday supporters took to the Norwegian and fully appreciated his commitment and work rate.

As a result of Shreeves's achievements, he was awarded a two-year permanent contract.

He said, 'It has been a very testing year for our supporters, mainly because we have lost a lot of home games and the overall standard has been less than what is desirable,' adding, 'Next season is going to be tough.' Shreeves had decided to keep 'a lot of the young boys in training over the summer', stating that they didn't need a full break of eight to ten weeks.

The start of the 2001/02 season was viewed with a degree of optimism – high-earning, low-achieving players including Gilles de Bilde and Wim Jonk had left the club, Des Walker had finished his eight-year spell at Hillsborough and the wage bill had been reduced.

Danny Maddix from Queens Park Rangers – soon to be made club captain – and Paul McClaren from Luton Town were recruited.

The financial situation at the club remained more than problematical – a £16.3m debt as the new season commenced. As the manager admitted, 'We are in trouble financially.'

Any optimism for the new season was misplaced – only one of the first 13 games resulted in a win. The last of those, a 2-1 home defeat to Preston North End, was Shreeves's final game in charge, the team next to bottom of the table.

Shreeves commented, 'With the limited resources available to the club, the last few weeks have been very tough. In the best interests of Sheffield Wednesday and myself, I felt the honourable thing to do was to offer my resignation.'

Assistant manager Terry Yorath observed, 'Peter's resignation came as something of a surprise to us all ... people can see from our league position that he had to do something about it, and Peter's way of doing that was being honourable in saying he couldn't take the job any further. I guess that is the ultimate sacrifice for the benefit of the club.'

In late 2001, Shreeves returned to London to become the assistant manager of Barnet in the fourth tier, before promotion to manager in 2002. A year later he left the club.

Subsequently he worked as an assessor for the Premier League and had short spells as director of football and caretaker manager at Grays Athletic in 2009 and returned to Underhill as a coach under then manager and ex-Wednesday player Ian Hendon in 2009. Shreeves left Barnet at the same time as Hendon in 2010.

Peter Shreeves achieved the Manager of the Month accolade for the First Division in March 2001.

Born: 30 November 1940, Neath, South Wales
Appointed: 12 February 2001
Departed: 18 October 2001
First game: 13 February 2001: Tranmere Rovers (h), First Division, won 1-0
Last game: 16 October 2001: Preston North End (h), First Division, lost 2-1

Record	P	W	D	L	F	A	Win%
League	38	13	9	16	46	52	34.2%
League Cup	3	3	0	0	9	5	100%
Total	**41**	**16**	**9**	**16**	**55**	**57**	**39.0%**

Includes games when Peter Shreeves was temporary manager

24

Terry Yorath

WELSHMAN TERRY Yorath's playing career started with Leeds United at the beginning of that club's most successful period, under manager Don Revie in the 1960s. The midfielder stayed at Elland Road for seven years before leaving to join Coventry City. A three-year stay at Highfield Road followed by a move to Tottenham Hotspur. Two years at White Hart Lane before he moved abroad to Vancouver Whitecaps.

Returning to the UK in 1982, he joined Bradford City for a three-year stay, then moved to Swansea City in 1986 where he made a single appearance before beginning his managerial career.

In addition to his total of 343 club career appearances and 16 goals, Yorath made 59 appearances for Wales, scoring two goals.

Yorath was at Valley Parade as player-coach when the Bradford fire took place in May 1985 – 56 people losing their lives in the tragedy. He was in the dugout when the horrific blaze engulfed the old wooden Main Stand late during the first half of their final game of the season, against Lincoln City. His parents, wife and children had been in the midst of the inferno – sitting in the directors' box in the centre of the stand.

In *Hard Man, Hard Knocks* he recalled running and shouting to everyone in the rooms and offices beneath the stand to 'get f*****g out'. Yorath found his wife and children – they had managed to get out of the stand. He could not find his parents.

'It was complete confusion. By this time, the fire had reached the roof and wood and molten felt were raining down all over the place. Then it hit the tunnel … It was an inferno – the flames had spread faster than a person could run … In the end, I had to throw a chair at a window in the players' lounge and then jump through it to escape myself.'.

Yorath's parents were safe. As creatures of habit they'd left their seats before half-time to have a cigarette – they were well away from the fire in the stand.

Others were not. Yorath remembered, 'After checking my parents were all right, I went back into the ground, where I saw all sorts of dreadful things.'

Leaving Bradford, his club managerial career started at the Vetch Field with Swansea City in 1986 followed by a return to Valley Parade in 1989 for a year, back for a brief stint at Swansea followed by a year in charge of Cardiff City. From 1988 to 1993 he was part-time manager of the Welsh national team. After leaving Cardiff he took charge of the Lebanon national team for two years until 1997.

Back in the UK, Yorath worked as a coach at Huddersfield Town between 1997 and 2000.

He joined Wednesday, supporting Paul Jewell, in the summer of 2000, following the new manager from Bradford. And he worked alongside Jewell's assistant, Peter Shreeves, who had been his assistant with Wales.

Arriving at Hillsborough, Yorath highlighted he saw a split in the squad – the homegrown British players and those players from abroad. The latter included Gilles De Bilde, Gerald Sibon, Petter Rudi and Wim Jonk.

Yorath observed the two groups did not talk with each other, and commented that the British players did not like the foreign players because of their apparent poor work ethic. Add to that the foreign players earned substantial sums from the club.

At the training ground there were two dressing rooms – one for the British players and the other for the foreign players, the decision taken to knock the two changing rooms into one – to ensure all the players mixed.

Yorath made reference to some of the contractual arrangements during this time – for example the cost of De

Bilde's two dogs being in quarantine when they came over was paid for by the club, and one of the foreign players – name not given – received £5,000 appearance money even if he didn't play, only failing to receive the bonus if the manager had dropped him.

Yorath was promoted to assistant manager when Peter Shreeves succeeded Paul Jewell.

After Shreeves's resignation, several names were mentioned in the media as possible replacements including Jim Smith, Trevor Francis, Nigel Worthington and Chris Waddle.

Yorath was put in caretaker charge of the team for a month before being offered and accepting the permanent role in November 2001 – reportedly doubling his annual salary from £90,000 to £180,000.

He said in his autobiography, 'I have to be honest, I didn't really want to be manager but it was there on a plate for me and I accepted the chance to run a big club with a great crowd and ground but very poor finances. The money troubles were a millstone around everybody's neck and they meant I couldn't bring in too many new players.'

His appointment as caretaker manager coincided with an immediate improvement in results, winning three of the next four games – albeit from that point the team struggled to the end of the season. The manager pointed to the signing of Shefki Kuqi in January as being 'decisive' in Wednesday's fight to stay in the division – which they did with a final-day draw with Wolverhampton Wanderers.

Wednesday finished in 19th, albeit with a notable run in the League Cup – reaching the semi-final stage for the third time in their history, losing in the two-legged tie to Blackburn Rovers, 6-3 on aggregate.

The 2002/03 season again produced a poor start, the first win not coming until well into October, albeit a win definitely worth waiting for, 2-0 against United in the derby at Hillsborough.

Yorath felt several players that season were not able to produce their best for Wednesday, and at Hillsborough in particular – including Lloyd Owusu, Leon Knight and Jon Beswetherick. His view that the club and ground were simply too big for them

– the expectations on them were too high. He described it as 'stage fright' – something he'd not seen before.

From that time, I recollect Beswetherick in particular struggling – and it was no surprise he made only 11 appearances for the club.

Interesting that Yorath reflected after the 3-1 home defeat by Burnley in October that he'd alerted his assistant manager, Willie Donachie, and goalkeeping coach Martin Hodge to make themselves scarce if they found there were no women in the boardroom when they went up there – Yorath's assessment was that in those circumstances his job would be the focus of discussion.

On arrival at the boardroom – no women present, Donachie and Hodge left. Yorath was given four games to sort it out. The first three produced a win and two defeats, the fourth losing 1-0 at home to Millwall and, 'Five minutes before the end of the Millwall game with defeat staring us in the face, I felt a tap on my shoulder. I turned round to find this woman looking at me.

'"Yes?"

'"Terry," she said. "You're a lovely man but please do the best thing for Sheffield Wednesday and resign."

'Her words haunted me through the night and I decided that she was right.'

Yorath resigned – Wednesday 22nd and in the relegation zone at the time. He observed, 'It was the first time I'd ever resigned because I felt I couldn't do any more. I respected the club so much that I had to do what was right.'

Yorath evidently pleased to be out of it – the pressure of managing a club like Wednesday 'nearly did me in', he admitted. At the time he thought he would not manage a club again.

Chairman Geoff Hulley stated, 'I must pay tribute to Terry, who managed the club with a dignity, and courage, right through to his resignation … he worked tirelessly on the training pitch to improve our fortunes. There is no doubt that Terry has left us with a better squad than the one he inherited.'

He went on to be assistant manager at Huddersfield Town the following year before a short stint as manager at non-league Margate in 2009.

Born:	27 March 1950, Cardiff
Appointed:	21 November 2001
Departed:	31 October 2002
First game:	20 October 2001: Walsall (h), First Division, won 2-1
Last game:	30 October 2002: Millwall (h), First Division, lost 1-0

Record	P	W	D	L	F	A	Win%
League	49	13	15	21	51	68	26.5%
FA Cup	1	0	0	1	1	2	0%
League Cup	6	3	0	3	10	8	50.0%
Total	**56**	**16**	**15**	**25**	**62**	**78**	**28.5%**

25

Chris Turner

THE CLUB were a reported £23m in debt as they embarked on the search for the successor to Terry Yorath.

Chairman Geoff Hulley, 'Our managerial appointment must be the start of a new beginning for Sheffield Wednesday ... we want someone who will win us football matches ... we must also take into account relevant factors such as experience, desire, professional conduct and financial requirements.' He went on to say that the squad is 'more than capable of a mid-table finish'.

The club's favoured candidate for the position was apparently Peter Reid, the Sunderland manager, but that interest came to nothing – 30 years earlier Wednesday had shown a keen interest in Reid the player in his early Bolton Wanderers days, before he joined Everton.

George Burley, recently departed as manager at Ipswich Town, was considered for the role at Sheffield 6. Other possibles mentioned in the newspapers included Chris Waddle and Ronnie Moore.

But it was Chris Turner, ex-Wednesday player and supporter, and manager at Hartlepool United, who became the fifth ex-Owls player to be appointed to the role.

As a player he'd progressed through the youth ranks at Hillsborough and made his first-team debut as goalkeeper in 1976, moving on to Sunderland, then Manchester United before returning to Wednesday in 1988 and making the move to Leyton Orient, the last club in his playing career.

He made a total of 166 appearances for Wednesday – surpassed only by his 195 appearances for Sunderland.

His managerial career started at Leyton Orient in 1994/95 – as joint manager with John Sitton. An unsuccessful campaign with the O's who were relegated at the end of the season – both men departed the club.

He went on to coach at Leicester City and Wolverhampton Wanderers, working under manager Mark McGhee.

Turner was appointed manager of the Football League's bottom club, Hartlepool, in February 1999. He guided them to safety – and changed the club's fortunes by finishing the next three seasons as defeated semi-finalists in the play-offs followed by promotion in 2002/03.

The interview process before Turner was appointed at Hillsborough was protracted – taking four weeks from interview to appointment.

In his first club programme notes he stated, 'I'm very proud to be the manager of Sheffield Wednesday and I know my family are proud for me as well. I'm under no illusions about the size of the task we are faced with for the rest of the season.' He felt that a switch back to a 3-5-2 formation would make best use of the team's most creative player, Gerald Sibon.

Turner was positive in his outlook that the club would make good progress, albeit Wednesday in the relegation places at the time of his appointment. His positive outlook was not reflected with results on the pitch – eight wins from 29 games, four points adrift of safety, finishing 22nd in the table and relegation to the third tier for the second time in their history.

His predecessor Terry Yorath later said in *Hard Man, Hard Knocks*, 'I felt partly responsible for their going down but not half as much as the board should have. The spectacular decline of Sheffield Wednesday as they've slipped from the Premiership to what is now League One in just three seasons is down to the club's directors. Just ten years ago the Owls finished seventh in the Premiership and runners-up in both the FA Cup and League Cup in the same season. The directors have been living in never-never land for far too long and mismanagement from the top level right the way down lies behind the sorry state of affairs at Hillsborough.'

Following relegation at the end of the 2002/03 season there was a keenness and belief that Wednesday could make a good fist of a return in one year from the Second Division. Turner observed, 'We need to be out of the Second Division in two years but hopefully we'll be out this year.'

For all the optimism, after a reasonably good start to the season Wednesday fell away and finished 16th in the table with only a run to the Northern Final of the Football League Trophy a real positive in the knockout competitions.

The start of the following season showed little improvement – supporters becoming frustrated by lack of progress, pressure put on chairman Dave Allen and Turner was dismissed after nine games following defeat at home to Bournemouth which left the club 14th in the table.

Allen commented, 'It was a very tough decision to part company with Chris Turner and Colin West [Turner's assistant]. We have had so many managers in recent years that I felt it was important to give them the best part of two years to put their own stamp on the playing staff here. But, although there is no doubt they improved the squad individually in the summer, by the time of the Bournemouth game it became clear to me that we were not making sufficient progress.'

Turner said in *Owls: Sheffield Wednesday Through The Modern Era*, 'When I took the job, I knew from Wednesday's track record there was a fair chance of not being successful. But I took it because I'm confident in my own ability. And I believe if we had more time, we would have achieved what we set out to achieve. We brought a whole new team in this summer, we've changed the culture and have left them with a lot of good players. We just needed more time.'

Captain Lee Bullen felt Turner was looking to succeed playing football and admitted in his autobiography, *No Bull: The Lee Bullen Story*, 'I was very sad to see Chris leave ... there was a sense of despondency in the changing room and also uncertainty.'

In August 2020 the *Star* had an interview with Chris Turner looking back at his time as manager at Hillsborough.

'I was told I had to run the club on a budget of £2.5m and we were at the time running at about £4.5m,' he said, describing the job throughout his time as Wednesday manager as 'hugely difficult'.

'Some players that were released I would have liked to have kept, but it's one of those things, I couldn't see much mileage in having players around who had been on £5,000 per week contracts that had been dropped to £2,000 or £3,000. They'd have been difficult to motivate. That's why I released so many.'

Out went Leigh Bromby, Derek Geary, Steve Haslam and Alan Quinn. Kevin Pressman's 17-year association with the club was over, Jon Beswetherick's less successful stay ended as well. Many youth players left and Wednesday were starting again on a shoestring.

'We sent [scout] Peter [Eustace] up to Scotland to look at JP McGovern, Steve MacLean, people like that,' Turner said.

'We had someone watching Boro's youth side and they said to me, "Chris, get this lad signed fast." So, we got Chris Brunt on loan and signed him within the first week.

'I spoke to Kevin Blackwell intensely about McGovern, he'd been at Sheffield United and Leeds on loan and hadn't really put a marker down. But we had no width in the team at the time and we envisaged him playing and putting crosses in for Lee Peacock and [Steven] MacLean. Some of them were risks, but it came together.'

Paul Heckingbottom, an experienced left-back, and goalkeeper David Lucas joined – a big personality – along with Sheffielder Chris Marsden, an experienced former Premier League midfielder whose injuries would cut short his appearances for Wednesday. All at a total reported cost of £230,000.

'You pick up the phone and you speak to people that have either managed or coached them,' Turner said. 'You look at their careers and look at what they've achieved, where they've been. They had to be able to handle Hillsborough.'

Lee Bullen was picked up on a free transfer from Dunfermline Athletic – a 33-year-old right-back, he would captain the team and in time under manager Paul Sturrock lift the League One play-off trophy and lead the club into the Championship.

Bullen remembered, 'Wednesday had gone through a rough time and were stuck in League One, so Chris made a huge, bold decision and rolled the dice, bringing in a whole boatload of players.

'Scotland at that time was going through some harder times money-wise and it was a good pond to be fishing in. I was at Dunfermline in the Scottish Premier League where the top wage was £2,500, so the average wage was about £1,000.

'For a club like Wednesday to come up to Scotland was brave, they signed myself, MacLean, McGovern. Then from elsewhere there were youngsters; Brunt, [Patrick] Collins, [Glenn] Whelan. It was a tough decision for Chris because he had to let go of some good players as well. But it worked.'

It did work in time – primarily for Paul Sturrock after he'd succeeded Chris Turner.

On holiday in New York, Turner didn't watch the 2005 League One play-off final against Hartlepool and was told the result by an excited supporter in Times Square. Seven of the 11 players who started for Wednesday were Turner signings, as well as three of the four goalscorers.

He looked back with pride when talking to the *Star*, 'I'd built both teams in that final, a large majority of the Hartlepool team were my players and obviously Sheffield Wednesday's team that year I'd put together.

'You feel frustrated that we'd worked for 18 months, I'd finally got a squad of players that I'd recruited and it was all over. But that's what chairmen and owners have got to make decisions about. There was a lot of pressure around at that time.

'Straight after the play-off final, Paul took the time to appreciate the work I'd done in collecting the players he had to work with, which I appreciated greatly.'

The financial challenges were underlined with off-field departures – chief executive Alan Sykes departed in January

2004, and commented to Yorkshire Live two months later, 'Relegation did not make for an easy time for the club.'

Separately, I'd arranged for the match ball to be sponsored for Dad's 77th birthday in October 2003 for the game against Blackpool – arriving early, we noticed in the seated area below the executive box in the South Stand Chris Turner talking to someone. I attracted the manager's attention, wishing him and the team good luck that afternoon – a friendly acknowledgement back. Good luck or not, Wednesday played poorly on the day and lost 1-0.

David Hirst, the legendary Wednesday striker of the 1980s and 1990s, was on host duties in the executive boxes that day and was critical of 'that lot' in blue and white stripes – he found it difficult to comprehend how the team had fallen so quickly from the Premier League. He was not the only one!

Chris Turner returned to management with Stockport County in December 2004 – then bottom of League One. He was unable to change their fortunes and they were relegated. The club struggled the following season and Turner left in December 2005.

He returned to Hartlepool as director of sport in February 2006 and took over as caretaker manager after the departure of manager Danny Wilson in December 2008. They finished the season in 19th position, and avoided relegation the following year on goal difference.

In August 2010 Turner resigned from his position at Hartlepool. He linked up again with Dave Allen at Chesterfield becoming chief executive of that club in 2011, switching roles to director of football in January 2017, before leaving two months later.

He later spent a year as sales and marketing manager at Port Vale.

Turner helped with the founding of a new football club – Wakefield AFC – in 2019 and was appointed their director of football.

Born: 15 September 1958, Sheffield
Appointed: 7 November 2002
Departed: 18 September 2004
First game: 9 November 2002: Norwich City (a), First
                     Division, lost 3-0
Last game: 18 September 2004: Bournemouth (h), First
                     Division, lost 1-0
Best league season: 2003/04 Second Division, 16th

Record	P	W	D	L	F	A	Win%
League	84	24	27	33	101	125	28.5%
FA Cup	4	1	2	1	7	6	25.0%
League Cup	2	1	1	0	3	2	50.0%
Football League Trophy	6	3	1	2	9	4	50.0%
Total	**96**	**29**	**31**	**36**	**120**	**137**	**30.2%**

26

Chat with Chris Turner

IN FEBRUARY 2025 I talked with Chris about his time as Wednesday manager.

'I was manager at Hartlepool United, then in the Third Division, and we were doing really well in the league. Out of the blue I had a call from [chief executive] Alan Sykes at Wednesday asking me if I'd be interested in the job – I met Bob Grierson a director at the club and later had an interview with chairman Dave Allen at a hotel in Wetherby.

'Three to four weeks later I was offered the job – I think the club interviewed other candidates in that period. The delay meant the team played six games between the time I was interviewed and joined the club – and the team lost five of those games.

'No question I was very keen to join the club as manager – I had supported Wednesday from boyhood and played for the club in two separate stints in the 1970s and in the late 1980s and early 1990s. I doubt I would have left Hartlepool for any other club. I had no reason to leave – at that time Hartlepool were 12 points clear in the division and would go on to gain promotion at the end of the season.

'At Hillsborough it was a very difficult job from day one – we were next to bottom of the table in the First Division "(now rebranded the Championship). The board had found itself under pressure and criticised since Trevor Francis's time at the club. Add to that the club were on the slide downwards and increasingly so since relegation from the Premier League.

'And because it was Wednesday, I put myself under that bit more pressure – I really wanted to do well.

'Overall, the squad of players were not strong enough for the level of football required, and many of them were out injured for a period. I had to beg, steal and borrow in the loan market.

'It takes time to stabilise and turn round a club like Wednesday from the position they had gotten themselves into. There was not enough time – not enough games left – for me to pull the team together and make the necessary changes that would give us a realistic chance of avoiding relegation in what remained of that season.

'An indication of the lack of team stability is a total of 40 players appeared in the first team that season.

'That said, we gave it our best shot – and won at champions-elect Portsmouth at Fratton Park 2-1 in April 2003 ... such was their confidence they had crates of champagne on ice before the game ready to celebrate promotion that day! And we followed that up with a 7-2 away win against Burnley at Turf Moor.

'At the end of the season 16 players were out of contract and 15 of those players were released. I would have liked to retain some of those players but such were the financial pressures that was simply not viable. I brought 12 players into the club for the new season. And the new players, the way of playing and my approach needed time to produce the goods.

'Add to that the expectations on a club of Wednesday's size and prestige – we were expected to win most games in the Second Division (then the third tier).

'To add more pressure Ken Bates was keen to purchase the club – and he'd made it very clear that he would bring in his own management team and make immediate changes and that included the team manager! Imagine that pressure.

'No question the results were not as good as we'd all have liked in my one full season in charge at the club and we finished a disappointing 16th in the league table.

'My tenure lasted for nine games from the start of season 2004/05.

'To the question was I surprised when the decision was made to part company? Yes and no. Yes, because I felt I'd brought the players in that would stand the club in good stead for a promotion push that season and they needed some time to bed down as a team. No, because I know the demands of the club and the expectations and we had not made a good start to the season.

'There was clear disappointment when the sack came but there was also a little bit of relief given the pressures. They were undoubtedly very trying times at Hillsborough.

'Looking back, Howard Wilkinson had mentioned to me after Peter Shreeves left the club that the next manager would have a very hard job – they would have to reorganise the playing staff and the structure. As we know Terry Yorath came in – he was not there long enough to complete what was needed. I had to carry that forward and action it. It needed doing.

'Before I left the chairman, Dave Allen, asked me who I would recommend as the next manager – other directors had evidently suggested to him several potential candidates including Bobby Robson and John Barnes. I recommended Paul Sturrock who had done a fine job at Plymouth Argyle and had recently lost his job at Premier League Southampton.

'And I appreciated Paul thanking me for recommending him for the job and also for recognising that many of the players who played in the play-off final against Hartlepool United were players I'd brought to the club – and by the way many of the Hartlepool United players that day had been brought to that club by me!

'Putting my time in the manager's job into context – when I came into the club the wage bill was something like £8.4m a year – a huge figure at the time – and a number of the players were clearly not performing at the level required. By the start of the following season the wage bill was down substantially to around £2.5m a year. I had to get the costs down because of the financial pressures on the club. And the players I brought in were better value for money.

'Those players included Lee Bullen, Glenn Whelan, Chris Brunt, and Steve MacLean among others. Whelan and Brunt arrived without the club paying a transfer fee and in time those two were sold by the club for about £5m.

'Overall, I have no doubt I left the club in a much better state than when I walked through the door in November 2002.'

I then took the opportunity to ask Chris about the managers he'd played for at Hillsborough.

'**Len Ashurst** – he did so well for me. He gave me my debut at the age of 17 at the beginning of the 1976/77 season. In the game against Mansfield Town at Hillsborough at the end of October I remember making a mistake – dropping a corner as it came over at the Leppings Lane end of the ground, the ball fell to their player who scored. The day before the next game – home to Rotherham United – Len said he was leaving me out of the team. I remember going home and crying – it felt like my whole world was falling in. That next game we lost 3-1 and Len restored me to the team and he kept faith in me. He was a very hard-working manager who had high demands. The training sessions were undertaken at match tempo all the time.

'**Jack Charlton** – in some ways he was before his time. Very technical in his approach – he introduced the "front sweeper" playing in front of the back four. Jimmy Mullen had that role. Nowadays it would be called a holding midfield player. He organised his team very well – knew what he wanted and ensured players worked to that system. On the coaching side he left that to Maurice Setters and Ian St. John – we might not see him down at the training ground until Thursday or Friday during the week. He decided he wanted a taller goalkeeper [Bob Bolder]. I left Wednesday in July 1979, moving to Sunderland, and joined up with ex-Wednesday captain Ken Knighton.

'**Howard Wilkinson** – I remember playing for Sunderland against his Wednesday team. I'd not seen a team run so hard, so quick and at such a tempo for 90 minutes. He brought me back to Hillsborough in September 1988 to play in the first team and he was pleased to hear that I was doing work for my coaching badges. He wanted me to push and promote two young keepers at the club – Kevin Pressman and Marlon Beresford.

'As a manager he knew the game inside out and made sure his teams were mentally strong. In training he worked on specific things – particularly set plays.

'I remember one time he asked me about the best strikers in the country – he was keen to recruit a top striker for the club. He showed me a list of names – the ones at the top of the list were either too expensive or not available. He highlighted the name of Lee Chapman. Lee had an excellent record at his first club, Stoke City, had not really lived up to expectations at Arsenal or at his then current club Sunderland. It was agreed that Chapman would be watched at Sunderland's last game of the season at Leicester City – he had a blinder. He signed for Wednesday and proved to be an excellent signing.

'**Peter Eustace** – he had the chance to go with Howard to Leeds United. He decided to stay as caretaker and was then promoted to permanent manager. For any manager it's hard taking over as a caretaker manager and then moving into the role on a permanent basis. It was a difficult time and the team were struggling. The club only gave him three months in the position.

'**Ron Atkinson** – he treated players like men. He understood people and knew how to get the best out of the players. He did not focus so much on the coaching side – he had Richie Barker, as his assistant, who took more of that responsibility.

'He wanted players who could pass a ball and defenders who could defend – he brought Peter Shirtliff back from Charlton Athletic to join captain Nigel Pearson at centre-back.

'His preparation for big games was second to none – the League Cup Final against Manchester United, his friend the comedian Stan Boardman on the bus to relax the players, and beers at dinner in the days before the final. It worked to perfection.

'**Trevor Francis** – He signed the England international goalkeeper Chris Woods before the start of the 1991/92 season. It was time for me to move on. I went to Leyton Orient initially on loan to play and then moved permanently to become assistant manager to Peter Eustace who had gone to Brisbane Road as manager.'

27

Paul Sturrock

SCOTSMAN PAUL Sturrock had most recently been Southampton's manager in the Premier League – albeit for a brief period; his appointment at Sheffield 6 seen very positively and greeted warmly by the supporters.

Given that Sturrock was born in a small farming community in Ellon, Aberdeenshire, a career in football seemed an unlikely prospect.

Unlikely or not, when the opportunity arose, he grabbed it with both hands – as a player spending the entirety of his career at Dundee United. In the 1980s he was one of the most revered strikers in Scottish football, reflected in his return of 170 goals from 571 games for the Tangerines, and he played 20 times for the Scottish national team.

His career at Tannadice came in a golden era for United – winning the league title in 1983 and breaking the Old Firm duopoly, two League Cups and reaching the final of the UEFA Cup, as well as the Scottish FA Cup Final on four occasions.

Known as 'Luggy' (also the title of his autobiography), he was forced to retire through injury in May 1989.

Once his playing days were over, he joined the coaching staff at Tannadice, staying there until November 1993 when he took his first manager's job in Perth at St Johnstone. An excellent first season, he led the club to the First Division title in 1996/97 before returning to Tannadice as manager for two years.

Taking his career south of the border, Sturrock became manager of Plymouth Argyle in October 2000 with the club at a low ebb struggling in the fourth tier. He transformed Plymouth's fortunes, gaining promotion to the third tier with a record points tally and leading them on the path to promotion to the Championship in 2003/04.

Sturrock was appointed manager at Premier League Southampton in March 2004 and was in the role less than six months before he left by 'mutual consent'.

His appointment at Sheffield 6 on 23 September 2004 came less than two months after his departure from St Mary's. Sturrock's own words in *Luggy*, 'I was very pleased to be appointed as manager of Sheffield Wednesday, who are with all due respect to my other teams and fans, the biggest club I have managed, certainly in terms of fan base … nothing prepared me for the level of support the club generated and the expectation and loyalty of the fans – it was awesome … Wednesday's fans were something else again – they were unbelievable.'

Sturrock said he was told the performance of his Plymouth team at Hillsborough in beating Wednesday 3-1 in October 2003 was a significant factor in him being offered the position.

Chairman Dave Allen commented in the club programme, 'There were other candidates to take the manager's job but I was extremely impressed with Paul's success at this level and his ideas on how he wants to run things. His training methods – with double sessions and specialist coaching for each area of the team makes perfect sense, and his results have shown that they work.'

Striker Steven MacLean recounted Sturrock's arrival in *Owls: Sheffield Wednesday Through The Modern Era*, 'Basically he laid the law down straight away and got stuck into us. It was very much it was going to be his way or the highway. If you weren't going to do what he said and tune in to his way of thinking then you were no longer going to be required. It was a bit of a shock to the system for a lot of us … a little bit of a kick up the backside.'

Playing in the unfamiliar left-back role for Sturrock's first game, Paul Smith remembered, 'The manager came in on

Thursday and told us he wants to play the game at a high tempo and to play football at the right times.' It worked – a 3-0 win at Wrexham.

Sturrock quickly utilised the loan market to good effect – bringing in Kenwyne Jones [Southampton], Joey O'Brien [Bolton Wanderers], and Alex Bruce [Birmingham City], all of whom integrated into the team very well. Sturrock particularly praised captain Lee Bullen, 'As a player and an inspirational captain he was fantastic.'

That campaign – Sturrock's first – Wednesday were in the hunt for a play-off position right to the end. The penultimate game of the regular season they played away at Hull City. Sturrock's superstition of not being at pitchside during injury time came to embarrass him at the end of the game. In the dressing room as the players trooped in he started to rant about how the team had let their lead slip and that a draw was not going to be enough – until he learned that Wednesday had scored a last-minute winner!

A convincing 3-1 win on aggregate over the two-legged semi-final against Brentford led to the play-off final against Hartlepool United at the Millennium Stadium in Cardiff. A final where Wednesday seemed to do what Wednesday often do best – putting their supporters through the mill and back again.

Sturrock reflected that to relax the players before the Brentford game they had been taken out to drink as much as they liked; and prior to the final the players relaxed by canoeing on a lake – the manager careful not to join them on the lake.

The team stayed in Cardiff the night before the final – as Sturrock observed, many Wednesday supporters had arrived early for the game and 'the noise was unbelievable'.

At half-time 1-0 Wednesday, supporters in good spirits, tables turned in the second half and Hartlepool scored twice: 2-1 after 65 minutes, the supporters' anxiety rising. Sturrock made three substitutions – including Steven MacLean who had been sidelined for weeks with a broken toe. MacLean had only been told 65 minutes before kick-off that he would be involved and on the bench. Evidently Sturrock liked to keep his cards close to his chest.

Within minutes of the substitutions, a penalty to Wednesday. MacLean – 2-2. Relief and an additional 30 minutes to play.

Extra time – and Wednesday on top during that period, running out 4-2 victors. Promotion in Sturrock's first season. The celebrations of supporters and players something to behold – 'the noise from the Wednesday fans was absolutely deafening' observed Sturrock.

Towards the end of that season, in March 2005 there had been a change in management structure at the club – commercial director Kaven Walker was appointed chief executive.

After the play-off final, Sturrock said it would be a greater achievement to stay in the Championship the following season. In the event Wednesday finished 19th, ten points clear of the relegation places – and supporters recognised the job the manager had done in stabilising and consolidating the club.

In the programme for the game at Crystal Palace that season, captain Lee Bullen provided these observations about Paul Sturrock, 'He calls a spade a spade. It's refreshing because the game could do with a bit more honesty and straight-talking – there's too much back-biting and whispering. But with him there's none of that – if you've had a bad game or he's not happy with you, he'll tell you in your face.'

Sturrock commented in his autobiography, 'Ahead of the 2006/07 Championship season, I was told by the chairman that the budget was going to be cut and that he wanted to have the side play a more open style of football.' Sturrock considered the club did not have the money to bring into the club the kind of players required to play that way.

Ultimately, there was a debate between manager and chairman over the players to be released, leading to a vote on the board 'and a furious row ending in me swearing a good deal as I left them in no doubt over my opposition to their plan and interference'.

Early results in 2006/07 were not promising – one win in the first ten games. Nonetheless, Sturrock was offered an extension to his contract – for a reported four years – and was sacked a week later following a 4-0 defeat at Colchester United. I'd been at the game – and certainly while Wednesday had not played well, everything had gone right for the home team and the scoreline flattered the hosts.

There was surprise and genuine disappointment when Sturrock was sacked after the game – he had done well for Wednesday and the supporters were certainly with him.

Dave Allen said in a club statement, 'Our league position says it all ... in spite of strengthening the squad this year, we have not made the desired progress, and, to that end, we need a change in the coaching staff.'

Lee Bullen later said in his autobiography that all the players were surprised by Sturrock's departure, and they were not aware of the level of pressure on him. He added, 'He was both liked and respected in the dressing room, which is not always a common combination.'

Steven Maclean commented about the 'horrible day' of Sturrock's sacking, saying in *Owls: Sheffield Wednesday Through The Modern Era*, 'Paul was a great manager ... I was really sad to see him go,'

Author Tom Whitworth went on to comment, 'Later, reports would emerge of Sturrock rowing with the club's chief executive, Kaven Walker.'

Following the announcement of his departure around 3,000 supporters turned up at Hillsborough to protest and to show their appreciation of their now ex-manager.

Kevin Summerfield, who was part of Sturrock's management team at Wednesday, said in *Luggy*, 'In terms of what we achieved at Sheffield Wednesday in gaining promotion from League One and consolidating their position in the Championship ... I know Paul still thinks that was one of his better jobs and that play-off final for drama and euphoria will stay long in our memories. It was a fantastic experience.'

John 'Sloop' Blackley, another member of Sturrock's staff, added in the same book, 'We were really what I would term, a working league side and had come on the rails to reach the final ...

if we ever needed reminding of just how big Sheffield Wednesday Football Club is, that day at the Millennium Stadium removed all doubt ... The key again was Paul's meticulous preparations and insistence on training and fitness and the players responded by doing everything that was asked of them.'

Ex-Wednesday player and captain Graham Coughlan, who rejoined Sturrock at Hillsborough from Plymouth Argyle in July 2005, also told *Luggy*, 'Wednesday were long odds to get back up into the first tier of the Football League when Paul was appointed, so, to get a club promoted that year via the play-offs was fantastic and proved once again that Paul Sturrock is a genius when it comes to strategy and planning a campaign.'

Paul Sturrock posted on the social media platform X after Wednesday hosted Sunderland for a Championship game on 28 February 2025, 'Firstly, thank you so much to the club [Wednesday] for inviting me back this evening to watch the game as the club's guest, it's a real honour.

'A little-known fact about myself and Sunderland is that my mother was the tea lady in the boardroom at Roker Park for many years!

'As you are probably aware I have Parkinson's which means my voice isn't as strong as it used to be so it would have been difficult for me to speak directly to you all, hence the pre-prepared script.

'I have to say, Sheffield Wednesday and you, the fans, gave me one of the greatest days I've ever had in football when we won in Cardiff back in 2005. I'm sure you don't need me to remind you which game I'm talking about.

'I watched the highlights of the game on YouTube on the way up on the train today and it brought great memories flooding back. I just can't believe it was 20 years ago.

'The penalty from Steve (what a substitution by the way), Glenn's third and Drew's goal to make it four (what a substitution by the way).

'The noise from you fans was absolutely incredible, quite honestly the loudest I've ever heard.

'The M4 conga by the players and fans still makes me smile. Magic. I still wonder what we could have achieved together if things had worked out but it wasn't to be and that's football.

'I loved my time here and I would just like to thank you the fans for being so fantastic to me, John Blackley and Kevin Summerfield during our time at the club. This is a special club with special fans.'

No question the Wednesday fans would more than reciprocate the warm words back to their former manager.

Paul Sturrock received the League One Manager of the Month award for November 2004.

Within weeks of his departure, Sturrock was appointed manager at League Two club Swindon Town, leading them to promotion that season. He left in November 2007 to return as manager of Plymouth for a second time. He continued in that role for two years before moving to a business support role at the club, leaving Argyle in April 2010.

He managed League Two Southend United from July 2010 before leaving the Essex club in March 2013.

A brief spell as manager at League Two Yeovil Town followed – his tenure ended in December 2015 after less than a year.

Later he was appointed chief scout in England for Dundee United, reportedly leaving that role in the 2018/19 season.

Born: 10 October 1956
Appointed: 23 September 2004
Departed: 19 October 2006
First game: 25 September 2004: Wrexham (a), League
                   One, won 3-0
Last game: 18 October 2006: Colchester United (a),
                   Championship, lost 4-0
Best league season: 2005/06 Championship, 19th

Record	P	W	D	L	F	A	Win%
League	95	31	29	35	113	113	32.6%
FA Cup	3	1	0	2	7	10	33.3%
League Cup	2	0	0	2	2	7	0%
Football League Trophy	1	0	0	1	1	2	0%
Play-offs	3	3	0	0	7	3	100%
Total	**104**	**35**	**29**	**40**	**130**	**135**	**33.6%**

28

Brian Laws

AFTER PAUL Sturrock's departure, academy director Sean McAuley held the reins and had done well in his four games in charge – three wins and a draw and for a time the retention of McAuley in the manager's role until the end of the season was considered.

In the meanwhile, it was reported that among those interviewed for the position were ex-Wednesday players Nigel Worthington and Gary Megson, as well as Bryan Robson, the ex-England captain and Middlesbrough manager who would later take charge at Bramall Lane.

It was an up-and-coming manager, Brian Laws, then at Scunthorpe United, who was offered and accepted the job.

As a player Laws had been an accomplished full-back, seeing service with Burnley, Huddersfield Town, Middlesbrough, Nottingham Forest, Grimsby Town, Darlington and Scunthorpe.

He'd taken his first managerial role at Grimsby, before moving on to Scunthorpe for the 1997/98 season.

Laws's managerial career was on the up, having twice led the Lincolnshire club out of the fourth tier, and now the opportunity to manage in the Championship.

In his autobiography *Laws Of The Jungle: Surviving Football's Monkey Business*, the chapter covering his time at Sheffield 6 is titled 'Safe Seat to Hot Seat: Surviving at Sheffield Wednesday'.

On the decision to move to Hillsborough he said, 'You have to stretch yourself and to do that you have to take a gamble. For me, it meant swapping a safe, secure environment at Scunthorpe for one of the hottest seats in football. Sheffield Wednesday had been chewing up and spitting out managers at the rate of nearly one a year.'

With Sturrock's departure there had been eight managerial departures in nine years. Laws saw the opportunity of turning round a 'sleeping giant' and the potential of one day returning to the Premier League.

Steve Wharton, the chairman at Scunthorpe, would not stand in the way if the opportunity was right, but pointed out, 'Be careful. The finances at that club are in a mess. It won't be an easy job.'

In his first programme notes since taking the job, Laws referenced 'dedication, hard work and determination to succeed'. Again, the Wednesday fans had impressed him at his first two away games in charge, 'The support at Coventry was absolutely tremendous, a backing that made the hairs on the back of my neck stand up – it was very emotional.'

Looking back, Laws had no regrets about his decision to take the job, 'Hillsborough was a wonderful learning curve for me and not without its rewards, not least achieving a spot of history and surviving longer than all the previous eight managers.'

And that history? The first manager to lead the club to a league double against their cross-city rivals for 95 years. And that's a long time!

I'd been at the most recent Wednesday victory at Bramall Lane way back in September 1967 – it was over 40 years since that milestone and the double in 2008/09 was particularly special, marked by a superb individual run and thunderbolt shot by Marcus Tudgay for the winner at Sheffield 2.

The achievement had gone down particularly well with Laws's wife Jane, a keen Wednesdayite.

The *Sun on Sunday* asked Laws about that double achievement on the eve of the derby at Bramall Lane in November 2024, 'I have a picture on the wall at home from that day – and Wednesday fans still speak to me about it. It is something I am really proud of. I can remember after the game I had media duties and things happening right, left and centre and you can't take it all [in]. It is hard to enjoy the moment and I had hardly spoken to my assistant, Russ Wilcox. We decided to meet up in a B&Q car park on the way home and spent about an hour there reflecting on the win.'

Laws puts his good relationship with supporters partly down to his record in the derbies (only one defeat in five) and the fact they recognised how much the rivalry meant to him, as well as his perspective that he always tried to be straight with them.

In taking the role, Laws reflected that a lot of people had warned him about the way chief executive Kaven Walker worked – the new manager wanted to find out for himself. His assessment, 'To say it became a challenging relationship would be an understatement.'

For the remainder of that first season Wednesday showed steady improvement in performances and results, finishing a creditable ninth in the table.

Laws was optimistic about the team's prospects at the beginning of 2007/08 – that optimism was dissipated when the club's debts resulted in the sale of key players. Debts of around £25m led to the sale of centre-back Madjid Bougherra to Charlton Athletic for £2.5m, goalscoring winger Chris Brunt to West Bromwich Albion for £3m and midfielder Glenn Whelan to Stoke City for £500,000.

All players of great quality, their departure ripped the heart out of Wednesday's team and certainly caused dismay and frustration among the supporters. Thoughts of a possible play-off target quickly turned to a scrap against relegation.

During the summer leading up to that new season Laws had been keen to retain Steven MacLean – a quality striker and a legend with the Wednesday fans for his penalty goal in the play-off final at Cardiff in 2005 – his contract had been allowed to run down. MacLean had more than his fair share of injuries and the chairman was not keen but ultimately sanctioned a new contract offer.

And then there was Kaven Walker to deal with – Laws reflected that contract negotiations were taken out of his hands and conducted by Walker, 'That's where the fun started. The offer made to MacLean was so lame it was obvious he wouldn't accept it. Steve was gutted because he wanted to stay but my hands were tied and I lost him.'

During that 2007/08 season Laws's old club Burnley expressed their interest in him joining them as their man at the helm and approached Wednesday – they were refused permission to talk with him, Laws evidently comfortable with that decision provided everyone was onside and he had the necessary support.

A week later Dave Allen resigned as chairman. A sudden decision and one that left Laws disillusioned – he felt he was left high and dry. 'No one wanted to take control of the club at the time and we were a rudderless ship,' he said in his autobiography.

Chief executive Kaven Walker was effectively in charge at the club.

Wednesday's season was deteriorating – it needed two wins in the last two games to escape relegation, and Laws observed, 'my overwhelming emotion was the feeling of being completely and utterly drained.' The club finished the season 16th in the table.

Laws reflected that the worst defeat of the 2008/09 season – 6-0 at Reading in September, a very poor performance – was not helped by Walker's tightness with the purse strings. He had refused the team the opportunity to stay in a hotel on the night before the game – a cost of around £1,500. The team travelled down on the day, got stuck in traffic for hours and grabbed whatever they could at a service station. Clearly supporters had no idea about these goings-on.

The Reading game and the lead-up to it was a significant turning point for Laws – it led to a huge fall-out between him and Walker.

The club was without a chairman or investment for ten months until Lee Strafford arrived in September 2008 – Laws highlighted the new chairman being well-intentioned, albeit he was primarily a supporter which did not necessarily aid the business side.

At the end of December 2008 Kaven Walker left the club by 'mutual consent'.

Aside from the derby double in 2008/09 there was an overall improvement in performances and results – finishing 12th in the table.

The end for Laws came in December 2009 – results had nose-dived after a steady start to the season, his last nine games had seen two draws and seven defeats, Wednesday sitting in 22nd in the table and in the relegation zone.

He had lasted in the Hillsborough hot-seat for just over three years – the longest since Trevor Francis's tenure.

Few supporters disagreed with the decision to part ways with the manager given the very poor run of results.

Lee Strafford commented, 'Parting company with Brian was not something taken lightly but we believe that change at this point will deliver fresh energy and direction into first team affairs.'

Brian Laws received the Championship Manager of the Month award for November 2007.

It came as a surprise to some that within a month Laws was appointed manager in the Premier League– at Burnley. The Lancashire club had the lowest budget in the top flight and having worked on limited resources at Sheffield 6 they possibly saw in their ex-player a style of football and a resourcefulness necessary for their circumstances.

Burnley were relegated at the end of the season; Laws continued in his role for the first few months of the new Championship campaign, leaving Turf Moor in December 2010.

In October 2012 he returned as manager of League One Scunthorpe, lasting in the role for a little over a year.

He has subsequently undertaken work in the media – particularly working for local radio, BBC Radio Sheffield and BBC Radio Nottingham.

Born:	14 October 1961, Wallsend
Appointed:	6 November 2006
Departed:	13 December 2009
First game:	11 November 2006: Ipswich Town (a), Championship, won 2-0
Last game:	12 December 2009: Leicester City (a), Championship, lost 3-0
Best league season:	2006/07 Championship, ninth

Record	P	W	D	L	F	A	Win%
League	143	49	38	56	180	192	34.2%
FA Cup	5	0	3	2	6	8	0%
League Cup	6	3	1	2	10	9	50.0%
Total	**154**	**52**	**42**	**60**	**196**	**209**	**33.7%**

29

Alan Irvine

CHAIRMAN LEE Strafford made it clear the club was looking for a manager who would 'drive success on the field' and 'who has the qualities of a genuine leader with a modern approach to the game'. Howard Wilkinson would be assisting in assessing the capabilities of candidates.

Whatever the expectations of supporters following the departure of Brian Laws, few anticipated that Alan Irvine would have been appointed his successor.

He'd been a coach at Newcastle United and Everton before taking his first managerial position at Deepdale with Preston North End. Two years at that club before his employment was brought to an end in December 2009, following a poor run of form.

Irvine's playing career as a winger had started with Queen's Park in his native Scotland, before moving to Everton, Crystal Palace, Dundee United and finally Blackburn Rovers.

The new manager was appointed on 8 January 2010 and lasted just over a year in the job – departing on 3 February 2011.

It was reported he had signed a three-and-a-half-year deal to take up the position at Hillsborough. He brought with him Rob Kelly as assistant manager, Bill Barr as first team coach and Andy Rhodes as goalkeeping coach.

On Wednesday's club website, this statement, 'Following a thorough recruitment process, involving a number of very strong candidates for the manager's position, the club is confident that they have secured the best possible candidate to drive forward Sheffield Wednesday's footballing operations, both out of our short-term position and also in the longer term.'

Irvine would have to work within a limited budget. *The Guardian* commented, 'Wednesday are still saddled with debts of around £26m, and appointed the American investment bank Inner Circle Sports last summer in a bid to find investors willing to inject £20m in return for taking control of the club. They remain confident of securing a deal.'

Irvine said, 'While the league table shows us that there is a lot of hard work in front of us between now and the end of the current season, it is a challenge I am relishing and I believe the squad here at Hillsborough is more than capable of pulling away from the current situation at the bottom of the Championship.'

Lee Strafford commented, 'He is a high-calibre manager, respected throughout football, who has proven he can make a team competitive at this level, and we feel very fortunate to have secured his services. When the manager's position became vacant at Sheffield Wednesday, we did not expect him to be available because of the commitment he had to his previous club.

'Alan did a very good job at Preston last season and West Brom were prepared to pay a substantial fee for his services in the summer. The fact that he turned down a club with one of the biggest budgets in the Championship at that time speaks volumes about his loyalty.

'While we had interest from a large number of candidates, and the calibre of those interested in the job was also very high, Alan Irvine stood out as a passionate leader who we believe can achieve success at Sheffield Wednesday in the coming years.'

Irvine's tenure at Sheffield 6 started well – he enjoyed success on the pitch, winning three games in his first month, four wins from his first five games.

The form was not maintained. The team's results went into an alarming decline – it ultimately led to a last-match relegation decider against Crystal Palace at Hillsborough (Palace having been significantly handicapped that season by a ten-point deduction). The game broadcast live on ITV – a Wednesday win and the club would stay up at the expense of Palace. A crowd of over 37,000, the match drawn 2-2 – Wednesday 22nd in the table, and relegated to the third tier for the third time in their history.

Relegation or not – Irvine appeared to be in the running for the vacant role at Championship Coventry City after the departure of Chris Coleman, quoted at 6/1 by the bookmakers for the role. He responded telling BBC Radio Sheffield on 14 May, 'I can assure people I'll not look for another job. I am not running away from the League One situation.'

The close-season following relegation saw a major restructuring of the playing staff – several experienced players joined to address the challenge of League One, including Clinton Morrison, Gary Teale and Nicky Weaver.

Wednesday were in dire financial straits – the club appeared in court twice appealing against winding-up orders. Howard Wilkinson stepped in as interim chairman in an attempt to steady the ship.

At the start of the season Irvine commented in the club programme, 'I am very pleased with the business we have done in the transfer market. We now have a very good squad, the players recruited tick the right boxes, not just in terms of ability but also character … I know they [the players] believe we have a squad that is capable of competing for promotion this season.'

Wilkinson observed, 'Alan needed to recruit a lot of new faces and he is to be congratulated on the rebuilding job he's done in a short period of time.'

A promising start to the season with the club there or thereabouts for the promotion places through to December.

In that month the club was sold to Milan Mandarić's UK Football Investments for £1, the substantial debt settled by a reported payment of £7m by Mandarić.

No question supporters saw him as the club's saviour. In my 60 years-plus supporting Wednesday no chairman has ever had his name sung to the rafters by the club's fans – except for Milan Mandarić.

That initial promising start on the pitch was overtaken by a downturn in results. Irvine's penultimate away game in charge was in the capital at Leyton Orient in January 2011, Wednesday poor on the day and soundly beaten 4-0 – playing for the hosts Harry Kane on loan from Spurs who promptly scored his first goal in senior football.

Much of the talk among the away supporters focussed on how long the manager had left after another unsatisfactory performance. The answer was not long.

In the *Daily Mail,* journalist Matt Barlow commented he thought Irvine could well be the next manager to be sacked in the Football League, 'Mandarić's reputation goes before him. Those Sheffield Wednesday fans who jeered the disappointing 2-2 home draw against Yeovil, which left the Owls tenth in League One, did so knowing the owner will not hesitate to fire a man he did not employ in the first place.

'Defeat at Peterborough on Tuesday may bring an end to Irvine's tenure after little more than a year and Mandarić will start the search for manager number 20 [at Mandarić's various clubs] but who does this help? It does not help a club craving stability.'

The 4-0 rout was followed by a 5-3 defeat at Peterborough United to make it a six-game winless run with the team 12th in the table.

For Mandarić, enough was enough. He commented, 'Changing the manager was the last thing I wanted to do when I bought Sheffield Wednesday. I supported Alan from the first day and I supported him significantly in the January transfer window … But the performances were not consistent and the results were bad so although it was such a tough thing to do, I had to make the change.'

Mandarić had indeed backed the manager in the January transfer window – players joining the club included Réda Johnson, Michael Morrison and Gary Madine. Quality players but the defeat at Peterborough had left Wednesday eight points adrift of the play-off places and only five above the relegation zone.

Former captain Darren Purse, who had left the club by mutual consent to join Millwall two weeks prior to Irvine's departure, told BBC Radio Sheffield, 'I'm gutted for Alan. I worked with him for a year and I have never known anyone who works as hard as him. It's a shame it hasn't worked out for him as we started the season really well but recent results haven't been good. The squad doesn't just deserve to be in the promotion places in League One, it should be in the Championship.'

Few supporters would have disagreed with the decision to part ways with the manager – at best the team were treading water.

Alan Irvine received the Championship Manager of the Month award for January 2010 and the League One Manager of the Month award for August 2010.

Assistant manager Rob Kelly was put in temporary charge of the team until a new permanent successor was appointed.

After leaving Sheffield 6, Irvine joined Everton as the manager of the club's academy in July 2011 and subsequently had a spell in charge at West Bromwich Albion in the 2014/15 season then as interim manager at Norwich City two seasons later, followed by a spell as assistant manager at West Ham United in 2017/18, later enjoying a return to the east London club as a technical advisor to manager David Moyes in 2019.

He teamed up once more with Moyes when taking the role of assistant manager at Everton in January 2025.

ALAN IRVINE

Born:	12 July 1958, Glasgow
Appointed:	8 January 2010
Departed:	3 February 2011
First game:	16 January 2010: Barnsley (a), Championship, won 2-1
Last game:	1 February 2011: Peterborough United (a), League One, lost 5-3

Record	P	W	D	L	F	A	Win%
League	49	17	12	20	65	65	34.6%
FA Cup	4	4	0	0	15	5	100%
League Cup	2	1	0	1	3	4	50.0%
Football League Trophy	4	2	1	1	9	7	50.0%
Total	**59**	**24**	**13**	**22**	**92**	**81**	**40.6%**

30

Gary Megson

EARLY FAVOURITES for the vacant role identified in the media included former Wednesday player Gary Megson and ex-Crystal Palace, Coventry City and Hull City manager Iain Dowie.

'It's Meggie' – my simple, straightforward reaction when news came through that Gary Megson had been appointed. Good appointment in my view. Steeped in the Wednesday blue and white – his father, Don, had made 442 appearances and been captain of the club. Gary played for Wednesday and now the manager. Very positive. It felt good.

It was reported that the new manager was on a three-and-a half-year deal. Chairman Milan Mandarić called Megson a 'top-drawer manager'.

Megson the sixth permanent manager to have played for and now managed the club, and of the five who had blue and white in their veins since boyhood, Megson undoubtedly the most demonstrative about his passion for the club.

As a player he began his career with Plymouth Argyle in 1977/78, moving on to Everton and then his first spell with Wednesday before a spell at Nottingham Forest – where he made no senior appearances under the idiosyncratic manager, Brian Clough – on to Newcastle United, a return to Wednesday, then Manchester City, Norwich City, Lincoln City and Shrewsbury Town.

The midfielder made a total of 489 appearances and scored 41 goals – of which there were 233 appearances for Wednesday and 25 goals.

His managerial career started at Norwich City before taking in Blackpool, Stockport County, Stoke City, West Bromwich Albion, Nottingham Forest, Leicester City, Bolton Wanderers and then Wednesday. His greatest success at The Hawthorns leading Albion to two promotions to the Premier League.

Megson added two new members to his backroom staff – assistant manager Chris Evans and coach Neil Thompson.

In his first programme notes, Megson said, 'What a privilege and an honour it is to be the manager of Sheffield Wednesday. This job is something I have always wanted to do, Wednesday is the club I have followed all my life, and the club that is closest to my heart.' I did not doubt one word of that.

Following his appointment there was no significant revival in fortunes and the club finished the season 16th in the table.

In his final programme notes of the season the manager said, 'The biggest entity of our football club that is admired throughout football is you, the supporters … I want a team that matches the quality of the support.'

Meggie had been brought in to do a job; he had a different style of football, he had a successful style of football and he was the chairman's choice for the manager's role at Sheffield 6. During the close-season he brought in the players to suit his playing style. Players who joined included midfielder David Prutton, centre-back and soon to be made captain Rob Jones, midfielder José Semedo, defender Danny Batth, full-back Julian Bennett, winger Ben Marshall and midfielder Chris Lines. Later, forward Chris O'Grady joined from Rochdale.

Outgoing players included Tommy Miller, Gary Teale, Richard Hinds, Michael Morrison, Tommy Spurr, Paul Heffernan and Darren Potter.

More than one away programme that season described Wednesday as 'a talented and physically imposing side'.

As a result of the incomings and outgoings it was claimed the wage bill had been reduced by £1.6m.

Evidently an important part of Meggie's selling of the club to potential new recruits was to take them up the steps from the bottom of the Kop to its summit – and let the players survey the stadium, drink it in, and appreciate the club they would be joining and all it stood for. Proud to be a Wednesdayite.

In preparation for the new season Megson put his players through five and a half weeks of fitness training, commenting, 'We've got to have the right base of fitness, so that when players are playing, if they don't put in the required amount of effort, it's not because they can't, it's because they won't – and that won't happen more than once.' The focus on fitness had clear echoes of Megson's time as a player under Howard Wilkinson.

Going into the new season Megson observed, 'There's a buzz about the place. I couldn't be more pleased with the players we've got.'

Not all the players were fans of the manager – one who left in the close-season was popular left-back Tommy Spurr. Speaking on the *Wednesday 'Til I Die* podcast, Spurr gave his perspective,

'It's something people don't get I don't think. The way I was treated in the end and how Megson made me feel as a footballer and a person, like I left with a bitter taste, even though I had all those good times, it tainted it.

'He never gave me a reason, he wouldn't speak to me, that's my big bug-bear. He couldn't even say to me, "You've got no future here, you can leave."'

An aspect of Megson's approach at away games, which I first saw at Wycombe Wanderers in the 2011/12 season, Wednesday supporters massed behind the goal. Before the game players warmed up on the pitch. A few minutes before kick-off the Wednesday players came together in a line, inside the penalty area, facing the Wednesdayites and walked towards them. The roar that went up was spine-tingling. The supporters fired up by their 11 gladiators – the passion, the engagement, the 'us' reinforced many times over. And no doubt the players taking on board the passion and support they'd unleashed by their actions.

As for the opposition? At the very least it must have been off-putting, quite possibly sowing seeds of doubt in their players' minds. It had to be unnerving for the opposition and their supporters.

For me, simply very, very impressive.

While the new 2011/12 season potentially offered a great deal, progress was good but not outstanding – the club there or thereabouts as far as the promotion and play-off places were concerned. But Wednesday were one of several clubs involved – including United.

There was much speculation about the manager's position before the season's second derby at Hillsborough in February 2012 – at that point the team had won only two games from the last ten.

Publicly, Megson appeared unconcerned about his future, stating, 'From the figures I read, about £1.5m was spent before I arrived. I've spent £425,000 and got the team up to third place. The gates are up as well and there's not been as much optimism among Wednesdayites for quite a few years.'

Come the derby – Wednesday the victors, 1-0, Chris O' Grady with the winner. Megson animatedly highlighting the club badge on his tracksuit to the home crowd and just for good measure making sure the away supporters congregated behind the Leppings Lane end goal could see it as well. The manager pumping with pride. Wednesdayite to the core – no better feeling than beating them in the derby. Supporters full of it and going home happy – a good day to be a Wednesdayite.

After the game, Megson commented, 'I've had some results at other clubs, where, looking back, they were big ones. But no match has ever meant more to me than beating Sheffield United in a derby game.' Every word of that sentence resonated with the supporters.

And then news like no other – Megson sacked. What? We've just won the derby. Must be a mistake. But no, it was true. I could not understand it. Why do you sack a manager after such a result and with the club set fair for a good run at promotion?

Yes, there had been some speculation about Megson's position after three consecutive defeats prior to the derby but that result surely meant Megson's position was secure? Certainly not as it transpired.

Milan Mandarić stated, 'This was a very difficult decision but one that has been taken with the best interests of Sheffield Wednesday at heart.

'We have 13 games to go of what is a critical season for our club, and this decision has been taken because I believe we have a better chance of achieving our key aim of promotion by making the change.

'I fully understand this may not be the most popular decision amongst our supporters but I ask them to trust me, as they have done so whole-heartedly during the time I have been at the club.

'Whilst we won what was a huge game last Sunday, I have looked at results before that to reach the conclusion which I believe is the right one for now and the future of Sheffield Wednesday.'

Baffled and hugely disappointed was my reaction, and I think that mirrored the reaction of many supporters. Megson had been in charge for little more than 12 months at Sheffield 6; BBC Radio Sheffield inundated with calls from supporters, social media weighed down with reaction and so it went on.

Megson was more than disappointed to lose his job, telling the station, 'It hurts more than any other disappointment I've had in my life.'

The League Managers' Association issued a statement on Megson's behalf, 'I am very saddened that I will no longer have the opportunity to manage my hometown club, Sheffield Wednesday. With just 13 games left this season and currently in third place in League One, it is very disappointing that I will not have the chance to guide this great club to promotion and back to the Championship. At some point in the future, I would like to come back to Hillsborough to finish the job I feel I had only just started. I am sure that many people are aware of the strong affection I hold for Sheffield Wednesday, not only from my playing days, but also my family connection with my father having served as club captain. One of the reasons why I took the job was to be able to work with the Sheffield Wednesday supporters. They have been terrific, a highlight of my career, and I would love to work with such great fans again.'

Having to accept that Meggie had departed the club, Wednesdayites had to focus their thinking on who would succeed him.

I was sorry to see Megson go. At the time it seemed the wrong decision – a baffling decision. And, of course, the game is full of ifs, buts and maybes – for my money with Meggie in charge he would have taken Wednesday back to the Premier League, but of course we'll never know.

I've only had one brief interaction with Gary Megson – an odd one at that. Dagenham & Redbridge away, March 2011. Before the game, entering the ground and walking among the seated sections of the away supporters – a voice from behind 'You can't go there' directed at my son Ben as he prepared to move into another section. Presumably a steward – no, Gary Megson! He was joking of course. Acknowledgements and smiles all round.

Megson's only managerial role to date since leaving was as the caretaker at West Bromwich Albion in 2017.

He is the only manager to have departed the club following a derby game against United.

Born: 2 May 1959, Manchester
Appointed: 4 February 2011
Departed: 29 February 2012
First game: 12 February 2011: Rochdale (a), League One, lost 2-1
Last game: 26 February 2012: Sheffield United (h), League One, won 1-0

Record	P	W	D	L	F	A	Win%
League	54	25	11	18	81	73	46.2%
FA Cup	6	3	1	2	5	8	50.0%
League Cup	2	0	1	1	1	3	0%
Football League Trophy	1	0	1	0	0	0	0%
Total	**63**	**28**	**14**	**21**	**87**	**84**	**44.4%**

31

Dave Jones

IN THE wake of Gary Megson's departure the name that soon came to the fore was that of Dave Jones – he was appointed within 24 hours of Megson leaving the club. Indeed, he'd watched Wednesday's defeat at Chesterfield prior to the Sheffield derby.

Dave Jones had played as a defender for Everton, Coventry City and Preston North End – 147 appearances in total, over half of those with the Merseyside club.

His managerial career began at Stockport County in 1995 – gaining promotion to the First Division at the end of 1996/97.

Leaving Stockport, he joined Premier League Southampton later in 1997 – staying for over 100 games in charge of the Saints. In January 2000 the club suspended him when he was arrested for alleged child abuse. Jones strenuously denied the allegations and was found not guilty at court.

Appointed manager at Wolverhampton Wanderers in 2001, he led the Molineux club to promotion to the Premier League in 2002/03 – albeit they were relegated after one season and Jones dismissed in November 2004.

A six-year spell in charge at Championship club Cardiff City followed – an FA Cup Final appearance in 2008 a highlight (losing to Portsmouth). After failing to achieve promotion, Jones departed the Bluebirds in May 2011.

Appointed on a reported three-and-a-half-year contract, Jones had the unenviable task of following Megson in the manager's chair – for many supporters that meant Jones had to deliver promotion to the Championship in what remained of the 2011/12 season.

At the press conference confirming his appointment the new manager stated, 'This is a fantastic football club and a fantastic challenge for me. Promotion is the first ambition and from there it is to try and get the Holy Grail, which is the Premiership, I've had a lot of calls asking why I have dropped down to League One but I don't see it that way. I look at the size of the club and think this is a club that can go places.

'After talking to the chairman and seeing what he wanted and what his plans are, I had no hesitation in choosing here because it is a huge club that should not be where it is now.'

For his part, chairman Milan Mandarić commented, 'It was essential that we made a swift appointment with 13 games to go this season and I am convinced we have the right man for this job. I like his style of football and his approach to the game but more than anything else, he is a builder of clubs and he will help to galvanise Sheffield Wednesday. His first objective is to get us out of League One and back into the Championship and then rebuild the club for the Premier League.'

Promotion – a tall order. But Jones met the challenge head on – in the space of three months it was achieved, as runners-up, much to the delight of the supporters, and Wednesday's success was achieved while edging out city rivals United into third place, the Blades consigned to fighting for promotion via the play-offs (they were not successful).

As the final weeks of the regular league campaign approached the Bramall Lane outfit were in pole position for automatic promotion – only to be pipped at the post by Wednesday.

Such was Wednesday's form under Jones in his first two months in charge that he received the Manager of the Month award in successive months.

Players released at the end of the 2011/12 season included goalkeeper Richard O'Donnell, defender Jon Otsemobor, midfielder Chris Sedgewick and striker Clinton Morrison. Ryan Lowe moved on before the new season began. Incomings included goalkeeper Chris Kirkland, defender Antony Gardner, midfielder Kieran Lee, striker Chris Maguire and forward Michail Antonio whose loan deal the previous season progressed to a permanent transfer from Reading for a reported £1.2m fee with the player on a four-year deal.

The new season was a difficult one for Wednesday – in and around the relegation zone for much of it and a last-day win against Middlesbrough ensured their Championship status. During the season seven consecutive defeats in November and December underlined the challenges of the Championship.

In the FA Cup and League Cup Wednesday exited the competitions at the third-round stages.

The game against Leeds United at Hillsborough in October 2012 made national headlines for all the wrong reasons – a visiting supporter entered the field of play and struck Chris Kirkland, in the face.

Dave Jones made his views clear, 'You can't let them get away with it. Leeds supporters should be banned from every away ground until they sort it out. I thought those days had gone.'

And in response to chants aimed at the manager by the visiting supporters, 'All the Leeds fans will be tarred with the same brush, and they should be, because from what I could hear it wasn't just one person chanting the vile things, it was quite a lot of them.'

On different matters, the Football Association had called Jones to account – he was given a two-game touchline ban in April 2013 after he was found guilty of misconduct following post-match comments after Wednesday's draw at Bristol City. Those comments included, 'All you ask is a fair deal from the match officials. We have had trouble with this referee [Darren Deadman] before. If he had done his job, we would have been going home with three points.'

This followed a £2,000 fine and a suspended one-game touchline ban earlier in the season – when he and the Brighton & Hove Albion manager Gus Poyet were sent to the stands late in the game.

Players leaving before the start of the 2013/14 season included goalkeeper Nicky Weaver, defender Julian Bennett, midfielder Chris Lines and striker Chris O'Grady. Incomings included defender Jérémy Hélan on a permanent deal, defender Kamil Zayatte and striker Atdhe Nuhiu.

The new season did not start well for Wednesday – by December they were bottom of the table with a solitary win. Jones's tenure was brought to an end.

Given the league position, the mood among supporters had turned against the manager.

The statement on the club's website was brief, stating that Jones had been '…relieved of his duties with immediate effect. The club would like to thank Dave for all of his hard work and wish him well for the future.'

For Dave Jones, an absence from football management ensued before he was appointed manager at League Two Hartlepool United in January 2017. A poor run of form over the next three months led to his contract being terminated by mutual consent in April 2017. Weeks later the club were relegated from the EFL for the first time since joining in 1921.

Jones later went on to work as a consultant at Bury – leaving the club after their expulsion from the EFL in August 2019.

Born:	17 August 1956, Liverpool
Appointed:	2 March 2012
Departed:	1 December 2013
First game:	3 March 2012: Rochdale (a), League One, drew 0-0
Last game:	30 November 2013: Blackpool (a), Championship, lost 2-0
Best league season:	2012/13 Championship, 18th

Record	P	W	D	L	F	A	Win%
League	74	26	21	27	97	95	35.1%
FA Cup	2	0	1	1	0	2	0%
League Cup	4	2	0	2	6	6	50.0%
Total	80	28	22	30	103	103	35.0%

32

Stuart Gray

IN THE wake of Dave Jones's departure, speculation grew about his successor and one man's name seemed to come to the fore more than most, Neil Warnock. And that caused a voluble and passionate reaction from supporters.

For many his allegiance and management of the Blades together with his well-known jibes about Wednesday made him persona non grata; for a smaller constituency of supporters a more objective assessment of Mr Warnock's achievements merited serious consideration and for some he was the man to come in and do the rescue job that was needed at Sheffield 6.

If football is anything it is a game of passions and emotions – I am firmly in the camp that believes Neil Warnock and Sheffield Wednesday do not mix. Thankfully, chairman Milan Mandarić recognised the scale of reaction and any interest there may have been in the ex-Blade ebbed away.

Stuart Gray had been hired by Dave Jones in December 2012 as a coach. He'd worked with Gray while manager at Southampton and Wolverhampton Wanderers.

Jones talked to BBC Radio Sheffield about recruiting Gray, 'I felt that getting in a bit of experience would help the players and the coaches. He'll lead the pack amongst the coaches and bring a new point of view. It's a long time since I've been down at the bottom [of the division] looking up and no disrespect but Stuart has experienced a lot of that over the last six or seven years.'

On Jones's dismissal as manager in November 2013, Gray took over as caretaker and embarked on a run of 11 games undefeated – that momentum grew as the weeks went by and he was confirmed as the club's permanent head coach on 25 January 2014.

In his first programme notes Gray commented, 'First and foremost I was saddened to see Dave and Paul [Wilkinson, assistant manager] lose their jobs, it is never a pleasant experience, but anyone working in football is braced for when these things happen in the game.'

There had been talk of Paolo Di Canio or Benito Carbone being in the running for the role but Gray had revitalised the team and his appointment was well received by supporters.

During his playing career, Yorkshireman Gray was often referred to as versatile – playing in defence or midfield.

Starting out at First Division Nottingham Forest under Brian Clough, he moved on to play at Barnsley, Aston Villa and Southampton with a loan spell at Bolton Wanderers. His career was brought to an end by a serious injury to his achilles tendon while playing for Southampton. He totalled 285 senior appearances scoring 35 goals.

Commencing his coaching career at Southampton, he took over as caretaker manager after Glenn Hoddle moved to Tottenham Hotspur in 2001. Confirmed as permanent manager, his tenure was short-lived – three months before he departed St Mary's; subsequent coaching roles at Aston Villa, Crystal Palace and Wolverhampton Wanderers – including taking the caretaker manager position at each of those clubs.

Two and a half years as manager at Northampton Town ended in September 2009 followed by coaching roles at Burnley and Portsmouth.

Taking over the reins at Hillsborough with the club at a low ebb, Gray made a very positive impact – lifting the team to 17th in the table by the end of the season coupled with progression to the fifth round of the FA Cup.

For the 2014/15 season incoming players included goalkeeper Keiren Westwood, defender Tom Lees, midfielder Sam Hutchinson and striker Stevie May.

Players leaving included defenders Réda Johnson, Miguel Llera, and Antony Gardner, and midfielders Jermaine Johnson and David Prutton. Striker Michail Antonio was sold to Nottingham Forest for a reported £1.5m.

In Gray's one full season in charge – 2014/15 – Wednesday finished 13th, their highest position for six seasons, and equalled their record for clean sheets, 17, in a season. Progress in both domestic cup competitions ended at the third-round stage by that season's Premier League runners-up, Manchester City. To all intents and purposes Gray had done a good job.

Perhaps the football played under Gray could best be described as functional – it was certainly effective in the context of Wednesday's resources.

I recollect having the chance to talk with Gray and he made the point that the nature of the pitch at Hillsborough conditioned the way that a team could best play – the floods in Sheffield in 2007 had caused significant damage to the pitch after the adjacent River Don had burst its banks and flooded the ground. The pitch had still not fully recovered some eight years later.

I met Gray on two occasions and he came across as a warm and personable man. The first time was at 'An Evening With....' at the DoubleTree Hilton Hotel on Chesterfield Road, Norton. From recollection there were about 100 diners, all keen Wednesdayites and keen to hear the words of the manager in a more relaxed setting.

An interesting evening – among other things he commented on Wednesday's recent performance at the Etihad Stadium against Manchester City, they'd played well albeit lost; and he made a separate observation about a Premier League referee who had been allocated a game involving Wednesday and it became clear this was not the level the official expected to be refereeing.

One anecdote that stayed with me from that evening – an incident when Gray was a young player at Nottingham Forest under Brian Clough.

The short version – the Forest team travelling on the coach down the M1 for the game against Tottenham Hotspur, Gray's first time travelling with the first team.

It was customary for the travelling party to have beers, lagers and other drinks on the coach, Gray deputed to ascertain the drinks the travellers would like to imbibe.

The legendary manager heard the question asked of the chairman, 'What would you like, Fred?'

An immediate reaction from Clough who instructed the driver to stop the coach on the hard shoulder of the motorway – coach stopped, Clough wanted a word with young Gray.

My recollection of the dialogue between manager and player went something like this.

'What did you call the chairman?'

'Fred?'

'Fred! It is Mr Reacher or Chairman to you.'

No doubt a suitably chastened Stuart Gray, albeit everyone was apparently known to call the chairman Fred.

At that point Clough invited his young player to disembark the coach on the hard shoulder. Having made his point, he allowed Gray to rejoin his team-mates and the journey continued.

The second time I met Gray was the result of winning the opportunity for my young grandson Charlie to watch the Wednesday players training at Middlewood Road. Keen Wednesdayite Charlie was unquestionably looking forward to the morning as was his dad. In truth I was probably the most excited of the three of us!

Half-term week and arrival at the training ground. Stuart Gray the perfect host – pulling the players together and introducing seven-year-old Charlie, and informing them he would be watching training.

The manager took Charlie to one side and asked him who his favourite player was – 'Stevie May' the instant reply.

Gray turned to me and made a joking aside, 'He's not mine at the moment' – perhaps not surprising given that he would have had high expectations of the striker signed for a reported £800,000 from St Johnstone in the summer. May's scoring prowess at Sheffield 6 had not yet taken off!

We watched the players train: stand-out recollections for me was a good discussion with assistant manager John Deehan (called 'Dixie' by everyone – probably after the legendary Everton striker Dixie Dean), a real togetherness about the squad and watching coach Lee Bullen directing activities on the pitch – and the Scot quite definitely taking no nonsense from anyone.

Gray's first (and only) full season in charge was set against the backdrop of speculation about a takeover of the club. That takeover arrived in January 2015 – Thai businessman Dejphon Chansiri purchasing the club from outgoing Milan Mandarić.

At the time Stuart Gray was asked his thoughts about the new owner – he commented on the club website, 'All I can do is focus on what I can do. If I'm not the right person for them I'm sure they'll tell me. But the most important thing I'll carry on doing my job until told different.

'But the pleasing thing is that they seem very enthusiastic, very keen to get Sheffield Wednesday going in the right direction. We all know we need investment both on and off the pitch and hopefully that's going to happen.'

Gray learned of his fate in the close-season – in June 2015 he was told he was no longer required as the club's manager.

That decision came as a surprise to many supporters and a disappointment to some – me included. Gray had done well for Wednesday.

Dejphon Chansiri told the club's official website, 'This is not a decision I have taken lightly but one that I believe is in the best interests of our club ahead of the 2015/16 season.

'The club will be taking a new direction next season and it is my belief that the appointment of a new head coach will help achieve my desire of bringing Premier League football back to Hillsborough.

'I would like to thank Stuart for his hard work and diligence on behalf of Sheffield Wednesday and wish him all the very best moving forward.'

Gray moved on to join Fulham as a coach later in the year and held the role of caretaker manager at Craven Cottage for six games in December 2015.

In May 2025 Fulham announced that Gray would be stepping down from his role as coach.

Born: 19 April 1960, Withernsea
Appointed: 1 December 2013 (initially as caretaker)
Departed: 15 June 2015
First game: 3 December 2013: Leicester City (h),
                   Championship, won 2-1
Last game: 2 May 2015: Watford (a), Championship,
                   drew 1-1
Best league season: 2014/15 Championship, 13th

Record	P	W	D	L	F	A	Win%
League	76	26	24	26	88	87	34.2%
FA Cup	5	2	1	2	9	7	40.0%
League Cup	3	2	0	1	4	7	66.6%
Total	**84**	**30**	**25**	**29**	**101**	**101**	**35.7%**

33

Carlos Carvalhal

FOLLOWING STUART Gray's departure there was early speculation about his replacement – names mentioned included Sam Allardyce, Benito Carbone, Steve Evans, Darren Ferguson, Dan Petrescu, Gus Poyet and Mark Warburton.

The *Star* commented, 'Glenn Roeder, who was appointed on a three-man sporting director committee in April, may also be in contention.'

That three-man committee, which also consisted of Gray and business adviser Adam Pearson, now consisted only of Roeder after Pearson left for a similar position at Leeds shortly after his appointment.

It came as a surprise to many when the appointment of Portuguese Carlos Carvalhal was announced, Wednesday's first foreign head coach. For the substantial majority of supporters, Carvalhal was an unknown quantity.

Starting his playing career as a centre-back with his hometown club Braga, he moved on to play for Chaves (two spells), Porto, Beira-Mar, Tirsense and Espinho. His playing career spanned 16 years from 1983 to 1999. For Braga he made the most appearances in three separate spells (100, with one goal).

His managerial career commenced at Espinho before spells at Freamunde, Vizela, Aves, Leixões, Vitória Setúbal, Belenenses, Braga, Beira-Mar, Vitória Setúbal (again), Asteras Tripolis, Marítimo, Asteras Tripolis (again), Marítimo (again), Sporting CP, Beşiktaş, and İstanbul Başakşehir;

15 managerial appointments in 15 years prior to arriving at Sheffield 6 and three years since his most recent managerial appointment.

On the face of it Carvalhal's CV did not immediately suggest the new manager would be a roaring success.

As always it would be performances and results the key to how the manager would be received.

For his part Carvalhal expressed his pride in being Wednesday's new head coach and said, 'I have every confidence that I am the right person for this job because my football philosophies match those of the chairman at Sheffield Wednesday.'

For that 2015/16 season incoming players included defender Jack Hunt, midfielder Barry Bannan and striker Fernando Forestieri. Outgoing players included goalkeeper Chris Kirkland, defender Lewis Buxton and strikers Gary Madine and Stevie May.

The season started well – performances and results showed real signs of progress, there was a verve and quality to the flowing football. Wednesday finished in sixth place on 74 points and qualified for the play-offs. Add to that they'd seen off Arsène Wenger's Arsenal on a memorable night at Hillsborough, 3-0 in the League Cup, before exiting the competition at the fifth-round stage.

The FA Cup saw modest progress to the fourth round before a disappointing defeat at Shrewsbury Town.

Progress in the Championship the clear priority for the club.

For his part Carvalhal was clear on his approach, telling the *Star*, 'It is very easy for me [to rotate] and the players understand not every team has the same characteristics. We are here to try and manage everything and if the first plan isn't working and we aren't playing as we expect then we must change things. You have to have a plan B, C and D.'

The season had developed into one of real belief and optimism for the supporters. The mood was captured perfectly in one of the supporters' favourite songs:

Carlos had a dream
To build a football team …
We're Sheffield Wednesday
We're on our way back

It was sung with gusto and belief – a genuine feeling that things were changing for the better; Carvalhal reported as saying 'I loved the song' after he'd first heard it at Brentford.

And the play-offs – he commented to the *Star* on 27 May, 'Since the first day talking to the players, I believed we would reach the play-offs. They looked shocked, at me talking about promotion, they were looking at me thinking, "Maybe this guy is crazy."'

Two-legged semi-final against favourites Brighton & Hove Albion – on a raucous and famous night at Hillsborough the hosts took the first leg 2-0; a 1-1 draw on the south coast meant Wednesday booked their place in the final against Hull City.

Wednesday's first visit to the rebuilt Wembley and their manager's first-ever visit to the national stadium.

On the day Wednesday second-best and the Humbersiders – managed by Steve Bruce – merited their 1-0 win. Perhaps their team with a smattering of experienced Premier League players and players who would go on to have excellent careers at the highest level (including Harry Maguire, Andy Robertson, Michael Dawson and Jake Livermore) had a bit too much in terms of knowhow and quality.

No matter – the Wednesday supporters had been energised and could see the Premier League dream being fulfilled with Carvalhal at the helm. Hopes were high as the 2016/17 season approached.

Incoming players included defenders Daniel Pudil and Morgan Fox, midfielder Adam Reach signed for a reported £5m, and striker Steven Fletcher.

Players leaving included defender Jérémy Hélan, and strikers Caolan Lavery and Sergiu Buș.

The season did not get off to a good start – striker Fernando Forestieri refusing to travel with the team to Carrow Road for the game against Norwich City in August 2016 amid much transfer speculation.

Forestieri apologised for his actions and was fined by the club but it raised questions about togetherness in the camp and how the head coach dealt with such difficult issues.

After that hiatus the Championship season developed well for Wednesday – finishing fourth on 81 points. Play-offs again – this time against fifth-placed Huddersfield Town. Hopes were high. Hopes were dashed: 0-0 in both legs – the visitors winning on penalties in the second leg at Hillsborough. Many supporters – me included – critical of what was seen as overly negative and defensive tactics in the first leg.

In both domestic cup competitions Wednesday were eliminated at the first time of asking. Disappointing, but supporters confident of further progress in the league in the forthcoming season.

Incomings included defender Joost van Aken, midfielder Joey Pelupessy, winger George Boyd and Jordan Rhodes signing on a permanent deal for a reported £8m fee.

Outgoings included popular Portuguese midfielder José Semedo, centre-back Claude Dielna and midfielder Filipe Melo.

The 2017/18 season failed to live up to pre-season hopes and expectations – a run of seven games without a win in the run-up to the festive period brought home how much Wednesday were falling away. Some poor recruitment and an exceptional toll of injuries played their part in the downturn.

In the EFL Cup, the club knocked out at the second-round stage and some supporters called for Carvalhal's dismissal as the run continued.

The parting of the ways eventually came on Christmas Eve 2017 following the 2-1 home defeat to Middlesbrough – the third loss in a row – to leave Wednesday 15th in the table. Interestingly, the Boro manager Garry Monk left his club after that game.

On Wednesday's website, Carvalhal commented, 'I am very sad at this moment because I have enjoyed my two seasons and a half so much with Sheffield Wednesday. We had two fantastic seasons and two play-offs on the row but unfortunately we have not managed to replicate these positions this season.'

He added, 'Finally, I say a big thank you to the chairman, who has been amazing throughout my time with Sheffield Wednesday. He is the best chairman I have ever worked with in my life in football.'

Chairman Dejphon Chansiri stated, 'Both parties believe the time is right to go our separate ways. I maintain a huge amount of respect for Carlos as a coach and as a person and he will always be welcome at Hillsborough.'

BBC Radio Sheffield's *Football Heaven* presenter Rob Staton observed, 'At the end of Wednesday's latest defeat to Middlesbrough, some fans chanted for Carvalhal to go.

'That felt like the tipping point. This was supposed to be the year Wednesday finally made it back to the Premier League, during their 150th anniversary celebrations. Instead, they're nearer the bottom three than the top six.

'Carvalhal hasn't had it easy this season. Several key players have been missing through injury, including Fernando Forestieri and Tom Lees. Even so, fans were unhappy not just with results but with performances.

'Too often Wednesday were slow to start games and they were on a seven-game winless run.'

Former Wednesday manager Brian Laws said on BBC Radio Sheffield, 'I'm disappointed for Carlos, we all need to recognise what a great job he did. But we all know when we go in as managers, we have to get results.

'The new manager will be backed. They're not looking for someone to do something on a shoestring, they want someone to spend and spend wisely. The money spent under Carvalhal has probably not met the expectations, signings were not as good as they could have been.'

It's worth noting that 18 players were brought into the club by Carvalhal during his tenure – Dejphon Chansiri had provided the funds for some expensive signings but in the end those investments had not provided the returns anticipated.

Looking back at Carvalhal's time at Sheffield 6, a feature of some of his press conferences was the unusual way he occasionally made his point– after defeat in the derby at Hillsborough in September 2017 he produced a £20 note, crushed it, banged it on the table asking the journalists what he was left with – 'still the same £20 note'. He produced it after the team had won and it was the same £20 note, essentially relating it to the team having the same squad of players.

Carlos Carvalhal received the Championship Manager of the Month award for March 2017.

After the head coach's departure, coach Lee Bullen took interim charge for the Owls' Boxing Day visit to Nottingham Forest.

Fast forward almost six years when Wednesday won promotion back to the Championship in May 2023 there was a keen supporter in Iberia. 'I celebrated with my family,' Carlos Carvalhal told Sky Sports. 'But I wanted to be at Wembley. I still love Sheffield Wednesday.

'I have had a lot of friendly messages from Sheffield Wednesday fans and someone asked if I had received an invitation to go back to Sheffield Wednesday this season. I have had no contact but there is something I will tell you.

'I was ready if Sheffield Wednesday did not go up to go back there and try to win promotion back to the Championship. I would have made myself a candidate for that job. I do not care about the money. If the club had needed me, I would have been there.'

After leaving Wednesday, Carvalhal managed Premier League Swansea City – being appointed within days of his exit from Hillsborough. He then moved on to manage several clubs – Rio Ave, Braga, Al Wahda, Celta Vigo, Olympiacos and Braga (for the fourth time).

Of all his managerial appointments, the 131 games in charge at Sheffield 6 was the most he managed in a single spell at any club.

Born:	4 December 1965, Braga, Portugal
Appointed:	30 June 2015
Departed:	24 December 2017
First game:	8 August 2015: Bristol City (h), Championship, won 2-0
Last game:	23 December 2017: Middlesbrough (h), Championship, lost 2-1
Best league season:	2016/17 Championship, fourth (defeated play-off semi-finalists)

Record	P	W	D	L	F	A	Win%
League	115	49	35	31	153	119	42.6%
FA Cup	3	1	0	2	4	7	33.3%
League Cup	8	5	0	3	13	6	62.5%
Play-offs	5	1	3	1	4	3	20.0%
Total	**131**	**56**	**38**	**37**	**174**	**135**	**42.7%**

34

Jos Luhukay

FOLLOWING CARLOS Carvalhal's departure, the *Daily Mail* reported that the bookmakers' favourite, the former Wolverhampton Wanderers boss Paul Lambert, was offered a six-month contract until the end of the season but turned it down because he felt more time was needed to turn things around. The newspaper commented, 'The club are now expected to look overseas for a replacement.'

And overseas it turned out to be. Alan Nixon in *The Sun* highlighted Jos Luhukay as Wednesday's next manager four days prior to his being appointed. Nixon referenced that André Villas-Boas, Paulo Fonseca and Bruno Labbadia had been considered; apparently Luhukay fitted the profile.

A surprise to supporters – a name unfamiliar to many, though perhaps in the same way that Carvalhal had not been well known at his appointment, the new manager could prove to be a success.

Luhukay was a Dutchman who had played as a midfielder for several clubs in the Eredivisie during the 1980s and 1990s – making senior appearances with VVV-Venlo, RKC Waalwijk, SV Straelen and KFC Uerdingen. Total number of appearances just short of 200 with more than half with Venlo, his first club.

His managerial career started with SV Straelen, then KFC Uerdingen, FC Köln (caretaker), SC Paderborn, Borussia Mönchengladbach, FC Augsburg, Hertha Berlin and VfB Stuttgart – all roles with clubs in the German Bundesliga. His successes centred on his achievements in getting promotion for three of those clubs to the German top flight – Borussia Mönchengladbach, Augsburg and Hertha Berlin.

His last managerial role had been at VfB Stuttgart which ended in September 2016 after four months in charge.

More than a year later 54-year-old Luhukay was appointed Wednesday's manager on 5 January 2018 – on the club's website he said, 'In Germany I have turned down offers from the Bundesliga and Second Bundesliga in recent months because I have been looking for an entirely new challenge.'

His first game in charge, the Sheffield derby at Bramall Lane – a baptism of fire. Overall Wednesdayites pleased with the outcome of that game – a goalless draw – given captain Glenn Loovens had been shown a red card and goalkeeper Cameron Dawson saved a penalty. Reaction from the new manager seemed a little odd with his double negative, 'I was not unhappy with our performance at Sheffield United.'

Wednesday, 16th in the Championship when he took over, improving slightly to 15th by the end of the season.

Progress to the fifth round of the FA Cup – defeated by ex-manager Carlos Carvalhal's Swansea City team at Hillsborough.

As the new season approached there was no great wave of optimism sweeping over the supporters.

Loan players were the core of the incomings including defender Michael Hector and midfielders Josh Onomah and Rolando Aarons.

Outgoing players included centre-back Glenn Loovens, defender Jack Hunt and midfielders Ross Wallace and Sean Clare.

The first half of 2018/19 saw no significant improvement, the team in the lower reaches of the table, and eliminated from the EFL Cup at the second-round stage.

Less than a year in charge and Luhukay departed Sheffield 6 on 17 December 2018 – having won one game in the last ten and the club 18th in the Championship, with *The Guardian* observing that 'Wednesday were drifting towards relegation'.

Chairman Dejphon Chansiri's statement included, 'I would like to place on record my thanks to Jos for the efforts he has given but now is the right time for both parties to move on and I wish him all the very best for the future.'

Coach Lee Bullen took caretaker charge of the team.

Sam Hutchinson – a talismanic player in his time with Wednesday – had this to say about the manager, when talking to the *A Wednesday Week* podcast in February 2025, 'With Jos he just didn't have a clue and I told him that.' Hutchinson went on to recount an away game at Leeds United where pre-match Luhukay said, '"We need to win this game because there's play-offs for relegation," and Glenn Loovens – and this was in front of the whole team – and Glenn Loovens went, "We don't do play-offs for relegation in England," and he'd been in the job for four months.'

Hutchinson recalled how in training the players were told to keep the ball below head height – because apparently that was the Dutch way – and the English style of playing had not been successful in international competitions for over 50 years. It seemingly did not go down well with the players.

Luhukay certainly did not help himself by sidelining Hutchinson and goalkeeper Kieren Westwood – both very effective players with Westwood arguably the best goalkeeper in the Championship at the time. Supporters were baffled by the exclusions.

Ross Wallace, a popular player in his three years at Hillsborough, was not impressed with how things worked out.

Speaking to the *Under the Cosh* podcast in March 2025, as reported in the *Star*, Wallace commented, 'He did me over to be fair. As the season [2017/18] went on we got injury after injury. Barry Bannan got injured, Forestieri got injured, we were decimated with injuries. I ended up playing left-back, left wing, right wing, centre mid. And then we went and played Millwall. I think it was towards the end of the season and I was out of contract.

'I said, "Listen, what are you thinking for next season?" He was like, "Yeah, yeah, I'm going to speak to the owner and get you a new deal. You're in my plans," all that stuff.

'We played Millwall, you know what they were like – land of the giants. I think he was trying to do a false nine thing, but we'd done no tactical work on it … I took a throw-in, bang, down the line, a big centre-half has come in down the side and snapped my medial.

'About two weeks later, he pulls me in, says, "Yeah, we're not offering you a contract any more." I was just like, "You p***k." I was I think 30 at the time. I think the right thing to say was to let me get fit, come in for pre-season and if I was fit then offer me a contract. That would've been the right thing … that's how ruthless football is.'

In fairness to Luhukay he was not helped by the club being placed under a transfer embargo between April and August 2018 for breaching Financial Fair Play Rules – the EFL's profitability and sustainability regulations that stated a club could not make a loss in excess of £39m over a three-year period. As a result, Wednesday made only one permanent signing and two loan signings before the transfer window closed at the end of August.

That said, his tenure will not be looked back on as being anything other than unsuccessful.

Having left Sheffield 6 Luhukay's next managerial appointment was with Hamburg's St. Pauli – he left the German club in June 2020.

The following season he took the reins for the first time in his home country, as manager of VVV in March 2021. He left the club at the end of the 2021/22 season – after a tenth-placed finish in the league.

Jos Luhukay is the only man whose first game in charge was the Sheffield derby.

Born:	13 June 1963, Venlo, Netherlands
Appointed:	8 January 2018
Departed:	21 December 2018
First game:	12 January 2018 Sheffield United (a), Championship, drew 0-0
Last game:	15 December 2018: Swansea City (a), Championship, lost 2-1

Record	P	W	D	L	F	A	Win%
League	42	13	12	17	57	66	30.9%
FA Cup	4	2	1	1	5	3	50.0%
League Cup	2	1	0	1	2	2	50.0%
Total	**48**	**16**	**13**	**19**	**64**	**71**	**33.3%**

35

Steve Bruce

FOLLOWING LUHUKAY'S departure the club again entrusted coach Lee Bullen with responsibility for the team – he fulfilled it admirably, two wins and two draws in his four games in charge.

Wednesday announced the appointment of Steve Bruce as their manager on 2 January 2019 together with his long-time coaching associates Steve Agnew and Stephen Clemence.

Bruce had been out of work since departing Aston Villa in October 2018 and evidently wanted to take a break from the game – in particular wanting to watch the England cricket team on their Caribbean tour. Unusually, therefore, Bruce himself would start the role almost a month later on 1 February – Agnew and Clemence would take charge of the team in the meanwhile.

The news of Bruce's appointment was received positively by supporters. He had a first-rate managerial CV – managing Hull City in their Championship play-off final win over Wednesday in 2016, and the support the Owls took to Wembley that day (40,000-plus) registered with him, 'I'll never forget the support in the play-off final, they bounced Wembley that day and I thought what an unbelievable club that would be to get moving.'

Add to that he had managed clubs in the Premier League. Most notably perhaps he'd achieved promotion to the top division four times – twice each with Hull City and Birmingham City.

His previous association with cross-city rivals United was put to one side by the substantial majority of Wednesdayites.

For his part, chairman Dejphon Chansiri must have been pleased with the appointment to allow the new manager to start his new role so much later after the announcement.

As a centre-back Bruce had a stellar playing career – starting at Gillingham before moving on to Norwich City and then achieving his greatest success as Alex Ferguson's Manchester United captain. After leaving Old Trafford he played for Birmingham before starting his managerial career at Bramall Lane as a player-manager.

Moving on from Sheffield 2, he was manager at Huddersfield Town, Wigan, Crystal Palace, Birmingham, Wigan (again), Sunderland, Hull and Aston Villa.

In his first programme notes, Bruce stated, 'This is a mountain of a club, a huge, traditional football club steeped in history. The fan base is incredible, it really is right up there, and I am absolutely delighted to be here. I had offers from elsewhere but nothing that rivalled Sheffield Wednesday.'

Bruce was interviewed by Sky Sports in the lead-up to the Sheffield derby in March, 'I've been given another wonderful job and I want to do the best I can, as I always try to do. If I do OK then, hopefully, I can be here for four or five years but you never know in management, I could lose my next six games and be out on my ear again!'

Ex-manager Gary Megson considered Bruce was the right man for the job – he told the *Star* on 22 March, 'There's got to be a big change, it needed changing when I was here, and there's no point bringing in a good manager and not letting him manage.

'So, the change has not only got to happen on the pitch – that has already happened with Jos leaving and Steve coming in.

'The change has got to happen off the pitch as well. I'm not on about money, but in terms of getting the structure right for the football club to go forward because it's not.

'This place is still not geared for going forward yet, but Steve will know that because of where he's worked in the past.

'It needs a real good sweep through and in Steve they've got the right person to do it but if they don't listen to him then there's no point having him here.

'I think when you go into management you have a fixed idea about how you'll do things, but within about 24 hours you realise it's not particularly like that. There are very few managers that go to a football club with fixed ideas and are actually allowed to do it.

'Usually, you've got your players and you've got the way the club works and you have to adapt to that and try to get the best out of it. The hours are really, really long if you do it properly. The demands you put on yourself are huge and it gets magnified.'

There was a positive run-in to the end of the season with the team finishing 12th in the table – a marked improvement in fortunes and supporters could see enough in performances and results to look forward positively and optimistically to the new season.

Central defender Dominic Iorfa had joined in the January transfer window, supplemented in early July with the incomings of central defender Julian Börner, full-back Moses Odubajo and midfielder Kadeem Harris.

Outgoings included midfielders Almen Abdi and George Boyd, winger Marco Matias, and strikers Gary Hooper and Lucas João – the latter reportedly sold to Reading for £3m.

And then came the bolt from the blue – news that Bruce had resigned, together with Steve Agnew and Stephen Clemence, reported on 15 July.

Sky Sports News said, 'It comes after he [Bruce] confirmed over the weekend that he had held talks with Newcastle to become Rafael Benítez's successor … Newcastle made an official approach for Bruce last week and on Saturday, Bruce told Sky Sports News, "It's in the hands of the two clubs at the moment. There is nothing really to talk about until the two clubs reach some sort of a compromise. I have had a conversation yes. It has happened so quickly that I have to take stock of the situation, it's in the hands of both clubs and I will see where it develops over the next 24 to 48 hours."

'Sky sources reported that Wednesday were holding out for a compensation fee far greater than originally expected by Newcastle, which held up the potential deal.'

The Guardian wrote, 'Sheffield Wednesday have reported Newcastle to the Premier League for their conduct during the appointment of Steve Bruce as their new manager.

'Wednesday insisted some legal issues were still outstanding when Bruce's appointment was announced and have now registered their discontent at Newcastle's behaviour with the governing body.'

In a statement, Wednesday said, 'Following Newcastle United's announcement on 17 July 2019 of its appointment of former Sheffield Wednesday staff Steve Bruce, Steve Agnew and Stephen Clemence, the club confirms that it has today reported Newcastle United's conduct to the Premier League.'

This whole thing felt grubby – months earlier Bruce had exuded about his 'wonderful job' at Wednesday and almost in the blink of an eye it seemed he was off. Wednesday supporters and the chairman had every reason to feel aggrieved by his actions.

Talking years later on the *Business of Sport* podcast, Bruce stated, 'I'm on a pre-season tour with Sheffield Wednesday and my lawyer rang me and said, "I've just had Lee Charnley on the phone who's the CEO of Newcastle, would you be interested?"

'I said, "Pardon? Would I be interested?"

'No disrespect to Sheffield Wednesday, which I had a really good four, five months there, they are a big club with a huge fanbase who really took to me.'

The opportunity to return to his hometown club was one Bruce could not resist – evidently Charnley came out to talk with the Wednesday manager while on the pre-season tour in Portugal.

Bruce discussing his future with Newcastle while managing Wednesday in Portugal did not sit at all well for many supporters.

The issue between the two clubs was ultimately settled. The *Star* reported on 9 March 2021, 'A mysterious figure in Sheffield Wednesday's accounts for the 2018/19 season could well indicate that the club received an eye-watering fee from Newcastle United in exchange for the services of Steve Bruce and his staff.

'It is suspected that the former Owls boss, who swapped South Yorkshire for his hometown club in a whirlwind of controversy in July 2019, is the subject of a "Confidential Compensation Package" totalling £6,475,000.

'The fee, which would also include compensation for the services of his assistants Steve Agnew and Stephen Clemence, would represent the highest fee ever received by the club, outstripping the widely reported fee received from Reading for Lucas João later that summer.'

Bruce stayed at St James' Park for two seasons becoming manager at Championship West Bromwich Albion in February 2022, later leaving The Hawthorns after 8 months in the role. He was subsequently appointed head coach at League One Blackpool in September 2024.

Born:	31 December 1960, Corbridge
Appointed:	2 January 2019
Departed:	15 July 2019
First game:	2 February 2019: Ipswich Town (h), Championship, won 1-0
Last game:	5 May 2019: Queens Park Rangers (a), Championship, lost 2-1

Record	P	W	D	L	F	A	Win%
League	18	7	8	3	27	17	38.8%
Total	**18**	**7**	**8**	**3**	**27**	**17**	**38.8%**

36

Garry Monk

LEE BULLEN was in interim charge as caretaker manager of Wednesday for their first six league games of the new 2019/20 season, winning three of them, leading to the club standing 11th in the league table.

Forty-year-old Garry Monk's appointment as manager at Sheffield 6 was announced on 6 September 2019. He had been out of work since leaving Birmingham City in June 2019 after 15 months in charge at St Andrew's.

The new man in charge said, 'My overriding feeling is excitement and what we can do here. We know we have a capable squad and it's about making us compete as hard as we can. I was a player here many moons ago and even though it was a short spell, I got a good grasp of how powerful and traditional this club is.

'There are big clubs in this league, like this one, with tradition and history and to be part of that history is an honour. You look at it like that as a manager. The overriding factor is I'm excited. I want to come here and get to work and get started with what we feel is a capable squad.

'We want to move it forward and see what we can do. When you look at it at the start of the season there's probably 13 or 14 [teams] that target promotion. The process has to be day-by-day improvement, improve the squad we have in terms of what we do on the pitch and take it step-by-step.'

For a fanbase pining for a return to the top flight the new appointment did not immediately signal that a return to the

Premier League was on its way. But no judgement could be made until the new manager had the opportunity and time to show his value.

As a player Monk operated as a centre-back – starting out with Torquay United before moving on to Southampton, Barnsley and Swansea City.

At Southampton he was loaned out to several clubs – back to Torquay, Stockport County, Oxford United, Barnsley and Wednesday.

His loan spell at Hillsborough in 2002/03 saw him make 15 appearances; relegation at the end of the season put paid to any hopes of a permanent transfer.

He made a total of 280 senior appearances, scoring three goals over a 16-year period – the bulk of those appearances with Swansea (220).

His move into management came as a player-manager with the South Wales club in 2014. Since his time there, he had managed Leeds United, Middlesbrough and Birmingham, all established clubs in the Championship.

Following his time in charge at Middlesbrough he was succeeded on Teesside by Tony Pulis.

At the press conference introducing him as the new Wednesday manager, Monk, flanked by chairman Dejphon Chansiri, was asked about getting to the Premier League and said 'that's the ambition' and it was a case of taking it 'step by step'.

As far as the Championship was concerned, 'The squad is more than capable.'

Chansiri was asked why Garry Monk had been appointed – 'I think he's the best choice at this time,' he replied.

Asked why the appointment had taken so long he said he'd seen several applicants for the post in July and that Lee Bullen had done quite well in the interim.

Central defender Julian Börner – a transfer during the summer from German club Arminia Bielefeld and a regular in Monk's back four – observed in the first weeks playing for Monk, 'Garry is a little bit German-like, he is a tactical man.

He has a philosophy. I love it, and the distance from player to player is short. The first step from Garry Monk was to work on our defence. We need time but we are going in the right way.'

Five months after Monk had departed Birmingham, Wednesday faced them in a league fixture at Hillsborough – up against his former assistant Pep Clotet, now in permanent charge at St Andrew's. At the end of the game there was no handshake between the managers.

At the end of February 2020 Wednesday were 15th in the table and clearly not making any significant steps towards the Premier League.

And then the whole perspective for football changed as a result of the global Covid-19 pandemic. Wednesday's last game with spectators present took place at Griffin Park, Brentford (that ground's last competitive game in front of fans) – it was not a good way to sign off for Wednesdayites, a woeful performance and a 5-0 hiding.

Monk and the players were left in no doubt as to how the supporters felt at the end of that game. At that point it felt to me at least that Monk's days in charge might be numbered, such was the abjectness of the performance.

When football resumed the exclusion of spectators meant the manager and players avoided direct scrutiny by the supporters.

Wednesday finished that elongated season 16th in the league table – at best treading water, progress in the domestic cups limited to a fifth-round exit in the FA Cup and elimination at the third-round stage in the EFL Cup.

Come the close-season, a substantial number of players left the club – not all were replaced (the global pandemic resulted in an attendant strain on club finances). Incomings included striker Josh Windass, central defender Chey Dunkley and midfielder Fisayo Dele-Bashiru who joined from Manchester City – a quality addition who would go on to play for senior clubs in continental Europe.

Outgoing players included midfielders Kieran Lee and Sam Hutchinson and strikers Steven Fletcher and Fernando Forestieri.

Incomings and outgoings to one side, Wednesday faced an uphill struggle before the season began – 12 points deducted by the EFL for financial irregularities (later halved to six points). It was against this difficult backcloth that Monk and his squad started the 2020/21 season.

And that start was not a good one – by early November the team second bottom in the Championship (albeit reflecting the points deduction).

In the *Star*, Wednesday reporter Alex Miller observed that Monk had been under pressure – and that it may not have been so much a concern that the manager could steer Wednesday clear of relegation, more that he may not have been the manager to lead the club to the play-offs.

The announcement of Monk's departure together with his staff was made on 9 November 2020. It followed a run of six games without a win, four of those defeats.

Dejphon Chansiri stated, 'I feel the time is right to make a change. I wish Garry and his team the best for the future. I would like to say thank you for the time and effort Garry and his staff have committed to Sheffield Wednesday.'

Monk's staff included Ryan Needs, James Beattie, Darryl Flahavan and Andrew Hughes – the latter three had only recently teamed up with the manager at Hillsborough at the beginning of the new season.

Following time out of management and after having apparently turned down opportunities to return to the game, Monk was confirmed as manager at League One club Cambridge United in March 2024 on a reported two-year contract. He left Cambridge in February 2025 with the team bottom of League One.

Born:	6 March 1979, Bedford
Appointed:	6 September 2019
Departed:	9 November 2020
First game:	15 September 2019: Huddersfield Town (a), Championship, won 2-0
Last game:	7 November 2020: Millwall (h), Championship, drew 0-0

Record	P	W	D	L	F	A	Win%
League	51	15	14	22	56	70	29.4%
FA Cup	3	2	0	1	3	2	66.6%
League Cup	4	1	1	2	2	4	25.0%
Total	**58**	**18**	**15**	**25**	**61**	**76**	**31.0%**

37

Tony Pulis

PULIS CAME into the role at Sheffield 6 full of positive words about the club and Sheffield itself – pointing out the city was a working-class one, and being similar to the one he had grown up in: Newport, South Wales.

For his part, chairman Dejphon Chansiri was reported as saying that Pulis was someone he had admired for some time.

With Pulis appointed during the Covid pandemic and the associated restrictions on non-attendance at sporting events, Wednesday supporters were not able to have first-hand eye-witness accounts of the team's performances under their new manager.

His appointment was not welcomed with open arms by many Wednesdayites – his style of football with a focus on the long ball, strong physical challenges and all energy around the pitch seemed for some to be out of time in the 2020s, with its increased focus on more skilful players and tactical flexibility.

Pulis's playing career spanned from 1975 to 1992, playing for Bristol Rovers, Happy Valley (Hong Kong), Newport County, Bournemouth and Gillingham – returning to Bournemouth as player-coach. He moved into management at Dean Court from that role and stayed for two years; subsequent managerial positions at Gillingham, Bristol City, Portsmouth, Stoke City, Plymouth Argyle, Crystal Palace, West Bromwich Albion and Middlesbrough.

He had great success in several of those roles, most notably at Stoke where he took the Potteries club to the

Premier League and consolidated them at that level – chairman Peter Coates reported as saying, 'Pulis is Stoke's greatest-ever manager.'

At Crystal Palace he was named Premier League Manager of the Season for 2013/14, guiding the Eagles to top-flight survival in their first year there after promotion.

Pulis left Middlesbrough in May 2019; the call came to take up the reins at Hillsborough 18 months later – announced as the club's head coach on 13 November 2020.

At Wednesday, the bottom line was that Pulis's tenure saw the club achieve one win and four draws in his ten games in charge.

His departure on 28 December 2020 after only 45 days in the chair was the shortest period in charge of any Wednesday manager, the team next to bottom in the Championship at the time of his exit.

Dejphon Chansiri said in a statement on the club website, 'The performances and results have not been of the level expected since Tony Pulis was appointed,' adding, 'There are also other issues which have had a bearing on the decision.'

No further explanation of the 'other issues'.

The *Daily Mail* on 1 January 2021 reported that the chairman had decided against appointing the Welshman in 2019 but a year on considered he had the credentials and experience to retain the club's Championship status.

He was quoted, 'This time I thought he had experience and we needed someone strong and we needed to stay up and then try to get into the play-offs if we could, but the priority was to stay up so I had an interview with him and he convinced me he could do that with the squad we had.

'I told him I don't like the old English style but he told me he wouldn't play like that, his tactics would depend on the opponents.'

It did not work out well for the club or manager. Chansiri continued, 'He said our players don't buy into his mentality. Our players are not a counterattack style, our players couldn't get used to him.'

Chansiri was not convinced by Pulis's style of play or his preferred 4-5-1 formation and acknowledged he had made a mistake in appointing him.

YorkshireLive interviewed Pulis on 8 March 2023, more than two years after his departure – referring to his 'doomed ten-game spell back in 2020'. The ex-manager said, 'I hold my hand up. It was during Covid and I found it very, very difficult to walk out at that stadium and the other grounds we went to, without any atmosphere and see it just empty. It was really difficult for me. It was my fault, nobody else's fault. I felt empty myself … I didn't feel right. It didn't suit me as a coach. I live off the crowd, the togetherness.'

Pulis's family was based on the south coast and the travel involved for the 62-year-old no doubt had its challenges.

He went on to comment, 'I still think the team was good enough to stay up, and should have stayed up – without a question.'

The *Star* reported that a shift towards a more rigid, defence-minded approach was a major source of frustration among players, some of whom politely said so in private meetings over a style of play many felt the squad unsuited for.

On 28 December 2021, to mark the first anniversary of Pulis's departure, sports writer Alex Miller provided an assessment of the manager's 45-day tenure at Hillsborough.

'"It was difficult from the start, to be honest," Pulis later said. "We'd [he and his wife] booked a holiday and because of the Covid it got cancelled. With the dark nights and everything else coming I thought 'go on then'. It was one of a few job offers that I'd been given."

'The squad trained more often than under Garry Monk, who preferred a recovery-based approach to fixture congestion … his assertion that Wednesday's was a changing room lacking leadership after a defeat at Huddersfield Town is understood to have ruffled feathers within the club.

'Alongside results, what appears to have finally pulled the plug on Pulis's time at Wednesday was a breakdown in his relationship with Owls chairman Dejphon Chansiri … He claimed Pulis had threatened to "call in sick" as the relationship soured.'

For many supporters the feeling was that it was the right decision to part ways and for some confirmation that his appointment at best was a significant risk.

On 31 January 2023 Pulis announced his retirement – his last managerial position having been at Sheffield 6. 'I'm 65 now. I had a really good run at it, management has passed me by now.'

Born: 16 January 1958, Newport
Appointed: 13 November 2020
Departed: 28 December 2020
First game: 21 November 2020: Preston North End (a),
                   Championship, lost 1-0
Last game: 26 December 2020: Blackburn Rovers (a),
                   Championship, drew 1-1

Record	P	W	D	L	F	A	Win%
League	10	1	4	5	6	12	10%
Total	**10**	**1**	**4**	**5**	**6**	**12**	**10%**

38

Darren Moore

COACH NEIL Thompson took caretaker charge of the team after Pulis's departure.

At one point a name strongly linked with the vacant managerial role was that of Paul Cook – any such link came to nought and he was soon appointed as manager at Ipswich Town.

Darren Moore's name first appeared as a potential candidate towards the end of January 2021, the appointment confirmed on 1 March – with Wednesday six points adrift of safety in the Championship. The club's third manager in 2021/22 amid the handicap of the points deduction.

No matter, Moore's appointment greeted positively by Wednesdayites, primarily because of the first-rate job he'd done in his first managerial post at West Bromwich Albion – narrowly failing to retain their Premier League status – and more recently at his current club, near neighbours Doncaster Rovers, where he'd overseen promotion from League Two.

As a player he amassed almost 600 senior appearances – as a centre-back – playing for Torquay United, Doncaster, Bradford City, Portsmouth, West Bromwich Albion, Derby County, Barnsley and Burton Albion.

Arriving at Hillsborough to take over the managerial reins, the disappointment expressed by the Doncaster Rovers supporters spoke volumes for how highly he was regarded.

Ex-Wednesday manager Gary Megson commented, 'Darren is one of the most genuine people I've ever met. Really enthusiastic and likeable. He knows what it takes and I hope he gets the time to put things right.'

Moore's appointment came during the pandemic and indeed the manager himself caught Covid in April and after a period of self-isolation quickly returned to work in his efforts to keep the club in the Championship.

That early return was to his detriment – his health deteriorated. He had pneumonia and then pleurisy, resulting in his hospitalisation for a week with 24 hours' oxygen. *The Mirror* reported, 'There was a 48-hour period when it was considered touch-and-go.'

He managed to recover to be in the dug-out for Wednesday's final decisive game of the season against Derby – a win to retain Championship status, in the event a 3-3 draw and relegation.

No one ascribed responsibility for relegation to the manager who had joined in March and had suffered those traumatic health issues.

As well as the relegation battle Moore found a club that was 'not together'. He pulled it together – players, supporters, staff all pointing in the same direction. And that was no easy feat.

In an October 2024 interview with Christie Scanlon on the *Mindset for Sport* podcast while Port Vale manager, he commented on the challenges at Sheffield 6, 'A club of that size and stature steeped in tremendous history and tradition in the football pyramid ... that was the next port of call for me in terms of can I get that real sleeping giant and reawaken it again.'

He went on, 'So many things had happened at the football club – the structure of the football club was messy, the environment was messy, the behavioural patterns were messy, the mannerisms in there were messy ... [I] had to heal a club that was broken and bring supporters back to the team and the team back to the supporters and that's what we did.'

Prior to the first season in League One there were a significant amount of player incomings and outgoings.

New signings included full-back Jack Hunt, left wing-back Marvin Johnson, midfielders George Byers and Dennis Adeniran, and striker Lee Gregory.

Departures included full-back Matt Penney, centre-back Tom Lees, midfielder Adam Reach, and strikers Jordan Rhodes and Elias Kachunga.

Moore was pleased with the rebuilding of the squad and with his backroom team, referring to a 'fantastic dynamic and wealth of experience'.

In his first full season, 2021/22, Wednesday finished fourth in League One and into the play-offs; a narrow defeat to Sunderland in the semi-finals brought the season to a close. It was a creditable first full campaign.

Disappointment in the knockout competitions – eliminated in the first round of the FA Cup and EFL Cup and in the second round of the EFL Trophy. Perhaps less attention was paid to the cups – the focus was clearly on the league and promotion to the Championship.

In the close-season prior to 2022/23 Moore observed on *Mindset for Sport* that there was 'such a determination and desire to get the club going again, the hurt pushed us and drove us'.

Player incomings included goalkeeper David Stockdale, defenders Ben Heneghan and Michael Ihiekwe and striker Michael Smith; outgoings included central defender Chey Dunkley, midfielders Sam Hutchinson and Massimo Luongo, and striker Saido Berahino.

For much of 2022/23 Wednesday looked set fair for automatic promotion, an almost unstoppable train – a club record 23 games unbeaten in the middle of the season underlined their credentials, complemented with a club record number of away wins, 16. But the team stumbled in the last two months and finished third on 96 points: a club record number of points and the highest number of points by a team not achieving automatic promotion.

Again, the lack of progress in the cup competitions was considered second priority to the task of promotion.

Into the play-offs – supporters understandably very disappointed that automatic promotion looked there for the taking and Wednesday had somehow conspired to finish third.

The first leg a disaster for Wednesday at Peterborough – seemingly everything that could go wrong did go wrong and Wednesday were on the end of a 4-0 defeat. Totally unexpected and unfortunate to say the least to lose by that margin – the home team had five chances, Wednesday more chances and a 'stonewall' penalty not given.

Wednesday supporters behind the goal were neither prepared for or expecting such a loss. For many it seemed that the season had evaporated in 90 minutes into the Cambridgeshire night air.

A substantial number of fans vented their frustration, disappointment and anger at the players and manager as they came to applaud their fans at the end of the game. It must have been a chastening experience.

One man for certain who knew it was not all over was Darren Moore himself, his mind focussed at once on the second leg and the preparation needed to make the comeback of all comebacks. Preparation that was absolutely meticulous.

Getting back to Hillsborough at 1am after the first leg, he stayed up all through the early hours until 7am. He'd watched a video of the game – the manager had developed a 'game plan' for the second leg.

A key element was psychology. The players had to be totally positive in their outlook and have the belief to win the game. No room for doubt.

At training the focus was on 'control of the mind' – the players watched videos of the goals they'd scored at Hillsborough that season; watched videos of great comebacks in a whole range of sports – football, boxing, athletics and more; they practiced penalties.

A real laser focus. Nothing left to chance.

Many outside the camp considered the task impossible. To overturn a deficit of four goals had never been achieved in play-off history.

On the night of the game, I'm sure most Wednesdayites arriving at Hillsborough were there more in hope than expectation. But the whole mood and tenor in the stadium changed minutes before the players came out on to the pitch –

the video screen flickered into life, Darren Moore up close and personal to over 30,000 Wednesdayites in the ground. His words were focussed and brief – on screen for less than a minute. He finished with, 'If ever we needed you, it's tonight.'

Cue a rumbling among all four sides of the stadium breaking out into a cacophony and tidal wave of noise and support. It enveloped the ground. Moore had lit the blue touchpaper. The supporters needed no second invitation – there was a developing belief that maybe, just maybe Wednesday could do it. For now it depended on the players – one thing was certain, they would not be lacking support.

Looking back and reflecting on the night it was that brief time of Moore on the video screen – calmly engaging with the supporters and making it crystal clear what their role had to be – that galvanised the supporters and kick-started the crowd into believing. The power and noise in the ground was special.

To use the video screen in this way was evidently the manager's idea – after the press conference preceding the game he asked for the cameras to keep rolling to let him produce his message for the supporters.

Game on and two goals to the good by half-time.

Moore commented on the special atmosphere at Hillsborough and said that after the second goal 'there was lift-off … when we went in at half-time the noise was deafening'.

The outcome of the game – a quite remarkable Wednesday win on penalties after bringing the scores level 4-4 at the end of normal time – the fourth goal slid in by Liam Palmer in added time – and then a further goal apiece in extra time.

Penalties. Jack Hunt, Wednesday win, Wembley.

Scenes after the game were incredible – supporters coming to terms with the fact that Wednesday had achieved the greatest of all comebacks in the play-offs. One of the best nights – if not the best night – for many supporters.

For his part Moore – as at every home game – was to the fore in supporting, singing and encouraging the home support when the Wednesday anthem, 'Hi Ho Silver Lining', came through the loudspeakers.

Back in the changing room celebrations to the fore, but not before the manager had these words for his players, 'Listen, come on boys, listen. I'm absolutely just so proud of every single one of you.

'We had a bit of adversity in the first game and we knew we didn't perform but listen lads, it just goes to show what preparation does.

'We've prepared all week the mindset, the mentality and in training I want to say this to you, the belief has been there from day dot, and I can't commend you all enough in terms of what you just produced out there.

'It's absolutely incredible, you really deserve it. I'm absolutely delighted, what we've had to come through this season.

'Listen boys, we've got one more, OK. Enjoy tonight but we've got one more, but I'm so proud, let's go!'

But before the dressing room erupted in celebration, Wednesday captain Barry Bannan wanted to make clear their appreciation of the manager.

Bannan responded, 'This last week, what you've done to change our mindsets ... You and the staff have been unbelievable.

'There were some people who were down and what you told us ... the work you and the staff have put in has been unbelievable. So, thank you.'

Now for the final – against Barnsley at Wembley. A poor game for the neutral. Riding their luck, Wednesday won the game in the most dramatic of circumstances – the only goal scored by Josh Windass in added time of extra time. No time for the opposition to come back. Promotion. And promotion on a wave of emotion.

On that last day in May everything looked rosy for Wednesday, for Darren Moore, for the players and the supporters.

And then totally out of the blue – in the middle of June – it was reported that Moore would be leaving Hillsborough by mutual agreement. What? Why?

By all accounts after the successful 2022/23 season Moore's agent was seeking a substantial increase to his remuneration package – some reports had it at four times the amount of his current salary.

Whatever was actually said between the chairman and representative(s) of Moore, the upshot was that apparently nothing was offered. You cannot but feel that Moore would not have wanted to leave.

As an individual Darren Moore came across as a decent man with a strong set of values. He had pulled the club together when it seemed in danger of tearing itself apart. He had made a very positive impact.

Moore's reflections looking back emphasise the club and its supporters – 'really good memories, good feeling', 'wonderful club, marvellous football club'.

And you can't help thinking with Darren Moore – what might have been? I for one was sorry to see him go.

Ex-Wednesday player and now broadcaster Clinton Morrison said it was a 'terrible decision' for Moore to be leaving after achieving promotion to the Championship

Speaking for the first time since his exit in an exclusive interview with Sky Sports News senior reporter Tim Thornton, Moore explained why he and the club parted ways and insisted it had nothing to do with contract demands.

Instead, transfer targets to support the club's step up to the Championship were a key issue when he met chairman Dejphon Chansiri to make plans for the new season.

'After Wembley and the dust had settled, we had a meeting, the chairman and myself, to continue what was discussed in the build-up to it,' he said.

'I'm clear on record saying irrespective of what division the club was in our targets were set in mind. When we had the meeting, the vision set at that timescale was just a little bit out of line. Amicably we came to an agreement at the time and decided it wasn't right. The decision was made for me to step away and the club to continue.

'That's why a lot of noise was made at the time, but I never said anything because my emphasis was to allow Sheffield Wednesday to continue and move forward and allow the chairman to bring in a manager of his choice that he felt would take the club forwards. I've got no grievance with that decision.

'It was a private conversation between me and him. I know there was a lot said about the salary – but it was never about the money side of it. It was purely and strictly about the football.

'Anybody who knows me, I'm energised by the football, I love the competition of the football. Ever since I've become a manager I've been energised by the job and I was really energised by Sheffield Wednesday.

'I didn't expect to be sitting here but we understand football and we wish the club well and I'm ready for the next adventure.'

Asked if, with time and backing, he could have taken Wednesday back to the Premier League – a division they have not competed in since 2000 – Moore was adamant.

'Absolutely,' he said. 'When I first had my interview with the chairman that was the desire. The size and capacity of Sheffield Wednesday, it's a club with a wonderful history and tradition of playing in the top flight, a fan base as big as anybody, a passionate fan base that wants top-flight football.

'We know nothing is done overnight but I felt ... going into the third season [of his reign], I think the club is perfectly poised to build on those solid foundations.

'The Championship is a hard league, some top players in there but at Sheffield Wednesday we have top players, a passionate, loyal support base and the club is back at the level they deserve to be at and I sincerely wish they're able to kick on from here.'

Having left Wednesday it came as no surprise that he was out of employment for only a short time – Championship club Huddersfield Town announced Moore as their manager in September 2023; it came as a surprise when he departed in January 2024 after only three wins in 23 games.

He was appointed manager at League One Port Vale in February 2024 on a reported five-year contract. After relegation in 2023/24, Vale achieved an immediate promotion back to League One in April 2025.

Born:	22 April 1974, Birmingham
Appointed:	1 March 2021
Departed:	19 June 2023
First game:	3 March 2021: Rotherham United (h), Championship, lost 2-1
Last game:	29 May 2023: Barnsley (Wembley), League One play-off final, won 1-0
Best league season:	2020/21 Championship, 24th (relegated); 2022/23 League One, third (play-off final winners, promoted)

Record	P	W	D	L	F	A	Win%
League	106	55	29	22	176	110	51.8%
FA Cup	7	3	2	2	7	7	42.8%
League Cup	4	2	2	0	6	1	50.0%
EFL Trophy	7	4	0	3	14	10	57.1%
Play-offs	5	2	1	2	6	6	40.0%
Total	**129**	**66**	**34**	**29**	**209**	**134**	**51.1%**

*Arthur Dickinson –
Wednesday's first manager
and the most successful – two
consecutive Football League
championships and two FA
Cup wins.*

*Bob Brown
– succeeded
Dickinson and
led Wednesday to
two consecutive
Football League
championships.*

Billy Walker – Brown's successor and in his first managerial role led Wednesday to the FA Cup triumph of 1934/35.

Eric Taylor – served Wednesday for 45 years and had a major impact at the club on and off the field.

CONSILIO ET ANIMIS

HILLSBOROUGH

GENERAL
ENQUIRIES

SHEFFIELD WEDNESDAY
FOOTBALL CLUB LTD.

*Harry Catterick – led
Wednesday to the runners-
up position in the First
Division in 1960/61. Lack
of financial backing resulted
in his departure and then his
subsequent success with Everton*

Alan Brown – appointed after the betting scandal of the early 1960s and regarded as a tough disciplinarian, he led Wednesday to the FA Cup Final in 1966.

Derek Dooley – the first Wednesday player to be appointed manager of the club, failed to achieve the success hoped for and lost his job on Christmas Eve 1973.

Jack Charlton – led Wednesday back from the abyss of the Third Division and came close to returning the club to the top flight.

Howard Wilkinson – ex-Wednesday player who made an instant impact leading the club to promotion and the First Division in his first season. Lack of financial backing meant he looked for pastures new – and achieved great success with Leeds United.

Ron Atkinson – charismatic and popular manager who had two spells at the club. His style of football was entertaining and effective. Led the club to League Cup success in 1990/91 and shown here with Swedish full-back Roland Nilsson celebrating that success in April 1991.

Chris Turner – ex-Wednesday player who left the club in a much better financial state than when he arrived. Brought in many of the players who went on to gain promotion in 2005.

Gary Megson – the fifth ex-Wednesday player to manage the club. His father Don had captained the club. Looked set fair to take the club forward – his departure after the Sheffield derby win caused dismay among many supporters.

Paul Sturrock – led the club to play-off final success at Cardiff in 2005. Popular manager – his departure resulted in protests from supporters.

Darren Moore – at the helm to mastermind the so-called 'miracle of Hillsborough' in the play-off semi-final and the triumph at Wembley. Shock departure from Sheffield 6.

Danny Röhl – inspirational manager who led the club to Championship safety against all the odds in 2023/24, and built on that progress the following season.

39

Xisco Muñoz

DEJPHON CHANSIRI had made the point that the new appointment 'must be the right fit' for the club following the departure of Darren Moore and intimated there would be a 'flexible' transfer budget. Xisco Muñoz was the apparent right fit – appointed on 4 July 2023.

There was a short statement on the club website announcing his arrival, 'Sheffield Wednesday are delighted to announce the appointment of Xisco Muñoz as our first-team manager. The Spaniard, who gained promotion to the Premier League with Watford in 2020/21, takes charge of the Owls with immediate effect.'

In some ways Muñoz was potentially on a hiding to nothing with his appointment as head coach at Sheffield 6.

Wednesday had been promoted to the Championship at Wembley on 29 May 2023; Darren Moore departed on 14 June.

By the time of Muñoz's appointment many clubs had returned for pre-season training. Player resourcing and transfers for the new season had been substantially progressed if not completed.

Inevitably, Muñoz started late in the pursuit of transfer targets. A range of new players came in – some on loan – and it was difficult to escape the view that many of the better players available would have been snapped up much earlier in the transfer window. Wednesday and Muñoz were playing catch-up.

Incomings included defenders Reece James, Pol Valentín and Di'Shon Bernard, and wingers Anthony Musaba and Djeidi

Gassama. Outgoing players included defenders Ben Heneghan and Jack Hunt, and midfielders Fisayo Dele-Bashiru and Dennis Adeniran.

As a player, Spaniard Francisco Javier Muñoz Llompart – Xisco Muñoz – had an 18-year career, representing Valencia, Real Betis and Levante in his native Spain before moving to Dinamo Tbilisi in the Georgian top flight, finishing his playing career at Gimnàstic. He was part of the Valencia squad, under manager Rafa Benítez, that did the double of winning the UEFA Cup and La Liga in 2003/04.

Muñoz had a pedigree in European football – his first permanent managerial role at Dinamo Tbilisi in Georgia, then Watford, Spanish club Huesca and Anorthosis Famagusta in Cyprus. Each of those spells had been relatively short.

The Watford connection caught the eye – Muñoz had been in charge of the Hertfordshire club when they last achieved promotion to the Premier League in 2021 – albeit his stay at Vicarage Road was for less than a year, with the Hornets 14th in the top flight when he departed.

It was noted that the new manager had been without a club since February 2023 having left Anorthosis in February 2023 following five defeats.

In the programme for the first game of the season, Muñoz commented, 'I am very happy with the players I already had in the squad and we have added some new players ... I am happy with our preparations. The players have given nothing less than 100 per cent.'

Against that observation was the apparent freeze-out from the squad of left wing-back Marvin Johnson and leaving the player to train on his own in Dubai. No explanation given but an apparent breakdown in relationships.

The PFA were instructed and as Wednesday reporter Alex Miller later noted in the *Star* on 18 May 2025, 'Muñoz ended up sarcastically inviting a BBC Sheffield reporter to play at left-back – some weeks after he had spikily invited media to "ask Marvin" why he had been left lame and unregistered from their EFL squad list.'

Very happy with the squad maybe but many supporters thought Wednesday looked lost in that first game of the season against Southampton at Hillsborough. Several times it looked like player communications were awry – perhaps understandable given the number of new players in the team. A 2-1 defeat and it could have been worse, albeit the victors went on to be promoted at the end of the season.

Results and performances did not improve. Each time that Muñoz appeared to give his thoughts in a post-match interview he looked increasingly like a rabbit caught in headlights.

The manager continued to be positive in print – in his last club programme notes before his departure he said, 'I have a big belief in this group of players. The spirit is high, the boys are fighting for each other and giving 100 per cent full power.' No question the manager was seeing much more positives in the team and their performances than the supporters.

After the tenth league game, Wednesday had recorded their worst start to a season in the club's history. Muñoz apologised after that match – a defeat at West Bromwich Albion.

On BBC Radio Sheffield he was asked how he felt about the club's start – 'Frustrated. Just frustrated.'

He went on, 'I am working every day at full power. We try to give the best for the team and I can understand the situation.

'All I can say is sorry, we will continue working and we need your support for the team. I can understand the fans. All I can do is say sorry.'

By this time supporters had turned against him in large numbers with chants for his dismissal being heard at games.

'We need to keep working and have the same attitude,' Muñoz added.

'We need to keep thinking about how we can improve. We tried playing 4-3-3, we tried to play 3-5-2, 5-4-1, 4-4-2 and we have this situation. We need to start thinking about clean sheets and we need to improve in the last third.'

It had been a torrid start to the campaign – team selection, formation and tactics had been questioned by supporters. With each game Wednesday were falling behind in the league.

A win on penalties and a defeat on penalties in the EFL Cup to lower-division opposition gave no cheer to the supporters.

At the time of his departure the club were seven points adrift of safety.

Xisco's backroom team of Miguel Muñoz, Miguel Gomila, Roberto Cuesta Roman and Antonio Brambilla departed with the manager.

The club made the usual statement of thanking Muñoz for his services and wishing him well for the future. Neil Thompson was put in temporary charge.

In the club programme, captain Barry Bannan observed, 'It's not been a pleasant week for me, personally. I liked working with the manager and his backroom staff. They gave everything and are really nice people and I will miss them.'

Muñoz's departure meant that Wednesday would be looking for their seventh manager in the past five years.

In February 2025, he spoke to the *Star* about his time at Sheffield 6, 'It was a completely different project to what we had had before. I think I made some mistakes as a manager there, perhaps signing players who were too young for what we really needed. They are now top players in the division, but at that time they still needed to take a step further.

'For example, [Djeidi] Gassama, an 18-year-old player at the time, is now at a very high level. We looked for young players with potential, but financially we couldn't afford everything we wanted. Also, the project came late, with signings being closed at the last minute.

'It was a very demanding situation, with a totally different system to the previous one. Adapting takes time and, when you arrive at a club, you need time to learn and make players assimilate the concepts.'

After leaving Hillsborough, Muñoz obtained his next managerial role with the Slovakian top-flight club FC DAC 1904 Dunajská Streda, leading them to a second-placed finish at the end of the 2023/24 season. He left his role in November 2024.

Born:	5 September 1983, Manacor, Spain						
Appointed:	4 July 2023						
Departed:	4 October 2023						
First game:	4 August 2023: Southampton (h), Championship, lost 2-1						
Last game:	3 October 2023: West Bromwich Albion (a), Championship, lost 2-1						

Record	P	W	D	L	F	A	Win%
League	10	0	2	8	5	18	0%
League Cup	2	0	2	0	2	2	0%
Total	**12**	**0**	**4**	**8**	**7**	**20**	**0%**

40

Danny Röhl

DANNY RÖHL had been a candidate and been interviewed for the role as part of the process that saw Xisco Muñoz appointed manager.

The German had clearly made a good impression and he was appointed on 13 October 2023 – ten days after his predecessor had departed. It was Röhl's first managerial role and at the age of 35 he was the youngest boss in the club's history.

As a player, Röhl had been a defender playing in the lower German leagues for FC Zwickau, FC Sachsen, Leipzig 11 and FC Eilenburg. His coaching career began at RB Leipzig, followed by roles at Southampton and Bayern Munich, followed by becoming assistant manager to the German national team.

His appointment as manager at Sheffield 6 came during the international break and afforded some time before the team's next game away at Watford.

Wednesday lost that 1-0; the team showed lots of effort and there was commitment in abundance, the organisation looked much improved but a cutting edge was lacking.

Wednesday had two points from a possible 33. The first win came at the end of October against Rotherham United; at the end of November Wednesday had six points from a possible 51 – the worst start in Championship history, the worst start in Wednesday's history. Bottom of the division by some distance but slowly Röhl's methodology and approach started to take hold and work.

Written off by many but not by the new manager – Röhl masterminded how his new team would scale the proverbial mountain, stamped his authority and will on the playing style, convinced and motivated the players to believe that against all the odds they could rescue the season and remain in the Championship.

The January transfer window produced three key loan signings – goalkeeper James Beadle from Brighton & Hove Albion, Canadian striker Iké Ugbo on loan from Troyes and Colombian winger Ian Poveda from Leeds United. All three played an integral part in the upturn in fortunes to the end of that season.

Going into the last six games of the season it was nip and tuck – Wednesday in the bottom three and facing the ignominy of relegation. But Röhl and his team had given themselves a fighting chance. Those last six games – the first three drawn, the remaining three all won. Safe. Röhl and the team had achieved the near impossible in footballing terms – from a place of apparent no hope, very much in the doldrums, they had emerged against all the odds to finish in 20th position.

Remarkable, miraculous, incredible, fantastic, spell-binding – take your pick from an array of adjectives, they all apply to what Röhl and his team had achieved.

In the week before the critical last game of the season, at Sunderland, Neil Thompson, a veteran of the Hillsborough backroom team, talked with the *Star*'s Joe Crann, 'It's been really impressive to watch. The detail, the way it's been bought into, the lines of how Danny wants to do things – and not just the game plans either, it's the training and everything. The gaffer challenges us, too. He sorts the training out, but we are the ones who have to go and deliver it. That's been really motivating for us, and it's been a real team effort.

'He's a really impressive young man. His detail, his work ethics, the staff that have been put in place and the way they've gelled together – and the players have really bought into what he wants … the meetings we have are very detailed, Danny does all that, and he's very clear – that gives players clarity on the way forward.'

Röhl was very clear on the approach to the last game of the season on Wearside – the team had to be on the front foot, had to go for the win, no time for considering playing for a draw. It underlined his philosophy and intensity of approach.

Backed by 2,600 Wednesdayites (the limit on tickets applied by the hosts), the Owls took the game to Sunderland. Definitely on the front foot from the off, pressuring the home defence.

On the sidelines I'd never seen a Wednesday manager so animated. His focus seemed to be on the organisation of the defence and midfield – getting the lines right to press forward when the time was opportune, while pressing and closing the gaps when the opposition had the ball. From the stands high up in the Wearside air Röhl's energy and focus evident for all to see.

Well worked and well-taken goals from Liam Palmer and Josh Windass saw Wednesday home 2-0. Just as well as all their relegation rivals won on the day.

Cue the most fantastic celebrations for players, manager and backroom staff and the supporters. You'd have thought Wednesday had won promotion never mind staving off relegation.

Scenes of jubilation and outright relief at the final whistle. Initially, Röhl held back from being at the centre of those celebrations as the players saluted the supporters and they responded in similar vein.

Soon the clamour came for Röhl from the supporters – 'Danny, Danny Röhl' the clarion call.

The song – lyric adapted from 'Daddy Cool' by Boney M – underlined the supporters' appreciation and great affection for their manager. For his part Röhl has said it gave him 'goosebumps' the first time he heard it.

At Sunderland he came forward and took the rousing applause and appreciation together with his backroom team. He led the by now familiar choreographed raising of both outstretched arms – shaking his hands to build the anticipation, the volume from the supporters reached new heights. Players and staff joined as one.

Within seconds Röhl and his team quickly raised their arms in unison – on repeat – as the supporters reacted with the loudest 'Hey' in response.

Röhl must have been running on adrenaline, he must have been both physically and emotionally spent given the afternoon's events and the culmination of the season's work. He'd achieved what many had thought an impossible task.

When interviewed by talkSPORT, Josh Windass made these observations about the impact of Röhl, 'Honestly, I think it was just belief in the way we were playing. When Danny Röhl came in he changed the style of play and showed us every day where we were improving. When we were losing games, he would show us why we've lost. The lads all bought into what he was doing and if he told us to jump in the air, I think they all would.'

Following the Sunderland game, the manager commented to Radio Sheffield, 'It's important we have a direction. I think I have an idea of how the direction could be like, but just to have an idea is not enough. We know this club has a high potential and you see what it means for the people in the city, I think all the people everywhere. We have a lot of Wednesday fans in the world. It's up to us, up to the club and we will see.'

Coach Chris Powell spoke on talkSPORT after the Sunderland game – he was asked about the future of Röhl and the club, 'There are discussions, and we know that happens at every club at the end of every season about which players you'd like to retain and which are going to move on – also what you'd like to bring in.

'My contract actually ends this June, I didn't sign until the end of next year like everyone else. That was just because when I came in in October with Dan – we'd only met a couple of times when I was with England and he was with Germany – we didn't really know each other, and I wasn't sure how it'd all go.

'But like I've said the club has got under my skin, and I love working with him. I think he's potentially a very, very good manager, higher up – whether that's the Premier League or Bundesliga, whatever he wants to do. I think he's got the makings of that … I really hope we can continue on this great journey that we've had, these seven months have been incredible.'

Barry Bannan told the *Star* on 6 May, 'We've got the right man in charge, there's no better man we could ask for, so as long as you keep him and give him what he wants, I'm sure the club will be on an upward spiral.'

Röhl's reaction to the win was reported in the *Star* that same day, 'I said on Saturday morning to the players that it was a final – and you go into a final to win. They showed the attitude I wanted to see. For me it is the biggest achievement I have had.'

The manager went on Instagram to express his thoughts and feelings. 'On 4 May 2024, we were able to make the impossible possible. After more than six months full of passion, commitment and togetherness, we were able to achieve our goal. Unbelievable, but true.

'I would like to thank my coaches, my staff, my players and above all our massive fans for your support. We could only achieve this together. At this point many thanks to our chairman, who gave me the opportunity and the trust to make me manager.

'This season will remain unforgettable for me forever and shows what belief, attitude, positive spirit and a plan can achieve. Thank you.'

Nonetheless, supporters remained concerned about the likelihood of their manager being at the helm for the new season.

In his *Sheffield Telegraph* column on 9 March 2024, Alan Biggs had observed, 'I think it demands a radical change of approach rather than just money … This calls for real football expertise in order to produce success on the field. And a definite plan, a real long-term strategy.

'I'd suggest both these things have been lacking in the running of Sheffield Wednesday … Röhl has seen the inside of Bayern Munich and Southampton for instance.

'He knows what clubs of a certain size should look like and how they should operate. Only in such an environment can he be confident of his future.'

The Athletic's weekly digest on 11 May was headlined 'Danny Röhl ticks all the boxes of a modern manager – can

Sheffield Wednesday keep him?' Every Wednesdayite had been asking that question.

In the body of the article there was a review of Wednesday's season and progress made under Röhl, the 4-0 defeat at fellow strugglers Huddersfield Town in February 2024 seen as a turning point for the manager. 'I showed a video that was four or five minutes that was about what it means to be successful, and then I showed the players the last 16 matches,' he said. 'Then we had a very emotional conversation with the players. Some players were really touched in this meeting, but then we looked forward. It was not easy to lift other guys up, but we did it as a team.'

On 24 May the *Star* reported that chairman and owner Dejphon Chansiri was 'delighted' that Röhl had accepted a new contract at the club – understood to be a three-year deal.

Chansiri said, 'The impact he made when he joined was immediate and was the foundation for preserving our place in the Championship. He has forged a special relationship with the supporters in the short space of time he has been here and now this journey continues.'

Ask any Wednesdayite where they considered Röhl's 'managerial journey' would take him and few would have doubted he'd go to the top – hoping that it would be with Wednesday.

During the domestic close-season Röhl tried his hand as a television pundit for ITV, covering the Euro 2024 tournament in his native Germany. All who watched and commented on the Wednesday manager's performance were impressed – insightful, lucid and articulate; another string to his bow.

On the return to pre-season training, Röhl told the *Star*, 'I think for the players that stay, or extended now or come back, they know the spirit we created last season, the high-performance culture we create, what I demand as a coach but also what I give them with my human side. Everybody knows we have a fantastic coaching team around me and we are building up something at the moment, you feel it building from the first day. The players are ready to go in pre-season and we should be working hard. Everybody is excited for the new season, we know this. It's a good thing. '

Add to this that the German's approach undoubtedly attracted players to come and want to play for him.

The manager showed his attention to detail in pre-season training. Alex Miller reported Röhl's observations in the *Star* on 24 July, 'We have to understand on which side we receive the ball and in which area we have to ask for the ball again. We have diagonal passing options which is a big, big topic, we need movement. Last season our running distance in ball possession was too small and this is exactly what we have been working on, we have to be active, to understand which is the pressing line of the opponent and in which position we have to be, to receive the ball, to speed up our game.'

Transfer activity before the new season produced significant changes in personnel.

Incoming players included full-backs Yan Valery and Max Lowe, midfielder Svante Ingelsson and striker Jamal Lowe, while Iké Ugbo's loan became a permanent transfer.

Outgoing players included centre-back Bambo Diaby and midfielders Will Vaulks, George Byers and Tyreeq Bakinson.

Plymouth Argyle at Hillsborough, first game of the season, expectant crowd. Boisterous, noisy, supportive. Expectations fulfilled – Wednesday bossed the game, won 4-0 and could have scored more. A more than satisfactory opener.

The manager was satisfied, pleased with the clean sheet, the fitness of the players and the way they had applied themselves.

Five words stayed with me from his interview with BBC Radio Sheffield after the game – 'Front foot, push, push, push'. It epitomised his style of play and the requirements on each player.

Daniel Storey for the *i* newspaper had been at Hillsborough for the game. He pointed out, 'Röhl performed the most remarkable job of anyone in English league football in 2023/24' – his transformation of no-hopers and relegation certainties to a club that remained in the Championship from the lowest ebb.

Röhl commented, 'From the moment I arrived here, I was convinced that I could bring something to this club: knowledge, personality, experience at different levels, hopefully success too.'

Storey observed, 'There were – and still are – two distinct strategies to Röhl's great escape. The first is a commitment to high-intensity pressing football … that style smacks you in the face. The energy levels of the Wednesday players without the ball are astounding.

'On the ball, the manner in which they drag opposition players out of position and then switch to quick passing football creates a supreme opening goal.'

The reporter highlighted the togetherness that Röhl had instilled in his team and this with a style of football and training that is demanding – it's double sessions and three hours straight on the pitch.

Röhl shared a slogan from basketball coach John Wooden that he 'sticks to' – 'A good coach can change a game; a great coach can change a life.'

The manager acknowledged that being away from his family in Germany was difficult, 'We have to find a way to make it work. It enables me to give my full energy to the club, but you have to find a balance between your work and family.'

At the end of the interview Röhl acknowledged that the expectations of supporters were growing. 'People will always dream for more,' he said.

Storey concluded on that point, 'He's right in one way – you felt that on Sunday. But Röhl is also wrong. Through the fallow years, the relegation, the two years in League One, they dreamed only of exactly what is happening now. Röhl is all they ever wanted, an outsider who seemed to understand the very essence of what made them sing and shout and stick with the team, and seemingly had all the tools to bring it to life.'

Wednesday's first away game of the season, at Sunderland, and an interesting observation about Röhl in Nick Barnes's column in the programme, 'I was very impressed with Danny Röhl last season … what impressed me most, followed Wednesday's win at the Stadium of Light last season when he came into the media lounge to do his post-match press conference. He made a point of going around the room to shake everyone by the hand. His English is excellent, and he spoke sincerely and humbly. He was very impressive and I have no doubt he will have a successful season.'

His way with the media at the Stadium of Light was an echo of his introduction to the media at the press conference confirming his appointment as Wednesday's new manager.

Despite the opening-day win, Wednesday had an unimpressive start to the 2024/25 campaign. Nonetheless, the bond between supporters, the manager and his team seemed as strong as ever as the year progressed.

The relationship between manager and chairman did not look so strong – at a fans' forum in mid-January 2025 Chansiri stated the pair had not spoken since December and confirmed an approach from Southampton for Röhl's services after the sacking of Russell Martin that same month.

It was later reported that Wednesday's demand for compensation – reported at £5m – had cooled the south coast club's interest.

On 25 January 2025 the *i* ran a feature headlined 'Wednesday fans full of woe after Chansiri summit'. It commented, 'On a bottom-six budget Röhl has worked wonders again, keeping the club on the cusp of the play-off places.'

And it added, 'The fear is Röhl will walk in the summer.'

Perhaps it was the game away at Norwich City in March 2025 that underlined the approach and impact made by Röhl – 2-0 down at half-time, Wednesday had a chastening first half; the manager used the break to adapt his tactics – he moved from a back five to a back four with a higher press and made two substitutions. An important in-game change that impacted the course of the match allied with the character and resilience of the players to come back and take the game to the opposition – resulting in a 3-2 Wednesday win.

Rob Staton of BBC Radio Sheffield commented, 'It is not very Wednesday to traipse into the dressing room 2-0 down at a place like Carrow Road and then flip the game on its head in the second half. This is the Danny Röhl effect.

'The German always seems to have a plan B. His tactical adjustments are sophisticated and filled with purpose. They aren't hopeful punts. He's legit. The real deal. Or the Röhl deal, if you like.

'Look at the scenes on Tuesday night. Players celebrating with fans as they roar their delight at another win on the road. Röhl having his moment, followed by Chris Powell loving every minute.'

Staton undoubtedly on the button – Röhl had transformed the team, the ethic, the culture, the approach, the connection with supporters. Nothing like it for 30 and more years at Sheffield 6 since the days of Big Ron in his first stint at Hillsborough.

Nonetheless, after the home defeat in the Sheffield derby in mid-March Wednesday seemed to go off the boil: eight games, one win, four draws and three defeats.

As added backcloth a temporary transfer embargo at the end of November 2024 following issues with HMRC coupled with players not being paid at the end of March 2025 because of reported cashflow issues brought concerns to the fore for supporters and players alike.

No doubt the manager had his own thoughts.

Following defeat at home to Hull City in the first week in April, Joe Crann in the *Star* stated Röhl was 'at his wits' end' following what was undoubtedly a bad week for the club.

At the time, talking to BBC Radio Sheffield, Röhl said, 'I will never forget these players in my future, I know this … Players with passion and character and the right attitude.' It seemed more than a hint that he may be leaving.

Before the season concluded Röhl stated he had made a decision about his future and informed the chairman. Would he stay or would he go? Nothing specific was said, albeit the general view was pointing towards his time at Sheffield 6 coming to an end.

Overall, the season had been more than satisfactory on the pitch - Wednesday finished 12th, and as Röhl pointed out, 'no longer are we the underdog.'

Danny Röhl was the veritable alchemist at Sheffield 6 – he transformed the style of play, the preparation for and the application in games. He'd given the team an identity and on any objective assessment, with the resources available, he had considerably over-achieved.

As the season ended the manager was being linked with jobs in the Premier League, Championship and Bundesliga.

In the time that followed it seemed like a whirlwind of chaos hit the club – players and staff not paid at the end of May and June, payments not made to HMRC, transfer embargoes and players' signing restrictions imposed by the EFL, the training ground not ready for pre-season training, no pre-season friendlies in place, the club in substantial debt with monies owed to other EFL clubs. Players were sold to raise revenue.

At one point it was an almost daily barrage of bad news.

Add to that the club was put up for sale by the owner, Dejphon Chansiri.

This was a summer like no other.

Meanwhile, no sign of Danny Röhl. He had not returned for pre-season training.

Out of the blue on 9 July BBC Radio Sheffield reported that the manager intended to return to the club. To say that was a surprise would be an understatement.

Against all expectations Danny Röhl returned to the Middlewood Road training ground on 14 July with a reported 'clear the air' meeting with the players. *The Star* reported, 'it's understood a frank exchange of views was aired.'

Two days later in the same newspaper, Joe Crann reported under the headline 'Question marks remain over Danny Röhl at Sheffield Wednesday' – 'Röhl coming back to Sheffield followed the decision to hand Henrik Pedersen a new contract after his last one expired, with the general understanding being that he would take over as manager once the incumbent manager – who was in talks to leave – had moved on.'

With the start of the new season little more than three weeks away, Crann concluded his article, '… it is far from certain that he (Röhl) will still be in his position as manager by the time the Owls head over to Leicester City on the opening day.'

As the new season came into view it was clear the club faced some of the greatest challenges in its history. The turbulence that had enveloped the club during the summer had to be addressed and resolved.

For his part the manager had to galvanise and motivate a reduced playing and coaching staff - 2025/26 would no doubt provide many challenges.

Born:	28 April 1989, Zwickau, Germany
Appointed:	13 October 2023
First game:	21 October 2023: Watford (a), Championship, lost 1-0
Best season:	2024/25 Championship, 12th

Record	P	W	D	L	F	A	Win%
League	81	30	18	33	99	119	37.0%
FA Cup	4	1	2	1	7	6	25.0%
League Cup	4	3	1	0	9	3	75.0%
Total	**89**	**34**	**21**	**34**	**115**	**128**	**38.2%**

41

Chat with Alan Biggs

I HAD the chance to talk with the well-known and respected Sheffield-based broadcaster and reporter Alan Biggs in February 2025. Alan has had dealings with every manager at Sheffield Wednesday since the mid-1970s and I spoke with him first about how things had changed since that time for the role of the football reporter.

'It has radically changed since the 1970s with the biggest changes coming in the early 2000s. In those earlier years the reporter's job was a lot easier in terms of access to managers – personal home numbers and later mobile numbers were exchanged once you had a good relationship with a manager. You could have off-the-record chats which provided good background to what was happening at the club – at Wednesday Ron Atkinson and David Pleat would be good examples of this.

'There's no doubt you had to work at the relationship with a manager and be persistent in following up but you had the opportunity to get closer to them in those days. Nowadays it's a lot more controlled and off-the-record chats are rare.

'And with many of the managers in those earlier years you had access to them during the week – nowadays it's confined to the pre- and post-match press conferences.

'The access to managers is controlled and channelled through the club – the media manager is present alongside the manager at press conferences. The media managers are invariably helpful to reporters but their presence inhibits any off-the-record comments. Compared to those earlier years I think it has resulted in greater blandness in communications.

'For instance, in recent years I find little value or anything of real interest coming out of the pre-match press conferences.

'And in more recent times with the advent of the social media platforms the club – understandably – wants to break any news story and that reduces the ability of the reporter to get to the stories ahead of time.'

I asked Alan about his recollections of the Wednesday managers since the mid-1970s.

'The first one was Steve Burtenshaw. I had just started with Sheffield Cablevision television and it was on the day he was sacked. The chairman Bert McGee brought the manager to a room to face the media – I recollect the manager looked forlorn. He was a nice guy but given the circumstances it seemed an unusual way for a manager to be treated. That was my first one and as subsequent dismissals took place it was clearly very unusual – unique in fact!'

We then talked about the individual managers.

Len Ashurst: 'He was a fearsome character – I was afraid of him. He arrived at the club pledging to put the players through the wringer. I think he and his assistant Tony Toms did just that. He had an impish sense of humour and liked to get one over on you – in those days, reporters from BBC Radio Sheffield, Radio Hallam and the press were invited into his small office for the post-match press conference. On one occasion he said to me "your flies are open" and everyone fell about laughing. Embarrassing – but my flies weren't open!'

Jack Charlton: 'What you see is what you get with Jack. He was a colourful character and a man of simple pleasures – I remember him being pleased to show me the drinks cabinet he'd had installed. He was also a "fag-cadger" – I made sure I had enough cigarettes when I was with him! More importantly he was not a man to bear a grudge – if he was upset with you, he'd tell you and then quickly move on. He brought a simple and effective style of football to the club.'

Howard Wilkinson: 'In my view the best manager for Sheffield Wednesday in my time reporting on the club – that is in terms of his achievement of promotion in his first season and then bedding the team down in the top flight as a first-rate and effective unit. Given the resources he had he did an exceptional job. You could talk to Howard – you might have to persist but you would get time with him. I recollect I was once invited to do pre-season training with the team at the training ground – Howard gave me a lift in his car back to Hillsborough explaining that the players would have their lunch at Middlewood Road and he had his at the ground. He said, "Players always talk about managers and it's easier for them to do that if I'm not there."'

Peter Eustace: 'I'd known Peter in his role as assistant manager to Howard and had a good relationship with him. Once he became the manager, he took on a different persona – to some extent of course you have to in that new role but he seemed to change so much. He became such a disciplinarian and I think he fell out with a lot of people.'

Ron Atkinson: 'A really colourful personality. At his first press conference he knew the name of every journalist in that room – and remember he'd just come back from managing in Spain. He had a presence about him that lifted everyone and that was just what the club needed at that time. He was a manager superbly attuned to the media's requirements – he was able to control the narrative, he steered it. At that first press conference he gave me his number and said he was available at 1pm – that's very refreshing and a little disarming at the same time! In his second spell he remained good to deal with. One thing that had changed from his first spell was that he no longer knew exactly when a player would be transferred, in or out. He was no longer in full charge of that process.'

Trevor Francis: 'He was a gentleman – a nice man to deal with. He did not take umbrage at criticism. You could get access to Trevor during the week. A class operator. I think everyone liked him. It became common knowledge towards the end of his final season in charge that he would be leaving the club – it was an open secret. He invited his family and a small number of reporters he dealt with to a farewell party in a suite at Hillsborough. This was before his departure was announced. The party was jovial and enjoyable. At one point I recollect chairman Dave Richards walking past the door and looking a little sheepish.'

David Pleat: 'He was the most intense and deep-thinking of the managers I've dealt with. I have a lot of respect for David. He had a difficult job – the team was ageing and he wanted to move on established stars. I see from his recent autobiography that he says this was the brief he was given. Perhaps he tried to change things a little too quickly. He brought in the two Italian players – Benito Carbone and Paolo Di Canio – excellent, skilful players.'

Danny Wilson: 'He had great success at Barnsley and had done a tremendous job there. He had sticky spells at Hillsborough and at times had a bit of a stand-off with the media. Some of his big-money transfers did not work out well. I recollect one game where Wednesday had been poor – losing to lower-division Cambridge United in the League Cup from memory – and at his press conference he had a go at "fancy dans" in the team. I interpreted his comment to mean the Italians – albeit Danny had mentioned no names. It caused an issue and looking back I think I went too strongly on referring to the two Italians. There's no doubt Danny was the manager at a difficult time for the club.'

Paul Jewell: 'A likeable, witty character but he can't have enjoyed his short time at S6. Came in on a remit to break up a squad of high-earning, under-achieving players and perhaps took it too literally. A difficult dressing room and he showed the strain.'

Peter Shreeves: 'He became manager at a difficult time and had to deal with issues following relegation from the Premier League at a time when the club had substantial financial issues. Peter, with all his experience, was a very relaxed bloke. Did well for a time.'

Terry Yorath: 'He inherited a club burdened by financial issues. I felt Terry, an honourable character, didn't enjoy the spotlight – he could be quite intense and sensitive at times. This was a difficult time for coaches rising up the pecking order, as he and Shreeves did, as opposed to hand-picked managers arriving from outside.'

Chris Turner: 'A very likeable character. He deserves an immense amount of credit. He signed some really good players – including Chris Brunt, Steve MacLean, Glenn Whelan and Lee Peacock. He did not get the benefit of being able to develop those players and the team as he intended. It was essentially "his team" that secured promotion under Paul Sturrock in the play-off final at Cardiff. He was unfortunate to be the manager when the chairman – Dave Allen – was in a takeover battle with Ken Bates for the club. Allen kept Bates out of Hillsborough, and I think at the time he wanted to appoint a more established manager who would be seen as someone to take the club forward quickly.'

Paul Sturrock: 'I liked him and he was an interesting character – and remember there is no right or wrong way to do the job. All kinds of characters are football managers. I recollect his Friday press conferences where he invited journalists to say who they would have in the team the following day! I'm sure he knew full well who would be in the team. I think he liked that interaction with the media. In the end the parting of the ways had more to do with his relationship with the hierarchy at the club.'

Brian Laws: 'An excellent communicator who was always a pleasure to deal with. It was clear he understood the media and its power. This, I feel, contributed to him having a good relationship with supporters – and to his relative longevity. Laws lasted more than three years in the job, which, at a challenging time, ranks as a considerable achievement in itself. A Sheffield derby double certainly didn't do him any harm! Later I enjoyed collaborating on Brian's book, *Laws of the Jungle*.'

Alan Irvine: 'He was an absolute gentleman. He was easy to talk to and very straightforward. I respected him. I think his main strength was as a coach rather than as a manager. I thought that, in Milan Mandarić wanting to make an impact, too many signings actually derailed a team looking good for the play-offs.'

Gary Megson: 'He was a firebrand, and I think in some ways he could be his own worst enemy. He had his own style of football and the players he wanted for that style. As I understand it, his exit was not results-driven. Words were exchanged behind the scenes. Regardless, he remains popular with fans to this day – rightly in my view. It should be remembered how much passion he had for the club and it was his team that went on to promotion.'

Dave Jones: 'As far as the players were concerned, he put round pegs in round holes. He was reasonable to deal with and was the right man at the right time – the club achieved promotion. I remember doing a piece about him – focussed on the person rather than the professional. He said he enjoyed scuba-diving which led to an interesting cartoon by Pete McKee accompanying the article.'

Stuart Gray: 'He was there for a brief time. He was straightforward and he steadied the ship. The football was not thrilling but the results were there. I think his strength was on the coaching side rather than as a manager. With the arrival of a new owner – Dejphon Chansiri – I was not surprised to see him leave the club. Many new owners want to have their own man in place.'

Carlos Carvalhal: 'Carlos is a colourful character and a real delight to work with. He's a very engaging individual who I really enjoyed talking to. He raised with me one time why he had not been invited to appear on my *Sheffield Live* television show – there had clearly been a breakdown in communications somewhere because we had invited Carlos on to the show. Subsequently, he appeared on it a couple of times and his thoughts and views were very interesting and good value.'

Jos Luhukay: 'His appointment came as a surprise. I was live on air with my *Sheffield Live* television show – BBC Radio Sheffield's Rob Staton was a guest on the programme – when a text came through saying that we might like to speculate that Jos Luhukay could be Wednesday's new manager. James Greig, a fellow presenter on the programme, quickly googled his name so that we had some background information. And while we in the media as well as the supporters were surprised by the appointment, I think Jos was surprised to get the job. As an individual Jos was perfectly agreeable albeit ineffectual in the role and his style of football was a little dull.'

Steve Bruce: 'Excellent with the media, as most journalists will tell you. But, as Steve knows, I didn't like the way he left. It wasn't so much that he quit to join Newcastle – attraction understandable – but the manner of his parting. Didn't say sorry or explain himself to fans who had been so supportive. That was poor, in my view. But we all move on, he's a good guy in my overall experience and has had a great career in the game, which staying at S6 could well have enhanced.'

Garry Monk: 'He'd done an impressive job at Swansea. He is an engaging character. I think in some ways he had a "poisoned chalice" following Carlos after those two play-off campaigns. His style of football was a little dull and I think he paid the price for being too cautious in his approach – after seasons challenging towards the top of the table Wednesday were in the bottom half. His expectations were more realistic than the club's at the time, in my opinion.'

Tony Pulis: 'At Stoke he had done a tremendous job – he had a particular direct style of football and it worked very well for him in the Potteries. I don't think his style of football fitted for Wednesday and certainly the results were not coming through. He was not helped that his tenure came in the Covid pandemic with no supporters allowed into the grounds – I'd seen him orchestrate the crowd very well at Stoke. He would not get that opportunity at Hillsborough.'

Darren Moore: 'One of the nicest guys you could ever wish to meet. He is a Christian and for example I never heard him swear. Overall, he did a good job – relegation in the season he joined was not down to him. In two seasons he managed to get Wednesday back into the Championship and he was looking forward to the challenge of taking the club forward. Certainly, he would have expected to be rewarded as a result of promotion and whatever the ins and outs of the contractual discussions that then took place with the owner I don't know – looking at it from the outside I think it may have been different perspectives on the whole negotiating process that led to a parting of the ways.'

Xisco Muñoz: 'He is an engaging man. I think the language barrier was not easy for him – I found it difficult to understand him at times. And I wonder whether the players might have found it difficult to understand him and more particularly what they were expected to do. I think he was unfortunate to come in at a time when the mood around the club was flat after the euphoria of promotion and the departure of Darren Moore. I have sympathy for Xisco. Ultimately, given all the circumstances I think he was a little out of his depth.'

Danny Röhl: 'As a manager he wears his heart on his sleeve – he does not disguise his feelings. He's a new manager, a passionate guy, a very bright guy. He is very refreshing to see and hear and he's very self-confident. For me he has made the biggest impact at Sheffield Wednesday in my time reporting on the club – taking them from a position of what seemed almost certain relegation from the Championship to play-off contenders for the Premier League in the space of little more than 12 months. Everything I see and hear says he has a very big future as a manager at the highest level.'

Appendix

Managers' Records Compared

	P	W	D	L	F	A	Win%
Harry Catterick	131	74	31	26	277	153	56.4%
Darren Moore	129	66	34	29	209	134	51.1%
Vic Buckingham	142	65	28	49	262	213	45.7%
Howard Wilkinson	266	120	69	77	405	333	45.1%
Bob Brown	589	264	134	191	1047	872	44.8%
Gary Megson	63	28	14	21	87	84	44.4%
Arthur Dickinson	922	394	188	340	1453	1329	42.7%
Carlos Carvalhal	131	56	38	37	174	135	42.7%
Jimmy McMullen	71	30	21	20	121	94	42.2%
Trevor Francis	216	89	68	59	326	264	41.2%
Alan Irvine	59	24	13	22	92	81	40.6%
Ron Atkinson	148	60	42	46	203	183	40.5%
Jack Charlton	298	118	93	87	407	341	39.5%
Peter Shreeves	41	16	9	16	55	57	39%
Steve Bruce	18	7	8	3	27	17	38.8%
Danny Röhl	89	34	21	34	115	128	38.2%
Len Ashurst	106	40	29	37	130	126	37.7%
Alan Brown	171	64	41	66	245	231	37.4%
Eric Taylor	539	196	128	215	932	946	36.3%
Stuart Gray	84	30	25	29	101	101	35.7%
Dave Jones	80	28	22	30	103	103	35%
Billy Walker	182	63	52	67	271	289	34.6%

Brian Laws	154	52	42	60	196	209	33.7%
Paul Sturrock	104	35	29	40	130	135	33.6%
Jos Lukahay	48	16	13	19	64	71	33.3%
Derek Dooley	137	44	35	58	170	200	32.1%
David Pleat	106	34	31	41	147	169	32%
Paul Jewell	38	12	5	21	48	68	31.5%
Garry Monk	58	18	15	25	61	76	31%
Chris Turner	96	29	31	36	120	137	30.2%
Danny Wilson	80	23	17	40	85	109	28.7%
Terry Yorath	56	16	15	25	62	78	28.5%
Jack Marshall	54	14	19	21	58	74	25.9%
Danny Williams	74	17	18	39	78	126	22.9%
Steve Burtenshaw	71	14	17	40	70	111	19.7%
Peter Eustace	21	4	7	10	21	32	19%
Tony Pulis	10	1	4	5	6	12	10%
Xisco Munoz	12	0	4	8	7	20	0%

The above figures reflect all Sheffield Wednesday competitive games – League and Cups.

I have stayed with the convention in cup games of reflecting the result at the end of any extra time

A number of the managers were in charge solely when the club were in the top flight – First Division or Premier League – including Vic Buckingham, Alan Brown, Trevor Francis and David Pleat.

Len Ashurst's tenure was solely when the club was in the Third Division.

Harry Catterick is head and shoulders above any other manager for win percentage. Darren Moore is the only other manager to achieve over a 50% win percentage.

Bibliography

Various matchday programmes – Sheffield Wednesday home and away games

Anderson, V., & Guest, L., *First Among Unequals* (Full Back Media, 2010)

Ashurst, L., *Left Back In Time: The Autobiography of Len Ashurst* (Know The Score!, 2009)

Atkinson, R., *Big Ron: A Different Ball Game* (Andre Deutsch, 1998)

Atkinson, R., *The Manager* (deCoubertin Books, 2017)

Bassett, D., *Settling the Score* (John Blake, 2002)

Bowler, D., *Shanks: The Authorised Biography of Bill Shankly* (Orion, 1996)

Bullen, L., & Biggs, A., *No Bull: The Lee Bullen Story* (Vertical Editions, 2013)

Charlton, J., & Byrne, P., *Jack Charlton: The Autobiography* (Corgi Books, 1997)

Chester, D., *Football – An Insider's Job* (Escafeld Press, 2022)

Cooper, A., *Eric Taylor: A Biography* (A. Cooper Publications, 2011)

Curran, T., & Brindley, J., *Regrets of a Football Maverick: The Terry Curran Autobiography* (Vertical Editions, 2012)

Di Canio, P., & Marcotti, G., *Paolo Di Canio: The Autobiography* (Collins Willow, 2001)

Dickinson, J., *Sheffield Wednesday FC: The Official History* (Amberley Publishing, 2017)

Dickinson, J., & Brodie, J., *The Wednesday Boys: A Definitive Who's Who of Sheffield Wednesday Football Club 1880–2005* (Pickard Communication, 2005)

Dickinson, J., & Brodie, J., *Sheffield Wednesday: The Complete Record* (DB Publishing, 2011)

Dixon, K., *Jackie Sewell* (DB Publishing, 2010)

Dooley, D., & Farnsworth, K., *Dooley! The Autobiography of a Soccer Legend* (Hallamshire Press, 2000)

Dyson, J., *Our Lowest Ebb?: A New History of Sheffield Wednesday's Darkest Times – 1973–76* (Vertical Editions, 2020)

Dyson, J., *Back In The Big Time: Sheffield Wednesday's Return to Division One 1984–86* (Pitch Publishing, 2022)

Giles, E., *Billy Walker: Once, Twice, Three Times a Winner* (Desert Island Books, 2010)

Gordon, D., *A Quarter of Wednesday: A New History of Sheffield Wednesday 1970–1995* (Wednesday Publishing, 1995)

Farnsworth, K., *Sheffield Wednesday: A Complete Record 1867–1987* (Breedon Books, 1987)

Farnsworth, K., *Wednesday!* (Sheffield City Libraries, 1982)

Farnsworth, K., *Wednesday Every Day of the Week* (Breedon Books, 1998)

Francis, T., & Dixon, K., *One In A Million: The Autobiography* (Pitch Publishing, 2019)

Huntley, E.J., *A Proper Player: The Career of John Sheridan* (youbooks.co.uk, 2011)

Huntley, E.J., *It's All About Winning: Gary Megson – A Life in Football* (youbooks.co.uk, 2012)

Johnson, N., *Sheffield Wednesday 1867–1967* (Tempus Publishing, 2007)

Laws, B., & Biggs, A., *Laws Of The Jungle: Surviving Football's Monkey Business* (Vertical Editions, 2012)

Lowe, S., *Match of My Life Stoke City* (Pitch Publishing, 2012)

McCalliog, J., *Wembley Wins Wembley Woes* (Langside Publishing, 2021)

McMenemy, L., *My Autobiography: A Lifetime's Obsession* (Trinity Mirror Sports Media, 2016)

Megson, D., & Olewicz, C., *Don Megson: A Life In Football* (Vertical Editions, 2014)

Mellor, I., & Buckley, A., *Spider: I Wish You All You Wish Yourself – The Ian Mellor Story* (independently published, 2024)

Metcalf, M., *The Remarkable Story of Fred Spiksley: The First Working Class Hero* (Pen & Sword, 2021)

Palmer, C., & Jacobi, S., *It Is What It Is: The Carlton Palmer Story* (Vertical Editions, 2017)

Platt, G., *When A Giant Stirred: Sheffield Wednesday 1976–1993* (DB Publishing, 2021)

Pleat, D., *Just One More Goal* (Biteback, 2024)

Ponting, I., *The Book of Football Obituaries* (Pitch Publishing, 2012)

Sawyer, R., *Harry Catterick: The Untold Story of a Football Great* (deCoubertin Books, 2014)

Scovell, B., *Bill Nicholson: Football's Perfectionist* (John Blake, 2011)

Sparling, R.A, *The Romance of the Wednesday 1867–1926* (Sir W.C. Leng & Co. Ltd, 1926)

Sturrock, P., & Richards, B., *Luggy: The Autobiography of Paul Sturrock* (Pitch Publishing, 2015)

Swan, P., & Johnson, N., *Peter Swan: Setting The Record Straight* (Stadia, 2006)

Thompson, G., & Howell, B., *Don't Believe a Word: The Garry Thompson Autobiography* (Curtis Sport, 2020)

Tynan, T., & Cowdery, R., *Tommy: A Life at the Soccer Factory* (Bud Books, 1990)

Wilson, D., & Mann, M., *I Get Knocked Down: But I Get Up Again* (Morgan Lawrence, 2022)

Whitworth, T., *Owls: Sheffield Wednesday Through The Modern Era* (Pitch Publishing, 2016)

Yorath, T., & Lloyd, G., *Hard Man, Hard Knocks* (Celluloid, 2004)